THE FAKE HUSBAND

The Other Voice in Early Modern Europe:
The Toronto Series, 75

Medieval and Renaissance
Texts and Studies

Volume 570

I0892661

The Other Voice in
Early Modern Europe:
The Toronto Series

SERIES EDITORS Margaret L. King *and* Albert Rabil, Jr.
SERIES EDITOR, ENGLISH TEXTS Elizabeth H. Hageman

Previous Publications in the Series

MADRE MARÍA ROSA
Journey of Five Capuchin Nuns
Edited and translated by Sarah E. Owens
Volume 1, 2009

GIOVAN BATTISTA ANDREINI
Love in the Mirror: A Bilingual Edition
Edited and translated by Jon R. Snyder
Volume 2, 2009

RAYMOND DE SABANAC AND SIMONE ZANACCHI
Two Women of the Great Schism: The Revelations *of Constance de Rabastens by Raymond de Sabanac and* Life of the Blessed Ursulina of Parma *by Simone Zanacchi*
Edited and translated by Renate Blumenfeld-Kosinski and Bruce L. Venarde
Volume 3, 2010

OLIVA SABUCO DE NANTES BARRERA
The True Medicine
Edited and translated by Gianna Pomata
Volume 4, 2010

LOUISE-GENEVIÈVE GILLOT DE SAINCTONGE
Dramatizing Dido, Circe, and Griselda
Edited and translated by Janet Levarie Smarr
Volume 5, 2010

PERNETTE DU GUILLET
Complete Poems: A Bilingual Edition
Edited by Karen Simroth James
Translated by Marta Rijn Finch
Volume 6, 2010

ANTONIA PULCI
Saints' Lives and Bible Stories for the Stage: A Bilingual Edition
Edited by Elissa B. Weaver
Translated by James Wyatt Cook
Volume 7, 2010

VALERIA MIANI
Celinda, A Tragedy: A Bilingual Edition
Edited by Valeria Finucci
Translated by Julia Kisacky
Annotated by Valeria Finucci and Julia Kisacky
Volume 8, 2010

Enchanted Eloquence: Fairy Tales by Seventeenth-Century French Women Writers
Edited and translated by Lewis C. Seifert and Domna C. Stanton
Volume 9, 2010

GOTTFRIED WILHELM LEIBNIZ, SOPHIE, ELECTRESS OF HANOVER AND QUEEN SOPHIE CHARLOTTE OF PRUSSIA
Leibniz and the Two Sophies: The Philosophical Correspondence
Edited and translated by Lloyd Strickland
Volume 10, 2011

The Other Voice in Early Modern Europe: The Toronto Series

SERIES EDITORS Margaret L. King *and* Albert Rabil, Jr.
SERIES EDITOR, ENGLISH TEXTS Elizabeth H. Hageman

Previous Publications in the Series

Dialogue with the Other Voice in Sixteenth-Century Italy: Literary and Social Contexts for Women's Writing
Edited by Julie D. Campbell and Maria Galli Stampino
Volume 11, 2011

SISTER GIUSTINA NICCOLINI
The Chronicle of Le Murate
Edited and translated by Saundra Weddle
Volume 12, 2011

LIUBOV KRICHEVSKAYA
No Good without Reward: Selected Writings: A Bilingual Edition
Edited and translated by Brian James Baer
Volume 13, 2011

ELIZABETH COOKE HOBY RUSSELL
The Writings of an English Sappho
Edited by Patricia Phillippy
With translations by Jaime Goodrich
Volume 14, 2011

LUCREZIA MARINELLA
Exhortations to Women and to Others If They Please
Edited and translated by Laura Benedetti
Volume 15, 2012

MARGHERITA DATINI
Letters to Francesco Datini
Translated by Carolyn James and Antonio Pagliaro
Volume 16, 2012

DELARIVIER MANLEY AND MARY PIX
English Women Staging Islam, 1696–1707
Edited and introduced by Bernadette Andrea
Volume 17, 2012

CECILIA DEL NACIMIENTO
Journeys of a Mystic Soul in Poetry and Prose
Introduction and prose translations by Kevin Donnelly
Poetry translations by Sandra Sider
Volume 18, 2012

LADY MARGARET DOUGLAS AND OTHERS
The Devonshire Manuscript: A Women's Book of Courtly Poetry
Edited and introduced by Elizabeth Heale
Volume 19, 2012

ARCANGELA TARABOTTI
Letters Familiar and Formal
Edited and translated by Meredith K. Ray and Lynn Lara Westwater
Volume 20, 2012

PERE TORRELLAS AND JUAN DE FLORES
Three Spanish Querelle *Texts:* Grisel and Mirabella, The Slander against Women, *and* The Defense of Ladies against Slanderers*: A Bilingual Edition and Study*
Edited and translated by Emily C. Francomano
Volume 21, 2013

The Other Voice in Early Modern Europe: The Toronto Series

SERIES EDITORS Margaret L. King *and* Albert Rabil, Jr.
SERIES EDITOR, ENGLISH TEXTS Elizabeth H. Hageman

Previous Publications in the Series

BARBARA TORELLI BENEDETTI
Partenia, a Pastoral Play: A Bilingual Edition
Edited and translated by Lisa Sampson and Barbara Burgess-Van Aken
Volume 22, 2013

FRANÇOIS ROUSSET, JEAN LIEBAULT, JACQUES GUILLEMEAU, JACQUES DUVAL AND LOUIS DE SERRES
Pregnancy and Birth in Early Modern France: Treatises by Caring Physicians and Surgeons (1581–1625)
Edited and translated by Valerie Worth-Stylianou
Volume 23, 2013

MARY ASTELL
The Christian Religion, as Professed by a Daughter of the Church of England
Edited by Jacqueline Broad
Volume 24, 2013

SOPHIA OF HANOVER
Memoirs (1630–1680)
Edited and translated by Sean Ward
Volume 25, 2013

KATHERINE AUSTEN
Book M: A London Widow's Life Writings
Edited by Pamela S. Hammons
Volume 26, 2013

ANNE KILLIGREW
"My Rare Wit Killing Sin": Poems of a Restoration Courtier
Edited by Margaret J. M. Ezell
Volume 27, 2013

TULLIA D'ARAGONA AND OTHERS
The Poems and Letters of Tullia d'Aragona and Others: A Bilingual Edition
Edited and translated by Julia L. Hairston
Volume 28, 2014

LUISA DE CARVAJAL Y MENDOZA
The Life and Writings of Luisa de Carvajal y Mendoza
Edited and translated by Anne J. Cruz
Volume 29, 2014

Russian Women Poets of the Eighteenth and Early Nineteenth Centuries: A Bilingual Edition
Edited and translated by Amanda Ewington
Volume 30, 2014

JACQUES DU BOSC
L'Honnête Femme: The Respectable Woman in Society *and the* New Collection of Letters and Responses by Contemporary Women
Edited and translated by Sharon Diane Nell and Aurora Wolfgang
Volume 31, 2014

The Other Voice in
Early Modern Europe:
The Toronto Series

SERIES EDITORS Margaret L. King *and* Albert Rabil, Jr.
SERIES EDITOR, ENGLISH TEXTS Elizabeth H. Hageman

Previous Publications in the Series

LADY HESTER PULTER
Poems, Emblems, and *The Unfortunate Florinda*
Edited by Alice Eardley
Volume 32, 2014

JEANNE FLORE
Tales and Trials of Love, Concerning Venus's Punishment of Those Who Scorn True Love and Denounce Cupid's Sovereignity: A Bilingual Edition and Study
Edited and translated by Kelly Digby Peebles
Poems translated by Marta Rijn Finch
Volume 33, 2014

VERONICA GAMBARA
Complete Poems: A Bilingual Edition
Critical introduction by Molly M. Martin
Edited and translated by Molly M. Martin and Paola Ugolini
Volume 34, 2014

CATHERINE DE MÉDICIS AND OTHERS
Portraits of the Queen Mother: Polemics, Panegyrics, Letters
Translation and study by Leah L. Chang and Katherine Kong
Volume 35, 2014

FRANÇOISE PASCAL, MARIE-CATHERINE DESJARDINS, ANTOINETTE DESHOULIÈRES, AND CATHERINE DURAND
Challenges to Traditional Authority: Plays by French Women Authors, 1650–1700
Edited and translated by Perry Gethner
Volume 36, 2015

FRANCISZKA URSZULA RADZIWIŁŁOWA
Selected Drama and Verse
Edited by Patrick John Corness and Barbara Judkowiak
Translated by Patrick John Corness
Translation Editor Aldona Zwierzyńska-Coldicott
Introduction by Barbara Judkowiak
Volume 37, 2015

DIODATA MALVASIA
Writings on the Sisters of San Luca and Their Miraculous Madonna
Edited and translated by Danielle Callegari and Shannon McHugh
Volume 38, 2015

MARGARET VAN NOORT
Spiritual Writings of Sister Margaret of the Mother of God (1635–1643)
Edited by Cordula van Wyhe
Translated by Susan M. Smith
Volume 39, 2015

The Other Voice in Early Modern Europe: The Toronto Series

SERIES EDITORS Margaret L. King *and* Albert Rabil, Jr.
SERIES EDITOR, ENGLISH TEXTS Elizabeth H. Hageman

Previous Publications in the Series

GIOVAN FRANCESCO STRAPAROLA
The Pleasant Nights
Edited and translated by Suzanne Magnanini
Volume 40, 2015

ANGÉLIQUE DE SAINT-JEAN ARNAULD D'ANDILLY
Writings of Resistance
Edited and translated by John J. Conley, S.J.
Volume 41, 2015

FRANCESCO BARBARO
The Wealth of Wives: A Fifteenth-Century Marriage Manual
Edited and translated by Margaret L. King
Volume 42, 2015

JEANNE D'ALBRET
Letters from the Queen of Navarre with an Ample Declaration
Edited and translated by Kathleen M. Llewellyn, Emily E. Thompson, and Colette H. Winn
Volume 43, 2016

BATHSUA MAKIN AND MARY MORE WITH A REPLY TO MORE BY ROBERT WHITEHALL
Educating English Daughters: Late Seventeenth-Century Debates
Edited by Frances Teague and Margaret J. M. Ezell
Associate Editor Jessica Walker
Volume 44, 2016

ANNA STANISŁAWSKA
Orphan Girl: A Transaction, or an Account of the Entire Life of an Orphan Girl by way of Plaintful Threnodies in the Year 1685: *The Aesop Episode*
Verse translation, introduction, and commentary by Barry Keane
Volume 45, 2016

ALESSANDRA MACINGHI STROZZI
Letters to Her Sons, 1447–1470
Edited and translated by Judith Bryce
Volume 46, 2016

MOTHER JUANA DE LA CRUZ
Mother Juana de la Cruz, 1481–1534: Visionary Sermons
Edited by Jessica A. Boon and Ronald E. Surtz. Introductory material and notes by Jessica A. Boon. Translated by Ronald E. Surtz and Nora Weinerth
Volume 47, 2016

CLAUDINE-ALEXANDRINE GUÉRIN DE TENCIN
Memoirs of the Count of Comminge *and* The Misfortunes of Love
Edited and translated by Jonathan Walsh
Volume 48, 2016

The Other Voice in Early Modern Europe: The Toronto Series

SERIES EDITORS Margaret L. King *and* Albert Rabil, Jr.
SERIES EDITOR, ENGLISH TEXTS Elizabeth H. Hageman

Previous Publications in the Series

FELICIANA ENRÍQUEZ DE GUZMÁN, ANA CARO MALLÉN, AND SOR MARCELA DE SAN FÉLIX
Women Playwrights of Early Modern Spain
Edited by Nieves Romero-Díaz and Lisa Vollendorf
Translated and annotated by Harley Erdman
Volume 49, 2016

ANNA TRAPNEL
Anna Trapnel's Report and Plea; or, A Narrative of Her Journey from London into Cornwall
Edited by Hilary Hinds
Volume 50, 2016

MARÍA VELA Y CUETO
Autobiography and Letters of a Spanish Nun
Edited by Susan Laningham
Translated by Jane Tar
Volume 51, 2016

CHRISTINE DE PIZAN
The Book of the Mutability of Fortune
Edited and translated by Geri L. Smith
Volume 52, 2017

MARGUERITE D'AUGE, RENÉE BURLAMACCHI, AND JEANNE DU LAURENS
Sin and Salvation in Early Modern France: Three Women's Stories
Edited, and with an introduction by Colette H. Winn. Translated by Nicholas Van Handel and Colette H. Winn
Volume 53, 2017

ISABELLA D'ESTE
Selected Letters
Edited and translated by Deanna Shemek
Volume 54, 2017

IPPOLITA MARIA SFORZA
Duchess and Hostage in Renaissance Naples: Letters and Orations
Edited and translated by Diana Robin and Lynn Lara Westwater
Volume 55, 2017

LOUISE BOURGEOIS
Midwife to the Queen of France: Diverse Observations
Translated by Stephanie O'Hara
Edited by Alison Klairmont Lingo
Volume 56, 2017

CHRISTINE DE PIZAN
Othea's Letter to Hector
Edited and translated by Renate Blumenfeld-Kosinski and Earl Jeffrey Richards
Volume 57, 2017

MARIE-GENEVIÈVE-CHARLOTTE THIROUX D'ARCONVILLE
Selected Philosophical, Scientific, and Autobiographical Writings
Edited and translated by Julie Candler Hayes
Volume 58, 2018

The Other Voice in
Early Modern Europe:
The Toronto Series

SERIES EDITORS Margaret L. King *and* Albert Rabil, Jr.
SERIES EDITOR, ENGLISH TEXTS Elizabeth H. Hageman

Previous Publications in the Series

LADY MARY WROTH
Pamphilia to Amphilanthus *in Manuscript and Print*
Edited by Ilona Bell
Texts by Steven W. May and Ilona Bell
Volume 59, 2017

Witness, Warning, and Prophecy: Quaker Women's Writing, 1655–1700
Edited by Teresa Feroli and Margaret Olofson Thickstun
Volume 60, 2018

SYMPHORIEN CHAMPIER
The Ship of Virtuous Ladies
Edited by Todd W. Reeser
Volume 61, 2018

ISABELLA ANDREINI
Mirtilla, A Pastoral: *A Bilingual Edition*
Edited by Valeria Finucci
Translated by Julia Kisacky
Volume 62, 2018

MARGHERITA COSTA
The Buffoons, A Ridiculous Comedy: *A Bilingual Edition*
Edited and translated by Sara E. Díaz and Jessica Goethals
Volume 63, 2018

MARGARET CAVENDISH, DUCHESS OF NEWCASTLE
Poems and Fancies *with* The Animal Parliament
Edited by Brandie R. Siegfried
Volume 64, 2018

MARGARET FELL
Women's Speaking Justified *and Other Pamphlets*
Edited by Jane Donawerth and Rebecca M. Lush
Volume 65, 2018

MARY WROTH, JANE CAVENDISH, AND ELIZABETH BRACKLEY
Women's Household Drama:
Loves Victorie, A Pastorall, *and*
The concealed Fansyes
Edited by Marta Straznicky and Sara Mueller
Volume 66, 2018

ELEONORA FONSECA PIMENTEL
From Arcadia to Revolution: The Neapolitan Monitor *and Other Writings*
Edited and translated by Verina R. Jones
Volume 67, 2019

The Other Voice in
Early Modern Europe:
The Toronto Series

SERIES EDITORS Margaret L. King *and* Albert Rabil, Jr.
SERIES EDITOR, ENGLISH TEXTS Elizabeth H. Hageman

Previous Publications in the Series

CHARLOTTE ARBALESTE DUPLESSIS-MORNAY, ANNE DE CHAUFEPIÉ, AND ANNE MARGUERITE PETIT DU NOYER
The Huguenot Experience of Persecution and Exile: Three Women's Stories
Edited by Colette H. Winn
Translated by Lauren King and Colette H. Winn
Volume 68, 2019

ANNE BRADSTREET
Poems and Meditations
Edited by Margaret Olofson Thickstun
Volume 69, 2019

ARCANGELA TARABOTTI
Antisatire: *In Defense of Women, against Francesco Buoninsegni*
Edited by Elissa B. Weaver
Volume 70, 2020

MARY FRANKLIN AND HANNAH BURTON
She Being Dead Yet Speaketh: The Franklin Family Papers
Edited by Vera J. Camden
Volume 71, 2020

LUCREZIA MARINELLA
Love Enamored and Driven Mad
Edited and translated by Janet E. Gomez and Maria Galli Stampino
Volume 72, 2020

ARCANGELA TARABOTTI
Convent Paradise
Edited and translated by Meredith K. Ray and Lynn Lara Westwater
Volume 73, 2020

GABRIELLE-SUZANNE BARBOT DE VILLENEUVE
Beauty and the Beast: *The Original Story*
Edited and translated by Aurora Wolfgang
Volume 74, 2020

FLAMINIO SCALA

The Fake Husband, A Comedy

Edited and translated by

ROSALIND KERR

Iter Press
Toronto, Ontario

ACMRS Press
Tempe, Arizona

2020

Iter Press
Tel: 416/978–7074 Email: iter@utoronto.ca
Fax: 416/978–1668 Web: www.itergateway.org

ACMRS Press
Tel: 480/965–5900 Email: acmrspress@asu.edu
Fax: 480/965–1681 Web: acmrspress.com

© 2020 Iter, Inc. and the Arizona Board of Regents for Arizona State University.
All rights reserved.
Printed in Canada.

Library of Congress Cataloging-in-Publication Data

Names: Scala, Flaminio, active 1620, author. | Kerr, Rosalind, 1941– translator.

Title: The fake husband, a comedy / Flaminio Scala ; edited and translated by Rosalind Kerr.

Other titles: Finto marito. English

Description: Toronto, Ontario : Iter Press ; Tempe, Arizona : Arizona Center for Medieval and Renaissance Studies, 2020. | Series: The other voice in early Modern Europe: the Toronto series ; 75 | Includes bibliographical references and index. | Summary: "English translation of a fully scripted dramatic work by the actor, theater manager, and playwright Flaminio Scala, based on his earlier scenario "The Husband," and featuring a lesbian marriage. The first actor/manager to publish commedia scenarios, Scala here translates the spontaneity of commedia dell'arte into a replicable theatrical document"-- Provided by publisher.

Identifiers: LCCN 2019034500 (print) | LCCN 2019034501 (ebook) | ISBN 9780866986281 (paperback) | ISBN 9780866987615 (ebook)

Subjects: GSAFD: Comedies.

Classification: LCC PQ4634.S224 F5613 2019 (print) | LCC PQ4634.S224 (ebook) | DDC 852/.5--dc23

LC record available at https://lccn.loc.gov/2019034500

LC ebook record available at https://lccn.loc.gov/2019034501

Cover illustration:
The Compagnia dei Comici Gelosi with Isabella Andreini (1562–1604), depicted giving a performance in Paris / oil on canvas / 16th century / Francken, Hieronymus (1540–1610) / Netherlandish / Comedie Francaise, Paris, France / Archives Charmet / Bridgeman Images CHT231072.

Cover design:
Maureen Morin, Information Technology Services, University of Toronto Libraries.

Typesetting and production:
Iter Press.

For my son Andrew and grandsons Quentin and Graham

Contents

Acknowledgments

I wish to thank series co-editor Margaret L. King for her vital support and encouragement. Her scholarly expertise, deep insight and critical acumen have brought this manuscript through the challenging editorial process. I would also like to thank the Editorial Board of the Other Voice series for their valuable editorial comments and support in publishing this manuscript. Iter Project Manager Margaret English-Haskin has been instrumental in steering the manuscript to publication with great care and consideration. I wish also to thank Maureen Morin for the cover design and Anabela Piersol for typesetting. My appreciation to Amyrose McCue Gill for her skill in preparing the index.

I am thankful to the staff at the Biblioteca Nazionale Marciana in Venice for their assistance in giving me access to the 1618 version of *Il finto marito.* Also, I thank the staff at the British Library in London for assistance in viewing their two copies of the 1619 edition. Above all, I thank Laura Falavolti for her 1982 modern edition which I have followed in my translation.

I am indebted to the Drama Department at the University of Alberta where I had translation assistance from Valerio Borchiellini. I was also fortunate to have the opportunity to workshop a production of *The Fake Husband* with a very talented graduate class in 2009.

I gratefully acknowledge the support provided by the subvention program of the Vice-President of the University of Alberta (Research Office) for assistance with this publication.

I also acknowledge the support I have received from the Centre for Reformation and Renaissance Studies, Victoria University in the University of Toronto. As a fellow, I have profited immensely from my access to library services and interactions with other scholars.

I thank the anonymous reader for The Other Voice series for helpful comments which led me to make important revisions. I also owe my colleague and friend Stefano Muneroni a great debt for his generous assistance in helping me with the translation and Scala's use of special idioms and local sayings.

I acknowledge that any errors are my own.

Introduction

The Fake Husband *as Other Voice*

Licinio, the fake husband, the epicenter of the play of that name, is a woman—in Counter-Reformation Italy, a thing absurd, shocking, and unthinkable. Licinio is actually Brigida, maidservant to the ingenue Porzia, the two women having concocted the phony marriage to save Porzia from a coerced marriage to a man she did not love, and so enable her marriage to Lepido, the man she did. The lesbian marriage, therefore, even as it introduces the intriguing theme of same-sex empathy, is chiefly a stratagem toward a heterosexual resolution that could only be attained by profoundly disruptive means. In it is heard the Other Voice: the voice of women, bonded across class lines by their resistance to male tyranny, in search of freedom to pursue their own desires.

As the play unfolds, Porzia is paired with Giulia, whose desire to marry Flavio is threatened by her aged guardian Demetrio who—hoping to facilitate his own access to her—has agreed to give her in marriage to Gervasio, another old man. Giulia's maidservant Ruchetta, disgusted by the designs of the *vecchi* (old men) on her mistress, and more generally by men's abuse of women, joined by the manservants Trapola and the Scaramuccia, will assist Giulia in evading the trap set for her. In the end, the two *innamorate* (women in love) win their two lovers, the *vecchi* are defeated and humiliated, and the wily *zanni* (the lowborn servants) triumph in a struggle that has pitted women against men, young against old, and servants against their masters.

Ripe with these explosive themes, enacted onstage with outrageous buffoonery, physical humor, and sexual ribaldry, *Il finto marito (The Fake Husband)*, published in 1618 by Flaminio Scala and translated here into English for the first time, was understandably a major success.[1] Scala, an experienced actor and director who had previously published in 1601 the play *Il postumio (The Posthumous Man)*, and in 1611 the important collection of *commedia dell'arte* scenarios, *Il teatro delle favole rappresentative (Theater of Tales for Performance)*,[2] expanded his authorial role to provide a fully written out script entitled *The Fake Husband*.

1. Flaminio Scala, *Il finto marito* (Venice: Andrea Baba, 1618; reprint Venice: n.p., 1619); modern edition in *Commedie dei comici dell'arte*, ed. Laura Falavolti (Turin: Unione tipografico-editrice torinese, 1982), 225–365. The 1982 edition is cited henceforth as Falavolti.

2. *The Husband (Il marito)*, in *Theater of Tales for Performance*, in Richard Andrews, ed. and trans., *The Commedia dell'Arte of Flaminio Scala: A Translation and Analysis of Thirty Scenarios* (Lanham: Scarecrow Press, 2008), Day 9, at 41–52; volume cited henceforth as Andrews, *Thirty Scenarios*. Original Italian text, *Il teatro delle favole rappresentative* (Venice: Giovan Battista Pulciani, 1611); modern edition by Ferruccio Marotti, 2 vols. (Milan: il Polifilo, 1976), containing *Il marito* at 1:101–9.

Scala's source text was the scenario, *Il marito (The Husband)*, one of the most enduringly popular scenarios of the fifty published in the *Theater of Tales* collection.[3]

The original creators of the play *The Fake Husband*, therefore, were not only Scala who provided the dramatic fiction, but also the actors who by their improvisations collaboratively developed the action and dialogue, drawing on their experience and the resources of their imagination, while adapting the message to different audiences and according to the capacities of the performers.[4] Among the latter, the female actresses were critically important; commedia actresses were the first professional women performers in the history of European theater.[5] Supreme among them were Isabella Andreini and Silvia Roncagli, of whom more below. In writing the scenario *The Husband*, and subsequently the play *The Fake Husband*, Scala revives and memorializes the voices of the actresses who had invented these roles and performed them throughout the last decades of the sixteenth and into the seventeenth centuries.

Scala's uncanny ability to capture the contribution of each actor to shaping the dramatic action enabled him to reveal the unique genius of each member of the ensemble. When he published the collection of scenarios, he defended not filling in the dialogue spoken by the characters on the grounds that he could not do them justice, since they all had their unique style of speech and gestures. As a result, because the scenarios were based on public performances, readers were invited to fill in the missing segments by recreating what they had seen performed on the stage. When Scala came to publish the scenarios, he put together a dream

3. The three-act scenario form used by the commedia dell'arte was created for the actors and provided a brief outline listing the characters and describing their entrances and exits, scene by scene, to indicate what actions they were to perform.

4. Commedia dell'arte troupes began to appear around 1545 when companies incorporated themselves to tour around to various Italian cities and perform in the piazzas. Typically, a troupe included two pairs of master-servant duos: the old patriarchs: the Venetian merchant Pantalone and the Bolognese doctor Graziano were paired against the crafty Zannis. Soon specialized Zannis such as Arlecchino (Harlequin), Pedrolino (Pierrot) and many others made their character masks famous. Later, the two pairs of young lovers called by names such as the male Flavio and Orazio and female Isabella and Flaminia made it possible to perform romantic comedies. The maidservant and the Spanish Capitano (captain) brought the troupe to the standard ten.

5. By the 1560s, female performers had become established members of the troupes and through their great talents and rhetorical skills revolutionized the commedia dell'arte stage. The appearance of women on the professional stage for the first time in western theater history seems to have happened for many reasons connected with the growth of a market economy and also the Counter-Reformation church's attack on the "honest courtesans" (refined female companions) whose training in the fine arts and rhetoric provided the new actresses with a model to follow. The actresses took over the roles of the young female lovers (*innamorate*), previously performed by young male actors, and quickly became dominant members of the troupes, often acting as company directors. The saucy maidservant role also became increasingly famous as female performers took it over from male actors.

team of all-star players, mainly from the company of the Gelosi.[6] For readers who had been frequent spectators over the years, several of the characters were associated with famous actresses who had included those roles in their repertoire. Such was the case with Isabella Andreini (1562–1604), the first great international *diva*, who not only played the *innamorata* and a transvestite page, but was also co-director of the Gelosi with her equally famous husband Francesco Andreini. Scala's inclusion of Isabella Andreini in so many of his scenarios provides an invaluable record of her acting range.[7] Unlike most of her fellow actresses, Andreini's stellar accomplishments also include published works: the pastoral play Mirtilla, two volumes of *Rime (Poems)*, and collections of lovers' speeches and stage dialogues in the *Lettere (Letters)* and *Fragmenti di alcune scritture (Miscellaneous Writings)*.[8]

Less known today but highly regarded in her time, Silvia Roncagli (1547–after 1603), having joined the Gelosi in the 1570s, became known for her bold interpretation of the cynical maidservant Franceschina, wise in sexual knowledge and the ways of the world. Scala includes her, as he does Andreini, as a vital character in many scenarios.[9] Married to the actor-playwright-scholar Adriano Valerini in 1583, she participated in performances at the Medici wedding in 1589[10] and in the Gelosi's last tour to France in 1603.[11]

By honoring the outstanding performances of trained actresses, and representing them as emotionally convincing subjects with self-knowledge and strong desires, Scala reveals how greatly he valued their contribution to making the commedia dell'arte into a "theater of excellence."[12] He strengthened the female voices in the scripted *Fake Husband* by providing them with full dialogue, paying tribute to the actresses who had developed these roles as members of an ensemble. The dialogue that Scala provides for individual actresses evokes their personal experi-

6. The Gelosi (1568–1604) were one of the most famous early companies who toured across Italy and France, performing for the public and the courts alike.

7. Isabella's versatility as an actress included her well-known performance of the transvestite page Fabrizio, who makes a sustained appearance in five of the fifty scenarios in *Theater of the Tales*, Isabella remaining in her male disguise throughout the entire play. It became a very common theatrical device to have female actors take on male roles. See "Transvestite Heroines" in Rosalind Kerr, *The Rise of the Diva on the Sixteenth-Century Commedia dell'Arte Stage* (Toronto: University of Toronto Press, 2015), 82–101.

8. See "The Making of a Diva," in Kerr, *The Rise of the Diva*, 102–46.

9. Franceschina appears in at least twenty of Scala's fifty scenarios. See *Thirty Scenarios*, 333.

10. For detailed coverage of this wedding gala, see James Saslow, *The Medici Wedding of 1589: Florentine Festival as Theatrum Mundi* (New Haven: Yale University Press, 1996).

11. M.A. Katritzky, *The Art of Commedia: A Study in the Commedia dell'Arte, 1560–1620, with Special Reference to the Visual Records* (Amsterdam: Rodopi, 2006), 246, 250–51.

12. Elena Tamburini uses the term "commedia di excellenza" as a more accurate translation of "commedia dell'arte." See *Culture ermetiche e commedia dell'arte: Tra Giulio Camillo e Flaminio Scala* (Rome: Aracne Editrice, 2016), 10.

ence while it universalizes their voices, which speak on behalf of the female sex by identifying the injustices from which women suffered. Despite the comedic tone, his play is full of social commentary concerning the treatment of women of different social classes as they try to escape forced marriages and unwanted sexual attentions.

Scala wanted *The Fake Husband* to serve many purposes: among them, to showcase the importance of the actresses; to portray everyday human behavior accurately by including actual women in female roles; to raise the standards of the commedia dell'arte; and to make it representative of contemporary Italian society. By providing a five-act script with a unified plot and well-developed characters speaking standard Italian, he also intended to prove that the commedia dell'arte could vie with the formal academic theater.[13] To bring the play closer to dramatic literature, Scala chose literary names for the characters that were not immediately identifiable with the commedia actors and actresses who had played them in the scenario: thus Isabella becomes Porzia, and Franceschina, whose male persona was Cornelio, becomes Brigida/Licinio.[14] While Porzia and Licinio are in ultimate control of the plot, Scala puts together a strong ensemble cast to work with them. Most notably, Pedrolino, the mastermind servant in the scenario, is replaced by Scaramuccia, who is in all likelihood a version of Scala himself in his role as *capocomico* (company director).[15] Assisting Scaramuccia in overturning the patriarchal oppressors and supporting the subterfuge is the cunning maidservant Ruchetta, who gives voice to all the injustices that she and other women endure.[16]

By including a version of himself as the director, Scala is able to show how the actors worked together to move the script forward, thus adding a metatheatrical dimension that requires the reader's participation in following the various subterfuges that are activated. The audience is also guided to realize that, although *The Fake Husband* is a fully scripted play, it is still connected to the performance text recorded in the scenario *The Husband*. In his two prologues, Scala invites

13. In *The Fake Husband*, Scala shows how the commedia dell'arte can respond to the convergence of oral, written, and print cultures, while he seeks at the same time to share his playmaking techniques with as wide an audience as possible and to respond to the increased demand for printed texts. Henry Jenkins discusses how media convergence flows across multiple media platforms involving cultural shifts owing to their competitive economies that encourage consumers to seek out new information and make new connections; see Jenkins, *Convergence Culture: Where Old and New Media Collide* (New York: New York University Press, 2006), 2–3.

14. See Andrews, *Thirty Scenarios,* xxxi and xxviii respectively.

15. I have chosen to keep the Italian *capocomico* instead of company director because it involves much more than the English term implies, since the *capocomico* was usually also a lead actor who had to keep the other company members in line as well as perform not only directorial tasks but also run interference with patrons, including renting halls and looking after booking and travel arrangements, and much more.

16. Ruchetta takes the place of Olivetta, the actress Isabella Cima; Andrews, *Thirty Scenarios,* xxviii.

readers and spectators to see what the differences are between the scenario and the play text, and so appreciate the living, breathing imitation of life that made the commedia dell'arte more emotionally powerful than most scripted plays.

By having Scaramuccia invent and orchestrate the immensely complicated series of bed tricks that will punish and reward everyone according to their deserts, Scala demonstrates the new commitment of the troupes to put the play's aesthetic cohesion ahead of individual star performers. Several times in the play, we are alerted to Scaramuccia's controlling influence as well as his difficulties in keeping the other characters on track.[17] By letting himself eventually be outmaneuvered by the lesbian couple of Porzia and Licinio, Scala's Scaramuccia shows that even the *capocomico* must submit to the demands of the plot, and bow to the even greater deception practiced by the female players. In this way, he celebrates the importance of both the carefully crafted buffoonery of the zanni and the refined eloquence of the *innamorati.* Scala's *Fake Husband* offers a play that preserves the full comic range of the commedia dell'arte while achieving a more disciplined and refined status in a scripted form that is still closely aligned with the vision of the actresses who first crafted its message.[18]

Flaminio Scala (1552–1624): Life and Works

Flaminio Scala was born on September 27, 1552,[19] to a noble Roman father, as evidence suggests, named Iacomo Scala.[20] Francesco Andreini, the husband of Isabella Andreini and himself a famous commedia dell'arte performer, refers to Scala's noble parentage in his Letter to the Readers prefacing the *Theater of Tales*:

> I shall just say this, that Master Flaminio Scala, known on stage as Flavio, in order to do justice to these aforesaid principles which have been so commended by great Philosophers, dedicated himself in his youth to the noble practice of the Stage (in no way detracting from

17. Domenica Landolfi, "Flaminio Scala," 1:441–42 in Giovanni Battista Andreini, et al., *Comici dell'arte: Corrispondenze*, ed. Siro Ferrone, Claudia Burattelli, Domenica Landolfi, and Anna Zinanni, 2 vols. (Florence: Le Lettere, 1993). Cited henceforth as *Corrispondenze.*

18. Siro Ferrone describes how after Scala's collection appeared, improvisation gradually came to be replaced with premeditated dialogue; see Ferrone, "Don Giovanni impresario," in Ferrone, *Attori, mercanti, corsari: La commedia dell'arte in Europa tra Cinque e Seicento* (Turin: Einaudi, 1993), 174–75.

19. This birthdate is confirmed by a comment he makes about turning sixty-six on September 27, 1618; *Corrispondenze,* 1:500–501; letter 38, note 1. His father's name is mentioned in a will he drew up in 1616: Archivio di Stato di Venezia, Notarile testamenti, Beacian Fabrizio, b. 56, n. 236, 3 cc. unnumbered; see *Corrispondenze,* 1:445.

20. Tamburini cites evidence that Iacomo was probably a relative of a nobleman Giacomo Scala who held an office in the Roman government, as documented in 1615 by Giovanni Pietro Caffarelli who wrote about the family; see Tamburini, *Culture ermetiche,* 201n 64.

> his noble birth), and made such progress in this profession that he deserved to be classed as a great actor, among the most excellent of his profession.[21]

Theater scholars have been inclined to see Andreini's parenthetical comment as flattery, especially since the noble birth Scala claimed did not provide him with an income, but recent scholarship suggests that some outstanding actors are likely to have had noble ties since their accomplishments are consistent with the erudition and refinement associated with elite status.[22] Certainly they were well aware of the need to acquire court patronage in order to enhance their status as performers and succeed economically and socially.[23] In his early years in Rome, Scala may have frequented elite academic and dramatic circles where artists of all kinds—architects, painters, sculptors, musicians and poets and writers—vied with each other to claim supremacy for their own art form, and engaged often in theater arts to try out their skills in imitating real-life action. Professional actors mingled with noble amateurs in the academies where many members were accomplished in more than one fine art.[24] While Scala had left Rome before the Accademia degli Umoristi was founded in Rome in 1600,[25] he was probably involved with other Roman academies in existence in the last quarter of the sixteenth-century, and hence well-prepared to thrive in Venice, where theater was enthusiastically supported.

Scala's activity is not documented until quite late in his career, after he had spent many years coming up through the ranks as a company member. It is not until May 1597 that, as a member of the Desiosi troupe, he obtained permission from the Genoese senate for a three-month performance contract.[26] His petition

21. English translations in Andrews, *Thirty Scenarios*, 2.

22. Tamburini cites the claims of Francesco Andreini, Isabella Canali, Vincenza Armani, Adriano Valerini to noble birth; see Tamburini, *Culture ermetiche*, 14, 201.

23. Scala was on the lookout for a secure court position at all times and maintained his connections with the Mantuan court even while under the patronage of Don Giovanni de' Medici. The records also show that in 1618, as the envoy Cosimo Baroncelli wrote to his master Don Giovanni de'Medici from Florence, Scala wanted above all to be given a permanent post in the Florentine court; see *Corrispondenze*, 1:494n6.

24. Tamburini mentions several examples in Rome and around Venice of intersections between academicians and theater artists; see *Culture ermetiche*, 69–78.

25. Elena Tamburini, "Dietro la scena: Comici, cantanti, e letterati nell'Accademia romana degli Umoristi," *Studi secenteschi* 50 (2009): 89–112. Although the Umoristi were not officially formed until 1600, there was already considerable crossover between the various literary and visual arts taking place in various circles under patrons.

26. For biographical details, I will rely mainly on *Corrispondenze*, 1:437–49. Other important sources are Marotti, "Introduzione" to *Teatro delle favole*, xiii–lxii; Ferrone, "Don Giovanni impresario," which details his close dealings with Scala and the Confidenti troupe during the period 1615–1621;

reveals his leadership role and ability to argue on behalf of comedy's classical merits.[27] The following April he was again in Genoa, negotiating on behalf of the Uniti for a similar contract.[28] In 1600 to 1601, he was with the Accesi troupe, performing in France with a group of outstanding actors who had developed individualized character masks: Fritellino (Pier Maria Cecchini), Arlecchino (Tristano Martinelli, the first to play that role), the prima donna (Diana Ponti), and Capitan Matamoros (Silvio Fiorillo). In January 1601, he published a play, *Il postumio*, in Lyon, identifying himself as author only by the initials I. S.[29] Although remaining anonymous in this instance suggests he still regarded himself as part of the ensemble, he allowed his stage name, Flavio, to appear on the frontispiece. In January 1606, he was in the employ of the Mantuan court, a connection he strove to maintain even after 1615 when, as will be seen, he came under the patronage of Don Giovanni de' Medici. What his position was at this time is not documented, since he seemed to move back and forth between different troupes with considerable ease. His difficulties with the authorities in one instance, however, is documented: in March 1610, he and his troupe were prohibited from performing in Mantua for an entire year by Cardinal Bonifacio Caetani, whom they had offended.[30] Although the offence is not spelled out, it had to do with something they did or said in a performance which the Cardinal considered to be unforgivable.

Scala's publication of *The Theater of Tales* the following year could be regarded as a counterstroke intended to silence his critics and cement his reputation as one of the foremost theater artists in Italy. Besides dedicating the volume to Count Ferdinando Riario,[31] Scala also drew attention to his connections to the Mantuan court by identifying himself as an actor in the employ of the duke of Mantua, Vincenzo I Gonzaga. The six dedicatory verses testify to the general esteem he had earned by his many accomplishments. In them, for example, the Mantuan state secretary Ercole Marliani compliments him on bringing to his

and Robert Henke, *Performance and Literature in the Commedia dell'Arte* (Cambridge: Cambridge University Press, 2002), 181–85.

27. Marotti, "Introduzione" to *Teatro delle favole*, xlvi. In his excellent treatment of Scala, Henke notes that Scala is referencing both Cicero's definition of comedy as an imitation of life, and Horace's praise for it as both teaching and pleasing; see Henke, *Performance and Literature*, 182n19.

28. These career details are from *Corrispondenze*, 1:445.

29. Flaminio Scala, *Il postumio: Comedia del signor I. S. posta in luce da F. S. detto Flavio, Comico Acceso* (Lyon: Appresso Jacomo Roussin, 1601). The mysterious "Signor I. S." is now thought to refer to Scala; they are the initials of his father's name, Iacomo Scala.

30. Scala's performance had offended the Cardinal to the point where the Cardinal felt "il maggior disgusto che possa darmi huomo della sua conditione" (the greatest disgust that a man of Scala's low rank could give him). See Henke, *Performance and Literature*, 183. The power of the Cardinal to legislate against commedia performances in Mantua reveals their opposition to the theater and their frequent interference.

31. Marchese di Castiglione di Val d'Orcia and Bolognese senator, an important patron.

writing the skills of a warrior, ruler, and lover, while his close friend Francesco Andreini lauds his exceptional powers of invention.[32]

The Theater of Tales contains scenarios of forty comedies and ten mixed-genre pieces, giving for each an outline of the dramatic action on the basis of which a performer could reenact the performance, or a reader imagine it. To claim authorship and preemptively protect his creations from being performed by others without acknowledgment, Scala put his stamp on them by including expository explanations that fill in background details, and by this expansion brought the scenarios closer to dramatic literature.[33] Groundbreaking as the only collection of scenarios to be edited and put into print by an author who was also an actor and impresario, it remains a foundational document that establishes the dramatic range and performative genius of the commedia dell'arte,[34] providing its readers with models for creating theater spectacles featuring characters from the different classes and regions of contemporary Italian society,[35] and dealing with the vagaries of Love as a never-ending game.[36] Imitating Boccaccio's division of

32. "Del Signor Ercole Marliani to Flaminio Scala"; "Di Francesco Andreini, Capitano Spavento." Scala, *Il teatro delle favole rappresentative*, ed. Marotti, 11, 12.

33. Marotti discusses several of these ideas and makes a comparison between Scala's "theatre of the knowable" offering us a universe of possible theater pieces with Giulio Camillo's "universe of the knowable" in his *Teatro della memoria*; see Marotti, "Introduzione" to *Teatro delle favole*, xlvi–liii. Although the great celebrity Camillo (1480–1544) belonged to an earlier generation, his vast influence continued to be felt and put into practice by visionaries like Scala whose goal was to use the art of memory to create a shared cultural heritage.

34. Scala might be considered to be ahead of his times in opting for print while most scenarios still circulated in oral and written forms, implying that he was aware that print was probably more efficient in spreading ideas and offering techniques that aided collective memory. Lisa Gitelman notes that we need to look for "meanings that arise, shift, and persist, according to the uses that media, emergent, dominant and residual familiarly have." See Gitelman, *Paper Knowledge: Toward a Media History of Documents* (Durham, NC: Duke University Press, 2014), 9.

35. In his defense of the theater, Giovan Battista Andreini described it as a mirror in which the public was offered the privilege of seeing human actions from a wise, informed perspective that offers remedies for many adverse conditions. See the excerpt from Giovan Battista Andreini, *La ferza contra l'accuse date alla commedia* (Paris: Nicolas Callemont, 1625), in Ferruccio Marotti and Giovanna Romei, eds., *La commedia dell'arte e la società barocca*, Vol. 2: *La professione del teatro* (Rome: Bulzoni, 1991), 489–534, at 490.

36. Scala mentioned a second volume that never materialized which would have brought the scenarios up to Boccaccio's one hundred. Lina Bolzoni proposes that Camillo's method of "making knowledge visible" through "the science of images" required the acquisition of a great deal of information on different topics that could be organized and remembered through certain techniques which often included memory games. Games became a big part of sixteenth-century culture, and such works as Baldassare Castiglione's *Book of the Courtier*, Pietro Bembo's *Asolani*, and Giovanni Boccaccio's *Decameron* are all examples of narratives that unpack literary and cultural conceits in the form of games. See Lina Bolzoni, *The Gallery of Memory: Literary and Iconographic Models in the Age of the Printing Press*, trans. Jeremy Parzen (Toronto: University of Toronto Press, 2001), xiv–xxi.

the one hundred tales of the *Decameron* into ten chapters, signifying the ten days over which the stories are told, Scala assigns a day to each scenario.

Not only did Scala write *Theater of Tales* to capture the range of the commedia dell'arte's repertoire, he also wanted his audiences to reimagine the gestures and dialogue used by the actors who had become known to a broad general public. Since troupe members had improvised their roles in highly individualized ways, shading them differently each time, Scala deliberately omitted providing written versions of their widely varying regional languages and dialects on paper. In his preface, he explained, saying that since language was not his specialty, he would leave it up to the experts.[37] Francesco Andreini's second preface explains more fully that Scala certainly could have supplied the words verbatim, but had decided that since the published scenarios were a brand-new product, he chose to "leave the task of adding the words to all the fine talents who were born with just such skill in language."[38] While this remark implies that both dilettantes and professionals who wanted to perform the scenarios were free to improvise their own dialogue, it also recognized that performers might make the texts their own through spontaneous gestures and speech. Such sentiments echo the belief of Giulio Camillo, an early theorist of the dramatic art, in the alchemic change that occurs when actions and words unite to make hidden meanings visible.[39]

Scala's artful method here is to write down his scenarios from the past quarter-century using an imaginary cast of famous players that he based on the greatest contemporary performers he had known. His goal in doing so was to celebrate their illustrious careers and preserve their particular acting skills in the memories of their audiences across Italy and Europe who had seen them perform their highly individualized characters, each represented by a distinctive mask. These include (Giulio Pasquato of Padua) who played Pantalone: (Ludovico da Bologna), Dottore Graziano; (Simone da Bologna), the Zanni; (Gabrielle da Bologna), Francatrippa; (Giovanni Pellesini), Pedrolino; (Orazio de' Nobili), Orazio; (Silvia Roncagli from Bergamo), Franceschina; (Isabella Andreini of Padua), Isabella, Prima Innamorata, and (Francesco Andreini), Capitano Spavento. To these famous Gelosi players, Scala added (Tristano Martinelli), who played Arlecchino, but was not listed as a Gelosi member.[40] The prominence in the cast lists of most of the scenarios of performers who were members of the Gelosi company—including the power couple, Isabella and Francesco Andreini—has led

37. "Original Prefaces to the 1611 Volume," in Andrews, *Thirty Scenarios*, 1.

38. Andrews, *Thirty Scenarios*, 1–2.

39. See Tamburini, *Culture ermetiche*, 208.

40. Francesco Andreini included this list of his illustrious company in *Ragionamento 14*, in *Le bravure del Capitano Spavento* (Venice: Giacomo Antonio Somasco, 1607); in Kenneth Richards and Laura Richards, *The Commedia dell'Arte: A Documentary History* (Oxford: Blackwell, 1990), 72. Andrews includes a discussion of the standard roles and their models in *Thirty Scenarios*, xix–xxxii.

to persistent rumors that Scala performed with the Gelosi. Capitano Spavento, made famous by Francesco, appears in all but four of the comic scenarios in the collection,[41] and Isabella, the ruling prima donna, appears in a wide range of roles, including the cross-dressed heroine. For several centuries afterwards, it was argued that Scala must have been a Gelosi member because of his close friendship with the Andreinis who were co-directors of the company from 1576 until it disbanded in 1604 on Isabella's tragic early death in Lyon.[42] However, although Scala included his Flavio mask as one of the male lovers in his collection, it seems unlikely that he ever performed with the Gelosi.[43]

The only significant mention of a Flavio is as the perfidious lover in the Gelosi performance of *La pazzia d'Isabella (The Madness of Isabella)* at the Medici wedding gala of 1589 held to celebrate the marriage of Tuscan Grand Duke Ferdinando I to Cristina di Lorena. Since Scala was the only *innamorato* using the stage name of Flavio, there is a distinct possibility that he performed with Isabella on this special occasion. The famous record of the unforgettable impression that Isabella Andreini made on the audience in her signature mad performance has led to a search for the scenario outlined by Giuseppe Pavoni, the envoy from Bologna, who was in attendance.[44] Although this scenario has never been found, similar ones confirm how familiar Scala was with the trope of madness. His scenario of the same name, "The Madness of Isabella" (*Theater of Tales*, Day 38), is very different from the one performed at the Medici wedding, but shows his facility for conveying madness through impassioned actions and heightened nonsensical speech.[45] This signature representation of madness demonstrates Scala's "poetic furor"[46] and suggests that he may have witnessed Isabella's mad turns in 1589, especially the second one capturing the bizarre range of languages that characterized each of these comic masks:

41. Andrews, *Thirty Scenarios*, xxxii

42. Marotti looks over the tradition that circulated in eighteenth-century theater history accounts but then shows that the archival evidence doesn't confirm Scala's membership in the Gelosi; see Marotti, "Introduzione" to *Teatro delle favole*, xviii–xxxii.

43. Although Scala continued to appear in the lover's role as Flavio well into middle age, he also added in another character role as Claudione, an Italianized Frenchman, who appears in Days 26, 34 and 37, despite the presence of Flavio as well. See Andrews, *Thirty Scenarios*, x.

44. Giuseppe Pavoni, *Diario descritto da Giuseppe Pavoni delle feste celebrate nelle solennissime nozze delli Serenissimi sposi il Sig. Don Ferdinando Medici e la Sig. Donna Christiana di Loreno Gran Duchi di Toscana* (Bologna: Giovanni Rossi, 1589).

45. Andrews, "The Madness of Isabella," in *Thirty Scenarios*, 225–38. He includes the Pavoni version for comparison as an appendix to Day 38.

46. The Platonic concept of "divine madness" as the source of poetic inspiration that took artists out of themselves and transmuted them to meld with the Divine was regarded as an alchemic mystery that led to the production of great art. For Isabella's performance, see Anne MacNeil, "The Divine Madness of Isabella Andreini," *Journal of the Royal Music Association* 120 (1995): 195–215.

> She then turned to imitating the speech of all her colleagues in the company, such as Pantalone, Dottor Graziano, Zanni, Pedrolino, Francatrippa, Burattino, Captain Cardone, and Franceschina—all with such natural conviction, and with such senseless utterances, that no tongue can express the power and talent of this lady.[47]

Scala and Venice

If Scala was present at the 1589 wedding gala and performed the role of the lover Flavio, it makes it possible to assume that he was familiar with the Gelosi performances during the 1580s and 90s. While we have scant evidence of his relationship with the Gelosi during those years, it is possible to comment on his life in Venice where he became a longtime resident. He based himself there because it was a cosmopolitan city with a vibrant and diverse culture, resistant to the papal Inquisition that elsewhere curtailed the activities of the professional theater condemned by the post-Tridentine church.[48] In addition to his busy life on the road as an actor and company director, Scala was the proprietor of a perfume shop located on the Rialto.[49] The Rialto was the hub of the mercantile life of the city, where native and foreign merchants mingled easily, and alongside of their commercial activity, exchanged ideas on literary, scientific, religious, and occult topics. Scala's perfume shop provided a place where artists, literati, and alchemists could gather to discuss the structure of the heavens as revealed by the newly-invented telescope, and delve into alchemy and other scientific and occult areas of knowledge. Scala may also have brought aspects of the secret knowledge he pursued there into his theatrical practice.[50] Interested in the complete sensory experience that theater offered, his knowledge of combining various elements to make perfumes and potions, as well

47. Andrews, *Thirty Scenarios*, 237. It is important for our purposes to note how dominant the zanni and related comic marks are here, including the maidservant Franceschina. Several of these masks are noted as performers involved with the Academy of the Blenio Valley (Accademia del Val di Blenio.) Since there is no direct evidence to tie Scala to the Academy of the Blenio Valley, this line of inquiry has not been pursued except for one further reference; see *The Fake Husband*, note 10.

48. In Venice such important political reformers as Paolo Sarpi were engaged in a long fight to keep Venice independent and powerful enough to resist interference from Rome. Sarpi was connected with Scala's mentor Don Giovanni de' Medici through the War of Gradisca, 1615–1617. For Sarpi, see David Wootton, *Paolo Sarpi: Between Renaissance and Enlightenment* (Cambridge: Cambridge University Press, 1983).

49. The first mention of the perfume shop occurs in a letter written in November 1615, but he may have owned it for some time before; see *Corrispondenze*, 1:454–56.

50. Landolfi mentions how knowing "secrets" dealing with the preparation of soaps, perfumes, etc., were foundational to Scala's profession, as is evident from a famous treatise published in Venice in 1555: Giovanventura Rosetti, *I notandissimi secreti de l'arte profumatoria, a fare ogli, acque, paste, balle, moscardini, uccelletti, paternostri, e tutta l'arte intiera* (Venice: per Francesco Rampazetto, 1555). See *Corrispondenze*, 1:582n1; letter 106, May 9, 1624.

as his search for ways to transmute metals into gold, fed into creating transformative theatrical experiences through living images.[51]

The likelihood that Scala's shop functioned as an academy of sorts is borne out by the insignia "Fame" that was hung over the door, as Francesco Andreini has the character Capitano Spavento describe it to Trapola.[52] Praising Scala as a beloved citizen of Venice, famous for his encyclopedic *Theater of Tales*, he remarks that Scala kept his shop open at all times for his friends. The Fame insignia probably closely resembled the image of fame as a goddess in flowing robes triumphantly sounding a trumpet who appears flanking one side of Count Riario's coat of arms on the frontispiece to the *Theater of Tales*.[53] This icon recalls Camillo, who had encouraged artists and poets to achieve eternal fame by mastering the art of eloquence, an achievement he believed restored mankind to its original divine nature.[54] A short-lived but vitally important Venetian Academy of Fame (1557–1561), dedicated to collecting and spreading knowledge for the benefit of mankind, had used as an emblem a similar winged goddess, her feet resting on a globe as she raises a trumpet in one hand and in the other holds a banner with the motto, "I fly to Heaven that I may rest with God."[55] Scala's choice of the Fame insignia to describe his own endeavors appears to have been a conscious decision connected to his belief in theater as high art.

Scala's Relationship with Don Giovanni de' Medici and the Confidenti

Scala's pursuit of fame was greatly aided when he came under the protection of Don Giovanni de' Medici (1537–1621) whose service he entered in 1615 as the

51. Scala's two professions were linked closely. As the Platonic philosopher Marsilio Ficino had noted, images and perfumes both influenced man's spirit, making it more receptive to receiving celestial knowledge; see Ficino, *Sulla vita*, ed. and trans. Alessandra Tarabochia Canavero (Milan: Rusconi, 1995), 266 (1.111, 20), quoted by Tamburini, *Culture ermetiche*, 204n72.

52. Francesco Andreini, *Le bravure del Capitano Spavento: Divise in molti ragionamenti in forma del dialogo* (1618); ed. by Roberto Tessari (Pisa: Giardini, 1987), 328–29. Marotti includes the quote in "Introduzione" to *Teatro delle favole*, xliv. The *Bravure* are a collection of fanciful dialogues covering a range of topics full of bizarre rhetorical twists, easily adaptable to the stage featuring the braggart Capitano.

53. On the other side of the coat of arms, there is a woman in classical Roman armor holding a crown of laurel to represent Virtue allied to Wisdom. See Tamburini, *Culture ermetiche*, 203.

54. Camillo depicted "good fame" as a woman sounding a trumpet and "bad fame" as a woman trying to blow into a horn made of broken strips of leather; see Lina Bolzoni, ed., *Il teatro della memoria: Studi su Giulio Camillo* (Padua: Liviana, 1984), 129. Isabella Andreini's depiction of herself as the goddess Fama on her memorial coin shows her blowing the "good fame" trumpet and holding the "bad fame" idle in her other hand.

55. "I fly to Heaven that I may rest with God," captures Camillo's belief that man could repair his relationship to God by learning how to use "the word" perfectly through the study of rhetoric and the pursuit of knowledge and wisdom. For the history and importance of the Academy as a model for others, see Bolzoni, *Gallery of Memory*, 3–22, with a reprint of the device at 4.

capocomico of the company of the Confidenti. Over the years until Don Giovanni's death in 1621, they developed a very close relationship and together shaped the Confidenti into a modern company. Their extensive correspondence of over one hundred letters provides a record of Scala's theatrical knowledge and his seasoned skills employed in keeping a troupe of actors on track as they endured all the complications of touring.

The important relationship between Scala and Don Giovanni as it evolved over the years is traced by Siro Ferrone, who shows how the prince applied his extensive knowledge of the battlefield to shape the troupe to behave as a well-disciplined ensemble.[56] Don Giovanni, a dashing entrepreneur, had made his reputation across Italy and abroad as a military leader and engineer, architect, theater scenographer and playwright, bibliophile, astrologer, chemist, and occultist.[57] As an illegitimate son of Cosimo I, grand duke of Tuscany, he was often on the periphery of Florentine inner court circles, acting as their representative rather than as a major player. Staying in the good graces of the archducal court proved more difficult, especially after he chose as his mistress the notorious Livia Vernazza, whom the Florentines detested.[58] He took on the prestigious position of commander-in-chief of the Venetian forces in 1610 and led them in battle in Friuli from 1616 until January 1618, when ill-health forced him to resign.[59] In Venice, both he and Vernazza were treated with the respect and reverence he desired and he was able to pursue his cabalistic and alchemical interests freely.[60] When he appointed the well-known and highly respected sixty-three-year-old Scala to be the company director of the Confidenti troupe, he knew that Scala was a perfect choice to help boost his reputation as patron of a premier company. In addition, he and Scala shared an interest in the pursuit of occult knowledge and alchemical experimentation, which Scala carried on in his shop with the assistance of his cadre of young assistants.[61]

Scala's extensive correspondence during these years with Don Giovanni, relating to the operation of the Confidenti but also including other aspects of

56. Ferrone, "Don Giovanni impresario," 143–99.

57. See Domenica Landolfi, "Don Giovanni de' Medici: 'Principe intendentissimo in varie scienze,'" *Studi secenteschi* 29 (1988): 125–62; also Brendan Dooley "Narrazione e verità: Don Giovanni de' Medici e Galileo," *Bruniana & Campanelliana*, 14, no. 2 (2008): 389–403.

58. For a fascinating account of their relationship, see Brendan Dooley, *A Mattress Maker's Daughter: The Renaissance Romance of Don Giovanni de' Medici and Livia Vernazza* (Cambridge, MA: Harvard University Press, 2014).

59. Dooley, *A Mattress Maker's Daughter*, 140–43.

60. Ferrone, "Don Giovanni impresario," 149.

61. Ferrone, "Don Giovanni impresario," 149nn26, 27. Scala also shared his interest in studying the stars using the newly developed telescope which he is eager to acquire. He mentions wanting to see the four famous satellites of Jupiter discovered by Galileo in January, 1610. See *Corrispondenze*, 1:511–12; letter 44. Scala reveals his obsession with telescopes in letters 46, 47, 48, 49, and 51.

their relationship, is deeply informative. A review of some key events can provide insight into Scala's theatrical practice over this time. The mature Scala shows himself to be deferential and gracious, frequently looking after Vernazza in the prince's absence and taking care of their lodgings and other personal matters.[62] Contributing to the history of the company, Scala provides a running account of the turbulent life on the road as they crisscrossed Italy to perform in such places as Genoa, Lucca, Milan, Bologna, Padua, Florence, Mantua, and, of course, Venice itself, to meet the demands of different patrons. Required to keep the highly volatile company members satisfied enough to not be tempted away by other offers, Scala worked tirelessly to balance the warring factions. In this endeavor, he served as Don Giovanni's lieutenant, working under him and his Florentine majordomo Cosimo Baroncelli, while always keeping Don Giovanni's relationship with the troupe members foremost. Their first task was to break up the ruling family dynasties of performers who attempted to manipulate the running of the company for their own ends, as well as disciplining star performers who had no qualms about breaking their contracts.

In addition, Scala's letters catalogued the ongoing feuds between the prima donnas and their families and followers. First, there was the rise of younger, prettier Lavinia (Maria Dorotea Antonazzioni) who took over the coveted *Madness* performance from her sister-in-law Valeria (Salomè Antonazzoni), who had reluctantly given it up as Don Giovanni had requested. Lavinia's great success in *The Madness* sparked the jealousy of Valeria and her husband who were being edged out, but within two years Lavinia faced a new rival in the form of the multitalented Celia (Maria Mallone).[63]

Scala's reports to Don Giovanni revealed the depths of his anger as he described the "whorish" behavior of Celia, and her "infamous" mother Virginia and "vituperous" brother Andrea. Since they were in Florence at the time, and

62. Don Giovanni's relationship with Scala, in the light of their status difference, may not have been one of complete respect. Benedetto Blanis, the great Jewish scholar, who was an intimate of Don Giovanni, describes an incident where Giovanni told him to chide Livia about being seen in public taking a gondola ride with a *buffone* such as Scala. Apparently, she burst into laughter when she heard the message. It is also true that such a comment may have merely been pointing out that Giovanni was well aware that he was known to keep a ménage which included "actors, whores and Jews" as part of his rebellious stance; see Edward Goldberg, *Jews and Magic in Medici Florence: The Secret World of Benedetto Blanis* (Toronto: University of Toronto Press, 2011), 162, citing Archivio di Stato di Firenze: Mediceo del Principato 5161, fols. 74v–75r.

63. The versatile Celia would eventually dominate as the prima donna because not only was she able to perform in any genre required, but she was also equally gifted as a performer of premeditated or improvised materials, so that she was able to perform new works immediately, whereas Lavinia and the other women would need a much longer time to prepare; see *Corrispondenze*, 1:503n1. Her increasing dominance as prima donna is a sign that premeditated scripts were becoming more popular than improvised scripts.

Scala's *The Fake Husband* was being launched to impress the court for both his benefit and Don Giovanni's, Celia's riotous actions threatened to discredit them all.[64] Scala requested that Don Giovanni ban Celia and her family from the stage, citing how Celia had used a gang of thugs to break up Lavinia's performance of *The Madness* to protest that she had not been allowed to do one herself.[65] Don Giovanni fully supported Scala, agreeing to announce his condemnation of Celia by publicly sharing his letter with the whole company. Unfortunately, the battles continued, with a fistfight on stage and injuries sustained on both sides. As his next letter shows, Celia's disruptive behavior was still infuriating him, although he blamed the riots on her mother's pandering to her daughter's male admirers, allowing them to mob her on stage. Over the course of this saga, Scala shows his dismay when the troupe, loyal to Lavinia, finds itself at odds with the city that was showering gifts on Celia.

Celia's scandalous behavior remained Scala's foremost concern since it affected the Confidenti's professional reputation. The battle lines hardened when Cardinal Carlo de' Medici, Don Giovanni's nephew, chose to side with Celia, supporting her in a positive letter. Scala described a scene on what is likely the Baldracca stage,[66] claiming it had been turned into the equivalent of a brothel when Celia's many lovers stormed the stage because they felt entitled to free admission, having spent their money on her while gambling at *riffe*.[67] Celia continued to play her lovers off against each other, and although the rest of the company opposed her, she still had the favor of the people of nearby Lucca.

Scala's admission that he felt "like Moses leading the Israelites out of captivity" as he struggled to keep the troupe together shows the depth of his

64. *The Fake Husband* is mentioned several times during these months in Florence and its apparent success with the archducal court seems to be in sharp contrast to the reaction caused by the scandalous behaviour of Celia. The play's production record is treated in the next section of this Introduction.

65. Don Giovanni's desire to ensure that the Confidenti were successful with the grand-ducal court was part of his plan to win recognition for patronizing a commedia dell'arte troupe, who because of their appeal to all classes, were highly sought after in aristocratic circles; see *Corrispondenze*, 1:501–3; letter 39, October 13, 1618.

66. *Corrispondenze*, 1:491; letter 31, August 12, 1618. The evidence that they were performing in the Baldracca is attested to by Scala talking about leaving for Florence to take up tenancy in the Baldracca which was the theater space traditionally rented to visiting commedia dell'arte troupes. The Baldracca or Stanzone delle Commedia (The Large Room for Comedies), built in 1576, was connected to the Uffizi. The Grand Duke and his retinue could enter unseen and watch the shows in a special box seat with grating in front.

67. *Riffe*, a kind of lottery that required its patrons to submit jewels and other valuables for betting purposes, is referred to as being played for several hours by Celia's admirers although it was against company rules. She insisted she needed the money, even at the expense of having her admirers get into serious fights. See *Corrispondenze*, 1:507 and note 5; letter 42, November 3, 1618.

frustration.[68] At this point, Don Giovanni took charge, writing a scathing letter to Celia in which he presented several harsh truths about her behavior and that of her infamous mother and brother.[69] After this standoff, Celia started to modify her behavior, slowly breaking with her family and committing to work with the ensemble. Shortly after, when Celia was being hissed off the stage, Scala defended her to the audience, an act that gained her undying affection.[70]

The combined efforts of Scala and Don Giovanni to bring Celia into line were part of a strategy to make the company self-governing and competitive with other great companies, such as the Fedeli, which had been founded by Giovan Battista Andreini, son of Isabella and Francesco.[71] Don Giovanni was committed to promoting the Confidenti so as to enhance his status as a Medici prince, often insisting on personally making arrangements with other rulers, as he did with the duke of Mantua who had tried to split up the company to take some of them on an all-star trip to France. Having built a highly disciplined professional company, as Don Giovanni wrote to the Mantuan secretary Ercole Marliani shortly before Don Giovanni's death, he could not consent to breaking up the company. Company members had come to him four times to insist that they not be disbanded, he wrote, pointing to the "manifest disaster that would befall them," since they recognized how much money they had made in the past year, money that Don Giovanni could not have given them. He explained that, unlike celebrity players who thought only of their own power and control, company members who had formed a fraternal association needed to stay together in order to function. This impassioned letter urged that the Confidenti be allowed to keep performing at the very successful level they had attained, noting that their success arose from their disciplined ensemble acting, with each member working to meet artistic requirements of the performance instead of showcasing their individual talents.[72]

Scala had played a key role in creating this disciplined and unified company, supervising them on the road for as much time as he could spare from his perfume shop. When the troupe was on the eve of leaving for Mantua after the hectic months in Florence, Scala described the ordeal as very troublesome since being in "perpetual motion" had almost "driven him crazy." He refers to this "perpetual

68. *Corrispondenze,* 1:510; letter 43, November 10, 1618.

69. *Corrispondenze,* 1:511–12; letter 44, November 17, 1618.

70. *Corrispondenze,* 1:517n4; letter 48, December 13, 1618. Scala's actual words (loosely translated) used to quell the crowd was to beg them, to excuse what the dog had done out of love for the master, suggesting that he was not fooled by Celia, but had learned to tolerate her.

71. Between May and August of 1619, in letters 66, 68, 73, 74, 75, and 77, Celia starts to work with the other women and sends homage to Don Giovanni; see *Corrispondenze,* 1:537–53.

72. For an English translation, see "A Patron's Difficulties with a Troupe, 1620," Letter from Don Giovanni de' Medici to Ercole Marliani, March 21, 1620, in Richards and Richards, *Commedia dell'Arte,* 76–79.

motion" in the two letters that follow, using it with multiple meanings all related to the functioning of his theater troupe. On one level, he is referencing their continuous travel from city to city, which in this letter seems to be a terrible chore,[73] but in the next, he is worried about how to keep the "perpetual motion" going when their contract runs out and they have to leave a city, in this case, Florence, at the height of their popularity.[74] In the same letter, Scala talks about another threat to maintaining forward momentum in the company when volatile star players like Arlecchino tried to entice Fulvio and Scappino away to serve the French court. Scala's worries about troupe members breaking up the company underlines how much importance he accorded to the laws of motion and gravitation, referencing the discoveries of Galileo and others. In the last letter citing "perpetual motion," Scala uses the term to apply to the feelings of the troupe following a poorly received performance, mitigated only by the largely enthusiastic support of the Mantuans.[75]

While Scala's amicable relationship with his patron can be contrasted with his great frustrations with his company, he was instrumental nonetheless in disciplining them to work as an ensemble. Sadly, the great success of the Confidenti was not sufficient to withstand the blow of Don Giovanni's death from throat cancer at Murano on July 19, 1621. After they disbanded, Scala, who had returned to his shop in Venice, scrambled to find a new patron, and in 1624 succeeded in getting an appointment as official perfumer to the Mantuan court. The aging Scala died just after moving back to Mantua on December 9, 1624. His death announcement read, "S. Flavio profumiere di S.A. Serenissima," an indication that he saw his theatrical and alchemical careers as complementary, allowing him to substitute one title for the other.[76]

The Fake Husband: *Publication, Production History, Plot, and Prologues*

Working hand in hand with Scala to shape the Confidenti into an outstanding theater company, Don Giovanni also encouraged Scala to enhance his reputation

73. *Corrispondenze*, 1:518n2; letter 49, December 22, 1618.

74. *Corrispondenze*, 1:518–19; letter 50, January 10, 1619.

75. Landolfi suggests that Scala is emphasizing the importance of "*moto*" to the actors' very existence as theater artists; see *Corrispondenze*, 1:521n4; letter 51, January 16, 1619. This echoes the importance of capturing "*moto*" that Lomazzo had stressed as the mark of the true artist. As an artistic term "*moto*" has a larger meaning than simply "motion." Its meaning it best conveyed as "movement" of the body and soul or "figurative expression." See Jean Julia Chai, "Introduction" to Giovanni Paolo Lomazzo, *The Idea of the Temple of Painting*, ed. and trans. Jean Julia Chai (University Park: Pennsylvania State University Press, 2013), 1–41, at 3.

76. "Signor Scala, perfumer to His Most Serene Highness," in Marotti, "Introduzione" to *Teatro della favole*, xlvii.

by catering to a sophisticated academic and courtly audience. He hoped, as well, that Scala's success in Florence could help to pave the way for his return to the court with Vernazza.[77] Scala's own reputation, meanwhile, firmly established with his 1611 publication, was enriched by his ongoing collaboration with his lifelong friend and fellow actor, Francesco Andreini. In 1617, Scala sponsored the publication of Isabella Andreini's *Fragmenti di alcune scritture (Miscellaneous Writings)*, which included models of lovers' dialogues, a work prepared for publication by Francesco Andreini to enhance her literary reputation and preserve her fame and that of the commedia dell'arte.[78] Early in 1618, Francesco brought out the second part of the *Bravure del Capitano Spavento*, which contains the tribute to Scala's "Fame."[79] Dedicated to Don Giovanni, it puts Andreini into their distinguished circle.

The publication of *The Fake Husband* in September 1618 was intended to establish that the commedia dell'arte could acquire legitimacy as a dramatic form by impressing the literati at the Florentine court where Scala's Confidenti were then performing. Earlier, in May 1618, Scala had discussed with Don Giovanni the possibility of dedicating the work to the latter's eccentric young nephew Cardinal Carlo de' Medici (1596–1666), who was well-known for his interest in the theater scene.[80] The choice of Carlo as dedicatee was likely deliberate, given Don Giovanni's affection for his nephew and his power to influence Scala's choice. Carlo's interest in the commedia dell'arte is evidenced by his rental of Don Giovanni's private box in the Baldracca from 1617 to at least the end of 1618.[81] His association with Don Giovanni, furthermore, is seen in his imitation of the latter's unconventional practices, such as his use of a secret theater box that allowed him to attend commedia dell'arte performances unseen by the public. It was through Don Giovanni's influence that Carlo, intended for the religious life, was encouraged to study Hebrew under Benedetto Blanis, the outstanding Jewish scholar

77. Don Giovanni married Vernazza hours before the birth in August of their only heir, Giovanni Francesco Maria. See Goldberg, *Jews and Magic*, 215–16, for the hostility felt toward her by members of the Florentine court and their boycott of Vernazza and Don Giovanni.

78. *Fragmenti di alcune scritture della signora Isabella Andreini Comica Gelosa, e academica intent; Raccolti da Francesco Andreini Comico Geloso, detto il Capitano Spavento, e dati in luce da Flamminio Scala Comico, e da lui dedicati all'illustrissimo Sig. Filippo Capponi* (Venice: Gio. Battista Combi, 1617). In his dedication, Scala describes Filippo, from the famous Capponi banking family, as having always been a generous benefactor and protector of the commedia dell'arte.

79. *Le bravure del Capitano Spavento: Divise in molti ragionamenti in forma del dialogo* (Venice: Somasco, 1618).

80. *Corrispondenze*, 1:486–87; letter 27, May 23, 1618.

81. Anna Maria Evangelista, "Il teatro dei comici dell'arte a Firenze: Ricognizione dello 'Stanzone delle Commedie' detto di Baldracca," *Biblioteca teatrale* 9, nos. 23–24 (1979):70–86.

with whom Don Giovanni had studied the occult and the Kabbalah.[82] Despite his religious responsibilities, Carlo took a lively interest in Don Giovanni's alchemical pursuits, even taking charge of Giovanni's laboratory in Florence where experiments were carried out.[83] Don Giovanni probably supported the choice of Carlo as the dedicatee of *The Fake Husband* in the hope that his nephew might help him stage a return to Florence with Vernazza. It is even possible that Don Giovanni himself wrote the dedicatory sonnet in Carlo's praise and passed it off as Scala's.[84]

For his part, Scala hoped that the publication of *The Fake Husband* might win him a court appointment in Florence.[85] On September 15, 1618, he was delighted by the arrival of copies of the play that were then delivered to the Cardinal.[86] Despite the problems caused by Celia and her family, the Confidenti troupe was enthusiastically received in Florence. Even the Grand Duke Cosimo II praised them highly and had them perform at the Pitti Palace.[87] *The Fake Husband* seems to have been associated with the Confidenti's repertoire, along with Don Giovanni's new tragedy, and Ridolfi's prologue.[88] If it was performed, however, the cast members might have been from the Incostanti Academy, since the Confidenti troupe members would not have needed the full script.[89] Clearly,

82. Edward Goldberg, in *Jews and Magic*, 19–21, discusses the close relationship of Don Giovanni with Benedetto Blanis, explaining the importance of Hebrew to an understanding of kabbalistic texts because of the numerical equivalents of Hebrew letters had been used to create numerological tables that revealed the hidden meanings of words and names in the cosmic scheme. Although Carlo never did take up Hebrew, he was later called upon to defend Blanis on different occasions against accusations of treachery and sorcery for which he was imprisoned.

83. Goldberg, *Jews and Magic*, 128–32.

84. Ferrone, in "Don Giovanni impresario," 180, suggests that Don Giovanni not only looked after the publishing but may well have composed the opening sonnet to Cardinal Carlo.

85. Scala mentioned his hope that when his comedy arrives, it would give him some leverage with Grand Duke Cosimo II. He hoped to be able to compete with Iacopo Cicognini whose group of young aristocratic amateurs from the Academy of the Incostanti had been performing scripts for him; see *Corrispondenze*, 1:493; letter 33, August 25, 1618. Baroncelli also wrote to Don Giovanni de' Medici the same day mentioning Scala's desire to get a permanent post in Florence; *Corrispondenze*, 1:494n6.

86. *Corrispondenze*, 1:498–99; letter 36, September 15, 1618. It is not clear whether Scala's reference to comedies in the plural refers to multiple copies of his play or to other works he had mentioned in an earlier letter which included a tragedy by Don Giovanni and a prologue of Atanasio Ridolfi's which he says he would like to see performed together; see *Corrispondenze*, 1:494–95; letter 34, September 1, 1618. Atanasio Ridolfi (c.1596–1655), a Florentine noble, was Don Giovanni's secretary and later stayed in Medici service.

87. *Corrispondenze*, 1:506; letter 41, October 27, 1618. Scala bragged that the Confidenti were more successful than any other company with which he had worked.

88. *Corrispondenze*, 1:494; letter 34, September 1, 1618. Scala writes about wanting them to be performed together.

89. We do know that Scala's reputation was greatly enhanced among the Florentine literati by having a fully scripted play, but there is no sure evidence who was performing it since none of the characters,

The Fake Husband circulated amongst the amateur court players and literati, and its success enhanced the reputation of Scala and the Confidenti who had a wide-ranging repertoire, including performances of *Aminta*.[90]

Such was the Confidenti's success in Florence during their extended run from August to the end of December 1618 that Scala himself lavished praise on the company, stating that they were so beloved that everyone from the nobles to the general public was devastated when they left.[91] When the troupe arrived in Mantua for carnival in January, they received an enthusiastic reception by the duke and duchess who had already seen them in Florence. Scala knew how much Don Giovanni valued this success, which automatically accrued to him.[92] Don Giovanni prided himself on having a famous commedia dell'arte company under his patronage at a time when the Florentine Grand Duchy did not have a troupe of its own. But not even this achievement was sufficient to restore him to the favor he had lost owing to his notorious consort.

The great prestige that the best commedia dell'arte troupes were held in by the courts stemmed not only from their artistry but also because they represented diverse social classes through their distinctive character masks and dialects modeled on specific regions. The nobility were aware of the need to pay attention to public opinion in an age when masses of impoverished citizens displaced by war, famine, and driven from the countryside were a force to be reckoned with in the cities.[93] The fact that all social types speaking in a range of regional languages and rustic dialects were represented in the improvised "comedy of the *zannis*" attracted the courtier audience, as did the bawdy humor and physical comedy that accompanied the representation of the servant and nouveau riche classes.

except for Scala as Flavio, could be tied directly to the Confidenti troupe. *The Fake Husband* is mentioned in several letters in the *Corrispondenze*: (27, 33, 34, 35, 36, and 37), but not much is said about performances.

90. *Corrispondenze*, 1:506; letter 41, October 27, 1618. Scala mentions getting Cardinal Carlo to attend a performance of *Aminta*.

91. *Corrispondenze*, 1:518–19; letter 50, January 10, 1619.

92. *Corrispondenze*, 1:507–8; letter 42, November 3, 1618. Scala describes to Don Giovanni the delight expressed by the visiting duke and duchess of Mantua for the performances of the Confidenti they had attended in Florence, at which Cosimo II and the Grand Duchess Maria Maddalena had been present. The duke of Mantua Ferdinando Gonzaga, who was hosting the Confidenti for Carnival, invited Don Giovanni to attend part of the festivities. However, there was considerable opposition to Vernazza's presence, especially from the grand duchess but also from Cosimo himself who warned his sister, the duchess of Mantua, about her bad reputation.

93. Cultural theorist José Antonio Maravell describes how all levels of culture grew in the seventeenth century, requiring the upper classes to pay more attention to middle and mass culture. The opinions of the common people became conflated with the concept of "taste" (*gusto*) which then became normative and hence something that the ruling classes felt the need to control. See Maravell, *Culture of the Baroque: Analysis of a Historical Structure*, trans. Terry Cochran (Minneapolis: University of Minnesota Press, 1986), 100–102.

While showing their apparent solidarity with the common folk, the aristocracy could enjoy their crude sexual antics while at the same time maintaining their sense of superiority, since such behavior usually characterized the lower-class characters in contrast to the *innamorati*'s refined displays of Neoplatonic love. The commedia dell'arte allowed the courts to seem to care about the body politic while it enabled the ruling classes to monitor public morality and social unrest.[94] So as not to offend these elite patrons, the performers could tone down their subversive social commentary when they presented at court. In Florence, as in many other cities, the grand-ducal family had a longstanding and enthusiastic relationship with commedia dell'arte performers, frequently attending their plays in the Stanzone (great hall) in the Uffizi, hidden from the vulgar masses behind their private screens. Cosimo II, an avid fan, followed his ancestors' habit by frequently attending commedia performances when the companies were contracted, particularly in the autumn season.[95]

The record of Scala's experiences in capably directing the Confidenti under the patronage of Don Giovanni and in enhancing his literary reputation by publishing his successful *Fake Husband*, provides us, according to Ferrone,[96] with evidence of the process that the commedia dell'arte was undergoing as it transitioned from improvised performances to enacting scripts requiring full memorization. Enjoying a moment of economic stability, evidently, the companies of the commedia dell'arte no longer needed to be ready to perform a varied repertoire on short notice and with minimal rehearsal time. *The Fake Husband*, along with other full scripts derived from commedia dell'arte performances, were intended for dissemination in courtly circles to wealthy collectors and theater dilettantes who wished to intermix court entertainment and popular theater. Scala sought to fulfill the demands of educated pan-Italian readers for a completed work in printed form, which would plainly establish the author's aesthetic preferences, in contrast to the incomplete and unstable messages conveyed by a performance or scenario.

The Relationship of the Play to the Scenario

Scala wanted *The Fake Husband* to be read as a finished dramatic product that possessed its own literary merit. At the same time, he made it clear to his readers

94. See Maravell, *Culture of the Baroque*, 132–43, for analysis of the important role that theater played in Spain and Italy in shaping baroque values under the guise of allowing certain excesses.

95. Domenica Landolfi mentions that the Medicean court began to hire young dilettante performers who could improvise commedia dell'arte scripts all year round to make up for the limited autumn season when the professional troupes were available for hire. She also notes that Don Giovanni had engaged such dilettante performers at his Florentine palace for private performances as early as 1611. See Landolfi, "Su un teatrino mediceo e sull'Accademia degli Incostanti a Firenze nel primo Seicento," *Teatro e storia* 6, no. 1 (1991), 68–69. It is significant that these dilettantes were most comfortable when they had access to full scripts from which they could turn back to partially improvised performances.

96. Ferrone, "Don Giovanni impresario," 180–83.

that the play was a scripted version of the scenario *The Husband* that had preceded it, even insisting that the scenario was probably superior to the play. Since the scenario version was in print, and was frequently performed, he could expect his readers to make their own comparisons if they so wished. Modern studies by Tim Fitzpatrick[97] and, more recently, by Richard Andrews,[98] have shown that the scenario and the play are very closely connected. They demonstrate that the playmaking processes used to develop the scenario's basic plotline involved input from all the actors, who built the scene-by-scene action and supplied the physical gestures and verbal discourse individuating their character masks. In the scripted version, in contrast, it is the playwright who supplies the motivations for the action, and gives all the characters their dialogue in standard Italian, with only a few variations in their speech patterns to denote class and status.

In the scripted play, the number of acts has been extended from three to the more usual five, and the character masks have been renamed or changed. The plotline is basically the same, although the play highlights the brilliant ruse of Brigida's reincarnation as the fake husband Licinio by postponing the revelation of her true identity until the denouement, whereas in the scenario many direct hints are offered early on.[99] Other differences may be noted between the two printed versions, scenario and play. Scala adds, for instance, extra expository notes to the argument of the scenario to explain how Brigida fakes her death, whereas in the full-length play, the back story is revealed as the dramatic action unfolds.[100] In the play, Scala signals the difference between the multiple versions—two printed, one remembered from performance—by including two prologues, one to be read and the other to be recited, to invite his readers to think about how we respond to oral, written, and print media.

Fitzpatrick's detailed analysis, which compares single scenes as they transition from the scenario to the play, demonstrates how Scala expanded them to produce structured combinations of performance units, in accordance with the rules for plot-building in practice at the time.[101] In suggesting the many places where

97. Tim Fitzpatrick, *The Relationship of Oral and Literate Performance Processes in the Commedia dell'Arte: Beyond the Improvisation/Memorisation Divide* (Lewiston, NY: Edwin Mellen Press, 1995), 223–93.

98. Andrews, *Thirty Scenarios*, 48–52.

99. Andrews notes three; *Thirty Scenarios*, 49.

100. Ultimately, the transparency of Licinio's male impersonation would be dependent on the contract made between the actors and the audience. The convention of maintaining her stage presence as the fake husband operates as a cypher, encouraging spectators to look for hidden truths.

101. Fitzpatrick includes two chapters on analyzing the points of convergence between the *Il finto marito* and *Il marito* with the goal of using the playscript to intuit the hypothesized "performance" of the original actors as they developed sequences of speech and action according to the subschemas and schemas notated in the scenario. After looking at how these generate formulaic structures, he then devotes the second chapter to examining ways in which these structures were amplified to move

the action allowed for expansion by the actors as they employed their "bag of tricks," he reveals the art of playmaking that Scala had practiced over the years.[102] While Scala does not remove all traces of the contribution that the characters had originally made to the scenario, he strengthens the role of the mastermind servant Scaramuccia, who also serves as a *capocomico*, giving him playmaking powers that Pedrolino (who had played that role in the original performance) did not have. As will be seen in the notes to the translation in this volume, Scaramuccia signals to the audience that he is driving the action and keeping the characters focused on moving the plot forward. Scaramuccia's control over all the bed tricks, except his own, is given far more emphasis in the play than in the scenario, as all the couples emerging from their bedchambers name him over and over again as the culprit who had tricked them.

Andrews takes Fitzpatrick's research further as he goes beyond speculating on possible points for the insertion of new material and instead shows the many instances where Scala brings scenes alive by using the embodied speech and actions of the character masks drawn from their extensive repertoire. Andrews points out many cases where, in the play, Scala supplies their set speeches to deepen our knowledge of their motivations. Borrowed from the popular stage, these speeches frequently include commentary on the social pretensions and bad behavior of those in power, and so add another dimension to the script. In taking over the authorial task, Scala also adds more cohesion to the plot by using the first scenes to portray Licinio's jealousy as so monstrous that it makes Porzia's betrayal inevitable. The exaggerated jealous husband scene enacted by Licinio and Porzia for Scaramuccia's benefit prepares us for the layers of deception that will have to be dismantled to expose Licinio's male impersonation as a fake and reunite Porzia with her first love, Lepido.

Perhaps the greatest difference between the scenario and the scripted play is that in the latter, all the dialogue has been put into standard Italian, although with several Florentine sayings thrown in for local color. Scala manages to convey class distinctions in Italian dialogue by giving highly ornamented romantic speeches to the elite lovers while assigning cruder language and often blasphemous insults to the exchanges between Scaramuccia and the servants. Here he departs necessarily from the approach taken in *The Theater of Tales*, in the preface to which he states that dialogue should be left to the actors. In so writing, he was defending the scenario as an improvisational art form that expected the players to fulfill the

---

beyond the formulae in inventive ways. See Fitzpatrick, *Relationship of Oral and Literate Performance Processes*, 223–93.

102. This "bag of tricks" refers to the set of flexible tools with which virtuosic performers approach any scene in the scenario: a set of schematizing techniques to deal with the action required, to enable it to be broken down into combinations of different stage-patternings and manageable sequences of action and dialogue. See Fitzpatrick, *Relationship of Oral and Literate Performance Processes*, 293.

aesthetic requirements of the plot by extemporizing the dramatic script collaboratively, and bringing the action to life through individualized vocal expressions and bodily movements.[103] In this way the performance text was brought into existence through the process of spontaneous invention by actors who engaged their audiences by involving them in shaping the action. When he scripts the play, in contrast, Scala approximates with the written word how the actors had developed their characters in performance, without wholly eliminating traces of the original performance that underlay the text.

The plot synopsis that follows will highlight some of the staging tricks Scala uses to make us aware that what we are seeing on stage is constantly being mediated by other characters who provide running commentaries, sometimes from concealed places, or on a split stage where alternative realities clash with one another. Such techniques intensify the stage meanings being created in sensorial ways, directing us to admire the virtuosity of the actors who are often sharing the joke with us, complexities that cannot be captured in the written text.

Plot Synopsis

Act One begins with the clandestine return of the banished young lover Lepido wearing a disguise to avoid being discovered by his father Demetrio. His first encounter with his friend Flavio leads him to explain that he has risked coming back to have one last meeting with his beloved Porzia, who has recently married Licinio, the fake husband impersonated by the presumably dead Brigida.[104] As spectators, we become complicit with Lepido's deception, and share the relief when he reconnects with his old servant Scaramuccia, who steps forward and offers to guide him.

The rest of Act One presents the subplot featuring the classic encounter between the old patriarchs Demetrio and Gervasio, who arrange to marry off to the latter the former's young ward Giulia.[105] Later, when Demetrio delivers the

103. Domenico Pietropaolo notes that in a scenario only the plotline is supplied and the actors have to create the scene-by-scene interactions filling in speeches and dialogue in accordance with the plot, as well as to bring it alive in the all-important gestural dimension both physically and vocally. See Pietropaolo, *Semiotics and Pragmatics of Stage Improvisation* (London: Bloomsbury Academic, 2016), 11.

104. The trope of the lovers who each believe the other has betrayed his or her vows occurs in Girolamo Bargagli's *La Pellegrina* (1579; first performed for the Medici wedding in 1589) and is used in many comedies and scenarios. See Bargagli, *La pellegrina* (Siena: Appresso i Florimi, 1618); modern edition by Florindo Cerrata (Florence: L. S. Olschki, 1971).

105. This echoes the similar plot line that appeared as early as 1531 in *The Deceived (Gl'ingannati)*, collectively authored by the Accademia degli Intronati, where in 1.1, the vecchio Virginio bargains off his daughter to Gherardo without her knowledge. See the English translation of *The Deceived* in *Five Comedies from the Italian Renaissance*, ed. and trans. Laura Giannetti and Guido Ruggiero (Baltimore: Johns Hopkins University Press, 2003), 205–84, at 210–12.

news to a stricken Giulia, the maid Ruchetta listens in and offers a barrage of brash asides expressing her disgust at the callous father. Her outpouring amounts to a fierce manifesto on behalf of women and their right to choose their own partners.[106] Speaking with the cynicism of a maidservant whose low status likely entails her providing sex on demand to her master Demetrio, she debunks the notion that women need to preserve their "honor"—that is, their chastity.[107] Instead, she advocates for sexual pleasure as a right that also belongs to women. Knowing that the best way for Giulia to avoid having to marry Gervasio is to give her "honor" to her young lover Flavio first, she plays matchmaker.

Act Two starts with Scaramuccia's attempts to gain access to Porzia on Lepido's behalf. A fearful Scaramuccia knocks at Porzia's door, then hides when Licinio, her newly espoused fake husband, answers. What follows is a three-way stage conversation, where Licinio and Porzia, pretending not to know that Scaramuccia is listening in, act out Licinio's extreme jealousy as he prohibits Porzia from appearing in public. As the unseen Scaramuccia gets in on the action by giving them suggestions as to what parts of the house she can enter—including the toilet—the scene acquires acoustic resonances that go far beyond what we can see.

When she and Lepido finally meet in Act Two, Scene Two, Porzia falls into a deadly swoon which leads to an extended "elastic gag" as Scaramuccia hold her up while Lepido addresses her supposedly dead body.[108] While Lepido mourns Porzia, Scaramuccia and the servant Trapola fight over how to carry her into the house.

As the scenes progress, Scala inserts Scaramuccia into all the intrigues that are developing. From the time he gets Ruchetta to fill him in on her plan to get Giulia and Flavio together, and learns that Ruchetta wants Trapola to marry her, he holds all the strands of the plot, so playing the *capocomico*. To identify Scaramuccia as such, Scala adds a scene (2.6) which winds up being extraneous:[109]

106. Ruchetta's comments on the ugliness of mismatching up young girls with men old enough to be their fathers and the unhappiness and likely adultery it fosters is also a familiar trope in Renaissance comedy, echoing Clemenzia's commentary to Virginio in *The Deceived*, 1.2, in Giannetti and Ruggiero, *Five Comedies*, 212–14.

107. Ruchetta, like Clemenzia in *The Deceived* (see previous note), is a maidservant who is sexually exploited by her master, in what became a comic cliché. The recognition that this was a very common social practice reveals the actual status of servants as being at the mercy of their employers. Ruchetta uses her relative lack of power and limited ability to attain respectability in marriage to attack the whole code of chastity as an invention designed to serve patriarchal interests.

108. This is one of many "elastic gags" where a sequence is set in motion and then the resolution is delayed for as long as possible depending on the particular performance and the audience's response. It can be used to tease, build suspense, surprise and sometimes give foreknowledge to the audience. See Andrews' discussion in *Thirty Scenarios*, xlv–xlvi and 50.

109. The commedia dell'arte was often accused of throwing together a mishmash of scenes that had no unifying theme. Here, Scala shows how that happens. He also makes sure it's a virtuosic showstopper

a classic misrecognition scene that Scaramuccia suggests to Lepido and Flavio as a way of getting them into Gervasio's house. They impersonate a ballet master and a musician who try to get Gervasio to hire them for the wedding. They insult him over and over again, claiming they are looking for a Master Castrone, rejecting his insistence that his name is Grifone. Although dropped later as a plot line, the scene stands alone as a brilliant farcical interlude, while thematically foreshadowing the upcoming deception of the *vecchi* (the old men) who will find themselves cuckolded and symbolically castrated.[110]

Access to Porzia's door becomes a central staging device that is repeated many times for maximum sensorial effects. Act Two, Scene Nine reprises the act's opening scene, only this time Trapola does the knocking and reveals that Scaramuccia is hiding nearby and wants Porzia outside. Once Porzia concedes she will talk to Lepido, Scaramuccia leaves and Porzia remains outside with Trapola. As Trapola goes over all the reasons why married women should take lovers as they wish, and become courtesans if it suits them, Licinio arrives in Scene Ten, and hidden from view, adds "his" commentary to Trapola's arguments in praise of female infidelity. Porzia's comment, "You have a great talent for making a good woman bad, but I don't know if you'd be as skilled at turning a bad woman good" (2.10), leads Trapola to respond with the same argument that Scala makes, as will be seen, in the second prologue to the play: since human nature is naturally inclined to the bad, it is not, therefore, the fault of comedy when the bad is chosen.[111] As social commentary, this scene suggests that, since women often find themselves treated as male possessions, they might as well take whatever power they can.[112]

Act Three, Scene Four repeats the scene at Porzia's door for the third time, as Ruchetta and Trapola make sexual jokes as they knock to come in. When Licinio answers the door, he maintains his masculine stance by flirting with Ruchetta and annoying Trapola. Together, the two servants persuade Licinio to take Gervasio off jewelry shopping, leaving the coast clear for Scaramuccia to repeat the knocking scene once again, this time with Lepido in tow, in order to set up the reconciliation with Porzia (which is delayed, however, until 3.6). Framed by Scaramuccia who listens from a distance and frequently interrupts them, we are reminded that this lovers' reunion is a set piece. In a prolonged piece of comic business, Lepido

---

that temporarily pauses the action.

110. In 3.5, Scala lets us know that this subterfuge has proved to be a blind alley. Scaramuccia tells Lepido that this plan to get into Gervasio's house has to be abandoned because it was taking too long.

111. The *Actor* concludes his longest speech by saying "that since the goal of comedy is to teach by example, it cannot be blamed for those who use it to wrong ends." See "Prologue to be Acted" in *The Fake Husband*, 49.

112. When commedia dell'arte was performed in the public squares, women from different social classes were in attendance and could profit from such advice.

prostrates himself before her, insisting that losing her has brought him to the point of death, while she puts him on trial over and over again, expressing her doubts about his love since he had stayed away beyond the agreed upon time. The romantic centerpiece of the play, their lovers' dialogue requires great virtuosity from both to find the point in the quarrel where they can forgive each other.[113] During this exchange, Porzia lets us in on the secret that her "husband" Licinio is really her maidservant Brigida; we now necessarily share in the task of maintaining the deception until the intrigue can be played out.

Act Four speeds up the action, creating the insanely complex circumstances that will allow the lovers to get into the right beds. The audience is invited to eavesdrop on Demetrio with Scaramuccia when he learns of the old man's uncontrollable lust for Giulia. As Demetrio vocalizes his wish to ravish his daughter, Scaramuccia, from a split-stage location, offers a series of asides expressing his revulsion; but when Demetrio questions him, he quickly turns his criticisms into support to get Demetrio into bed with Giulia before Gervasio can claim her. Scala does not shy away from having Demetrio perform his lust in Scene Two when he falls into spasms brought on by his jealousy and a painful erection that he tries to disguise as indigestion. Demetrio's enactment of his acute distress shows the audience that sexual urges, however grotesque, cannot always be concealed.

Driven by the exigencies of fitting this unruly dramatic fiction into the twenty-four-hour time period required by classical models,[114] and in keeping his promise to Demetrio, Scala's Scaramuccia starts to bring all the plot strands together by inviting Gervasio to have his first night with Giulia in advance of the wedding. Gervasio is given orders—the first to be so instructed—to have a special sound ready so that he can be identified and led to the bed of his lover. Gervasio's gullibility and lust-driven vanity make him easy prey as he agrees to cough three times. The darkened stage will be navigated hereafter by sounds and cries as Scaramuccia's stage magic unfolds, propelling the two pairs of young lovers, the two old lechers, and the servant surrogates to seek out the mates he has assigned them. He closes the scene by confessing that he has chosen to favor the young at the expense of the old. He mentions "the young" at other times as well, suggesting a metatheatrical referencing that a new kind of comedy is being born as the older more regionally-based improvised buffoon style begins to fade out.[115]

113. Isabella Andreini's examples of lovers' dialogues were collected by her husband in her *Fragmenti di alcune scritture* published by Scala; see 18. This complex exchange where they confess they have each other's heart in their bodies might well be from one of the Andreini's exemplary dialogues.

114. Scala observes the rules that a well-made play would observe the unities of place, time and action, even if with great difficulty because of the messy details in the background story. See section on "Renaissance Italy," in Bernard F. Dukore, ed., *Dramatic Theory and Criticism: Greeks to Grotowski* (New York: Holt, Rinehart and Winston, 1974), 119–55.

115. When Scaramuccia mentions favoring the young over the old, information he repeats on other occasions, he may be nodding to the new direction that commedia dell'arte was taking: a move, that is,

In Act Four, Scene Four, Scala adds another ingenious plot twist as Scaramuccia gets Trapola to agree to dress as a woman in order to be put in bed with Ruchetta. When Trapola responds by insisting that if he puts on women's clothes, he won't be able to make proper love to Ruchetta, Scaramuccia chides him for believing in the dated notion that biological sex is mutable and that wearing the clothes of the other can cause a change to occur.[116] However, such awareness that the deception may no longer work, makes us aware how precarious Scaramuccia's next bed trick is when he will put Trapola in bed with Demetrio. Scaramuccia asks Demetrio to whistle three times as the signal that he will lead him to Giulia's bed under cover of dark but Demetrio is clever enough to wonder how Giulia can be in two places at once and Scaramuccia finds himself inventing a whole sequence of the most improbable details as to how to fool Gervasio by substituting Ruchetta. Demetrio, to his credit, wonders if Scaramuccia will be punished for the intricate spider web he is weaving, while Scaramuccia, taking credit for Scala's authorship, brags about how good he is at being a master plot maker.

In Act Four, Scene Six, a great showdown ensues between Porzia and Scaramuccia over who is controlling the intrigue, and involves a surprise twist when Porzia forces Scaramuccia to follow her plan to get her in bed with Lepido. In a slow buildup, she plays him along by getting him to agree to do anything to accomplish this, and catches Scaramuccia in a trap similar to the one he has laid out for the old men. She insists that he bring Lepido to her, and then take her place in bed with Licinio so that she and Lepido can have an uninterrupted night together. An apparently shocked Scaramuccia runs through all the possible scenarios that could ensue if Licinio woke up, painting in the most graphic terms versions of sexual contact between an unsuspecting male with another in female clothing. In this standout comic scenes, Scaramuccia's detailed descriptions of actions that usually happen off stage titillate our imaginations even though we know the danger doesn't really exist, since Licinio is not a man. Eventually, he

---

away from improvisation and buffoonery to the more refined scripted romantic comedies.

116. See Falavolti, 329n1. Trapola is likely referencing plays from the early sixteenth century such as Bernardo Dovizi da Bibbiena's *La Calandra (The Comedy of Calandro)*, written and first performed in 1513, in Giannetti and Ruggiero, *Five Comedies,* 1–70; here it was possible for Fannio, Santilla (Lidio femina's) servant to argue that Santilla had miraculously transformed from a man to a woman when she dropped her male disguise and dressed in woman's clothing. Fannio's claim that "he/she" is an hermaphrodite and hence able to play both sexual roles as the situation required (3.7.47). This medical belief that hermaphrodites could switch back and forth as they wished came under scrutiny with new scientific anatomical research, and Bibbiena is already playing with its improbability by mixing it up with magic. When Scaramuccia dismisses Trapola's fears as no longer operative on the seventeenth-century stage, he is recalling the earlier tradition as a comment on the popular practice of female transvestism in the past and possibly alluding to its presence in the *The Fake Husband*, where Licinio's male impersonation seems to have fooled almost everybody, or at least must be played as if it has.

tries to dissuade her by suggesting every other combination he can think of to fool Lepido, including the insolent classbreaking idea of putting Lepido in bed with Licinio and coming to sleep with him.[117] At this point he has to give the victory to Porzia and concede that he will put on a nightshirt and bonnet and do her bidding.

In Act Four, Scene Seven, Scaramuccia draws attention to his central importance as the *capocomico* by disappearing from the stage, thereby highlighting his control over the other characters who are helpless without him, but doubt his competence. Giulia and Flavio worry that the plot is going off the rails when they can't locate him and start to doubt his abilities to pull off the plan. Giulia, in particular, panics because she has been married to both Gervasio and Flavio and is now caught in limbo. Although the characters express their lack of trust in him and try to think of other options, they have to concede their dependence on Scaramuccia's return.

In Act Five, Scaramuccia's ingenious master plan is held up by a momentary glitch as Trapola gets so excited in his transvestite disguise that he arrives early and decides to pimp himself out as a female prostitute. Scaramuccia has to intervene and shake him out of his trance in order to keep the plot moving. But it is also under the cover of night, signaled by the actors stumbling about and carrying lanterns, that Scaramuccia is able to fool Demetrio into believing that Trapola is actually Giulia. He pulls off this trick by swearing both of them to silence, a huge risk that reminds us how far we too have been pulled in. Moreover, he repeats the trick when Gervasio arrives on cue with his coughing signal, substituting Ruchetta for Giulia by similarly swearing her to silence in order to play a trick on Trapola, whom she thinks she will be bedding.

Having sacrificed the two servants Ruccheta and Trapola to the "old rodents" Demetrio and Gervasio (5.4), Scaramuccia now services his young lovers, bringing first Flavio and Giulia, then Lepido and Porzia together. Porzia, in particular, is represented as undertaking her night of lovemaking with Lepido with the gusto of a soldier about to face an equal opponent in combat. Scaramuccia's signature monologue sums up his fear about the outcome to follow when the old men find out who they are in bed with, but then talks himself through having to play the woman himself—even conjecturing as Trapola had before him—of falling into believing that putting on women's clothes means he has become a woman. The follow-up Scene Six ends with his disappearance into Licinio's bed, for he must swallow his own medicine as the *capocomico*, as he reluctantly admits.

The inevitable fallout from Scaramuccia's deceptions start exploding in the next few scenes as, first, Demetrio appears in a towering rage, chasing Trapola in

117. This transgressive act of letting a servant sleep with a noblewoman actually occurred in Bibbiena's *La Calandra* where Lelio femina (Santilla)'s servant Fannio substitutes himself at the last minute for Santilla in the dark as a bed partner for Fulvia (4.4.58). See note 116, above.

his woman's dress; then Flavio and Giulia turn Demetrio's accusations back on him. Next, Ruchetta appears trying to flee Gervasio, who keeps insisting that she is Giulia. All reach the conclusion that they have been tricked by Scaramuccia and all attention turns on him, foregrounding his pivotal role as the master manipulator. However, when he appears in his nightdress and bonnet, being chased out and held at the end of Licinio's sword and taunted by Porzia and Lepido, he claims that he is at everyone's mercy.

There is one more stage deception to unravel as Scaramuccia appears to have spent the night making love to another man. He begs for time to take a really good look at Licinio whose long braid has fallen down under his nightcap.[118] Once she has identified herself as the "dead" Brigida, she gets to fill everyone in on her male impersonation and collusion with Porzia. As Porzia then slowly unravels all the details involved in pulling off such a ruse, the *vecchi* eventually bow down to the new order and give their blessings: Porzia gets her Lepido; Giulia expresses her absolute right to marry Flavio and accuses Demetrio of planning to assault her; Ruchetta gets Trapola as a special reward for his having been Demetrio's maidservant. The *vecchi* have been caught red-handed and exposed as near criminals. Gervasio agrees that they should stay away from the young women and Demetrio admits his unlawful lust and greed and supports all the marriages. Scaramuccia gets the last word, arguing that having to take on a wife again will be his punishment. *The Fake Husband* has proven that Scala's adage "talk is cheap, actions speak" is absolutely true, since anything can happen on the stage.[119]

The Two Prologues

Scala's two prologues are modeled on those of the Roman poet Terence, who often defended his play to the public in the voice of one of his actors. In Scala's case, since he also acted, the *Actor* of the prologue at times seems identical with Scala himself. As such, he adds another level of metatheatricality to the prologues, heightening the engagement of the reader or spectators. The longer, formal prologue intended for readers is followed by a shorter, less formal one that is supposed to be performed, but both are in print form so that readers and spectators get to compare them for readability and performability. Scala, aware of the criticisms levelled at the commedia dell'arte, devotes the first prologue to the dramatic rules required for great comedy, and the second, to comedy's moral effects. While Scala derived authority from having produced a literary masterpiece in *The Fake Husband*, he also had the *Actor* admit that it had originated as a performance based on the

118. Scaramuccia recognizes his "dead" wife through her long braid. Recognizing a disguised person's identity through physical signs is the first method of discovery in Aristotle's list of ways unknown characters are found out; see Aristotle, *Poetics*, trans. Kenneth McLeish (London: Nick Hern, 1999), 22.

119. See *The Fake Husband*, 45, quoting from the *Actor*'s major speech in the First Prologue.

scenario known as *The Husband.* If the scripted *Fake Husband* proved that the performance text could be reproduced as an aesthetically unified work of art, capable of earning Scala a court position in Florence, Scala still wanted to show that his play was more than dramatic literature, in that it also reenacts the spontaneous performance from which it had evolved. He uses his prologues to demonstrate that speech alone fails to convince by avoiding the standard monologue form; instead, he has the *Actor* defend the commedia in a duologue with a *Stranger*, who stumbles onto a stage set in the piazza where a play is about to begin. The highly critical, erudite *Stranger* acts as a mouthpiece for the snobbish Florentine theater elite as he voices all the arguments against the commedia, which the *Actor* will then refute.[120] Dragging the *Stranger* into the piazza, the *Actor* forces him to acknowledge the commedia's fluid boundaries between stage and audience and the necessary involvement of the spectators in interpreting the action-based plot. By the end of both prologues, the *Actor* has convinced his skeptical *Stranger* to sit through a performance before dismissing the commedia dell'arte as scurrilous buffoonery.

When the *Stranger* utters all the usual complaints about the haphazard, crude, and undisciplined quality of the improvised commedia, the *Actor* is quick to insist that his actors are offering an imitation of the lives of ordinary people, behaving and speaking naturally in their respective dialects. The *Stranger* counters that, without dramatic objectives, and the instruments of oration and locution to develop them, there can be no art. In agreeing with him, the *Actor* goes on to note that good actors learn to imitate the emotions and actions of their characters through their daily artistic practice. Troupe members choose a character mask to portray and are in charge of bringing that character to life by inventing gestures and speech drawn from memory and imagination to capture their character's emotions and actions. In suggesting that his actors are practicing the art of conveying emotional knowledge to their audiences, Scala endorses Lomazzo's theories of the value of good art.[121]

120. Inviting the aristocrat to mingle with the crowds and share a dramatic experience with them may have had the markings of a democratizing event where, in watching a commercial comedy, the population could react as one. Maravall notes that this kind of open-air shared commedia event gave the illusion of community cohesion but went no further, as once the crowds had dispersed all persons resumed their normal class position. He sees popular theater as an institution the ruling class wanted to censor in order to consolidate their superior status. See Maravall, *Culture of the Baroque*, 204. Scala would have understood the need to cater to both the noble class and the general public as the occasion required, but was also willing to characterize the *Stranger* as a rather closed-minded intellectual snob.

121. Scala seems to be referencing Lomazzo's theory that the marvellous quality of a work of art will depend on the artist's "knowledge of the movements of the soul." This knowledge will come from firmly imprinting the emotions to be represented in the memory, creating a network of correspondences between body and spirit, a sort of living archive. See Bolzoni, *Gallery of Memory,* 176.

Scala claims that his actors' ability to portray their characters' lived experiences gives them authority over the rules governing comedy, far more than the learned playwrights whose polished rhetoric and faultless elocution fail to move their audiences.[122] The highest point of the argument comes when he insists that actions, nuanced with even the smallest gestures, are far more effective instruments in transforming the hearts and minds of the spectators than words alone. Insisting that spectators need a great deal of persuasion, sometimes even the threat of violence, to be genuinely changed, he rests his case by stating that the great commedia actors had mastered the art of conveying the emotional depths that their characters were experiencing:[123]

> And consider how it is with lovers who are moved and drawn to submit more by a beloved's teardrop, gaze, or kiss and suchlike, to go no further, than by the persuasion of any great moral philosopher, who with well-composed writing, perfect concepts, excellent locution, exquisite words, and finest arguments, praises virtue and urges putting sensuality aside. The senses are more easily moved by the senses than by anything abstract, just as like is drawn to like. (First Prologue to *The Fake Husband*, 46)

In his concluding speech, the *Actor* addresses his remarks to the entire audience, apologizing for having lost so much time convincing the *Stranger* to stay, and it is here that he confesses that this play really comes from a famous performance text. He explains that he, the author, chose to write out *The Husband* in full because his patron Don Giovanni de' Medici—"a great prince, worthy of immortal fame" considered it to be "the Queen of Comedies."[124] He then undercuts his own position, admitting that despite all his fine arguments, the author really only cares about making them laugh at what will be "a saucy, buffoon-style comedy," since that is his trademark. Having forced the *Stranger* to conform to his will, he

122. Scala's arguments line up with Camillo's description of a theater practice which encourages users to treat their subjects with passion. "Passionate subject matter" makes use of the entire range of expressive gestures from the theater of memory in order to "engrave these gestures on the face of language"; see Bolzoni, *Gallery of Memory*, 178. Scala's reference to the power of gesture recalls almost to the letter the Roman rhetorician Quintilian's observations on the emotional effectiveness of physical expressions designed to stir the mind. See Quintilian, *Institutio oratoria* 9.1.21, quoted in Bolzoni, *Gallery of Memory*, 177, and in the following note.

123. Quintilian, *Institutio oratoria* 9.1.21 "Further, there is no more effective method of expressing the emotions than an apt use of figures. For if the expression of brow, eyes and hands has great efficacy in stirring the mind, how much more effective must be the face of our discourse itself when disposed to produce the result at which we aim?" *The Institutio Oratoria of Quintilian*, trans. Harold E. Butler (Cambridge, MA: Harvard University Press, 1920), 3:359; quoted in Bolzoni, *Gallery of Memory*, 177.

124. First Prologue to *The Fake Husband*, 47.

carries the joke further by admitting that the *Stranger*'s original disparaging label is true and that *The Fake Husband* is in fact a Buffoon Show.

The second prologue, although it concentrates on addressing the charge against the immoral message that comedy conveys and its corrupting influence on the spectator, also plays with ironic ambiguities. Ferrone sees it as a gratuitous add-on to the first, and only understandable as further pandering to the refined sensibilities of the Florentine literati, probably at the behest of Don Giovanni.[125] While this may be true, the second prologue also augments the first prologue's argument about the power of comedy to move its audiences by underlining what its purpose is in doing so. The *Stranger* condemns the trashy subject matter of comedy as dangerous to everyone involved, leading the *Actor* to maintain that comedy holds up a mirror to a middlebrow audience by portraying average human beings with all their weaknesses as well as virtues. Where the *Stranger* cites historical cases where actors had been banished by the state, to which the *Actor* responds with the citation of different cases, as when in ancient Rome, the actor Roscius had argued that acting, as much as rhetoric, promoted civic virtue.[126] He builds the case that comedy has to show humans being tempted to act badly so that they can confront good and evil. Thus, the second prologue is best seen as a continuation of the first in that it is stressing the need to not only entertain, but also to instruct audiences to make their own choices in the face of bad behavior. Although he gets the *Stranger* to admit that the evil men do cannot be blamed on comedy, he has to answer a follow-up question concerning the moral position of the actors who continue to perform comedies even where they have been prohibited. The *Actor* speaks on behalf of his actors when he insists that they are willing to risk their reputations and suffer censure wherever necessary in order to practice their art truthfully. His reply reveals his awareness of the dilemma facing actors trained to depict the range of human physical and emotional behavior, and admits that actors knowingly fly under the radar and risk transgressing increasingly strict censorship laws. When the *Stranger* agrees to take his chances and attend the performance, the *Actor* again emerges victorious, having succeeded in getting the *Stranger* to see the show, and increasing the possibility that he will be changed by it.

Conclusion

Scala wrote *The Fake Husband* to establish to his own and future ages that commedia dell'arte, as an improvised art form that emphasized embodied spontaneous

125. Ferrone, "Don Giovanni Impresario," 180. He regards it as a palinode denying the arguments of the first prologue.

126. The actor Quintus Roscius was not only a performer but also ran a school for acting and prepared a manual for actors. Cicero defended him in *Pro Quinctio Roscio comoedo* against the lawsuit brought by Gaius Fannius Chaerea. See Falvolti, 238n6.

action, enriched the development of the theater. Its goal was to employ art to imitate life so skillfully as to penetrate to its essence and thereby move spectators to experience viscerally what they were witnessing, and so undergo a process of pleasurable transformation. An art form that could vie with painting and poetry in capturing the deeper truths of human existence, it stressed spontaneous vitality above all.

Having in 1611 introduced the public to the scenario form, Scala showed the artistic and scholarly world with his 1618 publication of *The Fake Husband* that the scenario on which it was based already contained all the aesthetic elements of scripted drama. In the scripted play, he approximated the individual contributions of the actors who had made the scenario famous by supplying their dialogue, which, although stripped of its regional dialects, could be appreciated by a wider pan-Italian group of readers and spectators. In so doing, he constructed a play that demonstrates that a commedia dell'arte performance offers a complete, aesthetically unified experience no different from a fully scripted text. The two prologues to the play, furthermore, express Scala's theoretical position, leaving an invaluable commentary on Italian dramatic theory that was then put into practice in *The Fake Husband*.

Note on the Translation

Adding an English version of *The Fake Husband* to Italian dramatic literature already available in English makes possible a broader understanding of how commedia dell'arte developed from its beginnings as buffoonery to its maturity as a disciplined dramatic art form. The English translation is intended to provide a workable play script that can be performed,[127] and to give English-speaking scholars access to Scala as both a theoretician and a practitioner.[128] It aims to create a text that is accessible to readers and performers today, which has required a search for equivalent modern idioms to capture seventeenth-century expressions while staying faithful to Scala's text and preserving the flavor of the original. Since the dialogue he supplied for his characters is given in standard seventeenth-century Florentine Italian, it has been relatively easy to translate into English. Class distinctions, which in the original performance would have been conveyed by the use of varied dialects, still remain: the lovers speak in overblown Neoplatonic romantic conceits full of rhetorical embellishments, while the servants—Scaramuccia but

127. I have already put on a workshop version of *The Fake Husband*, which was highly successful, with a cast recruited from a graduate class.

128. Other important recent studies in English include Natalie Crohn Schmitt, *Befriending the Commedia dell'Arte of Flaminio Scala: The Comic Scenarios* (Toronto: University of Toronto Press, 2014), and Erith Jaffe-Berg, *Commedia dell'Arte and the Mediterranean: Charting Journey and Mapping "Others"* (Farnham, Surrey, UK: Ashgate, 2015).

also Trapola and Ruchetta—use pithy local sayings, often about sexual functions and other intimate household matters, and the *vecchi* reveal their nouveau-riche obsessions with their money and sex. Since all the characters deliver monologues in order to share their desires with the audience, they acquire a certain emotional depth.

I have followed Falavolti's modern edition with its systematic modifications to orthography and punctuation. I have also kept the formatting changes she has made to the 1618 publication where she has attempted to help the reader follow transitions from asides to normal address, or for changing address to a different speaker.[129] I have kept all the parentheses from the original, although they are only partial guides to who is intended to hear a particular aside. Still they are valuable signs to make us aware that no action goes unobserved by someone.

As a rule, I have not added stage directions to explain scene changes, exits or entrances, or major shifts in the action, as it felt truer to the text to let the reader pay full attention to the words on the page to discern what is happening since there are constant changes as speakers enter, exit, hide themselves, eavesdrop, speak in asides intended for the audience and/or other different characters. However, I have where necessary changed the order in which the characters are listed in certain scenes to reflect the modern practice of listing characters in order of when they speak rather than appear. In a few cases, I have indicated that a character has exited in order to make it clear who is left on the stage to hear a final speech. Occasionally, it has been necessary to explain why a character is listed as present, even if silent. It is hoped that readers can learn the clues needed to understand what is happening, as Scala's script can best be followed in an interactive way which speaks to the audience as well. I hope the script will give contemporary readers and performers a sense of the ensemble effort that characterizes commedia dell'arte performances.

I have also had to pay special attention to indicate very frequent use of the vocative "O" since it is often not spelled differently from the exclamatory "Oh" which is also often used. In addition to keeping this now archaic use of the vocative to highlight the importance of dialogue between the characters, I have also retained the titles and forms of address used by the characters to address one another. Since titles were of great importance in Baroque culture, it would not be accurate to omit these important class markers. The servants Trapola, Ruchetta, and Scaramuccia are never given titles, and are often crudely insulted by each other and their social superiors by being referred to as "filthy beasts" or in similar derogatory terms. While the commedia dell'arte delighted in drawing attention

129. Fitzpatrick suggests that Falavolti's use of new paragraphs to capture deictic changes offers a "false impression of the extent to which Scala was catering textually to performance pragmatics." See Fitzpatrick, *Relationship of Oral and Literate Performance Processes*, 234n4. Fitzpatrick has worked exclusively from the 1618 edition, regarding it as truer than later versions to Scala's intentions.

to these artificial distinctions and often showed the servants as superior to the masters, the social commentary depended on maintaining a class hierarchy.

I was challenged at times to find swear words and curses that would ring true today for the servants but found that references to animals were the most common. The *vecchi*, Demetrio and Gervasio, are usually referred to as *messer* which I have translated as "Master." The *innamorati* Lepido, Flavio, Giulia, and Porzia are given many different titles including "Signore," "Madonna," "Padrona," "Signora;" and although they are all the children or wards of the *vecchi*, they are regarded as of higher rank. I have used "Sir," "My Lord," "My Lady," "Lady" with their names, although such titles might convey a higher class than it should. I also chose to keep the Italian names for all the cast members to preserve Scala's foray into separating his characters from easily identifiable known actors.

On a final note, I have often wondered if Don Giovanni de' Medici loved *The Fake Husband* so much because it was a theme dear to his heart. His attempts to get Livia Vernazza's first marriage annulled so that he could marry her legitimately might have attracted him to this play where a fake husband steps up to save Porzia from having to marry against her will. Vernazza's first marriage to a much older man speaks of the terrible injustice of forced marriage that is dealt with in *The Fake Husband*. Don Giovanni wished to legally marry Vernazza to avoid being considered a fake husband himself. Sadly, after his death she became the prisoner of the Medici and lost her status. However, the play endures.

FLAMINIO SCALA

The Fake Husband, A Comedy

The Fake Husband, A Comedy
by Flaminio Scala, Venice 1618[1]

Dedication

To the most illustrious and most reverend lord
My lord and patron
The Signor Cardinal de' Medici[2]

What more can I do, my most illustrious and reverend lord, as a sign of my respectful and humble servitude, than give to you the tribute of the fruits of my profession, as a remembrance of the innumerable favors and kindnesses received from your most generous, great father of glorious memory? Here it is then, my comedy, *The Fake Husband*, not yet worthy to make future comparisons to, but as a vehicle to show to an even greater extent just how magnanimous you are; perhaps not unworthy to be presented to you, and so much the more as you most illustrious and reverend lordship, the model of every heroic paternal virtue, are without fault amongst your fellow humans. I sincerely regret that my poor comedy faces such a great test, because such brilliance overshadows everything. But, I give it to you, your luminous self, your most illustrious and reverend lordship, as I beg you with reverence, that you will have the goodness to make even such a small thing worthy of your regard and accept me as your most humble and true servant, with thanks.

From Venice, September 15, 1618.
Your most devoted servant Flaminio Scala offers reverence to your most illustrious lordship.

To the most illustrious and most reverend
Lord Cardinal de' Medici
His most esteemed Lordship
Flaminio Scala humblest servant
Glorious splendor of royal offspring
Supreme ornament of our century

1. The 1618 date appears on the frontispiece of the first edition preserved in the Biblioteca Nazionale Marciana. It was reprinted in 1619 with a different frontispiece, but the 1618 date remained on the dedication letter. Copies in the British Library confirm the 1619 reprint.

2. For Scala's dedication of *The Fake Husband* to Cardinal Carlo de' Medici, see the Introduction, 18.

In whom blazes, from the heavenly choir,
The divine ray of my blessed sun.
As a humble tribute simply offered
From my pen with its impure ink,
Not a jeweled crown, of gold, or purple,
But a garland of flowers it wishes to offer you.
Truly you deserve to be decorated
With both purple and gold circling your forehead
With a double diadem of equal worth.[3]
But to place this little gift amongst the great offerings
Will make its words ready for your praise in
Your magnanimous heart an immortal prize.[4]

3. Falavolti, 226, notes the reference to his double merit as a Medici and a cardinal. The frontispiece for *Il finto marito* (1618) shows two figures holding up a diadem poised over a Medici shield. On the left side, the winged figure of FAME appears holding her trumpet and, on the right, another winged figure holds a palm branch indicating Victory.

4. Falavolti, 226, refers to Scala's plea to the Cardinal to protect his comedy from censure. Falavolti errs in confusing the Cardinal with Don Giovanni.

Two Prologues

First Prologue

Actor and Stranger

Actor: Hey, hey, sir, where are you going? You can't go this way.

Stranger: What way then?

Actor: This way here, damn it!

Stranger: Hey, slow down! Isn't this the set, the stage, and the place where the comedy is going to be performed?

Actor: And that's the place where the audience sits, and not this. You can't go this way either.

Stranger: Well then, we'll go this other way; but what kind of Buffoon Show is being put on here?[5]

Actor: Oh, this man is annoying: it's *The Fake Husband* by Flaminio Scala.

Stranger: By whom?

Actor: By Scala, yes, who in his day wrote a thousand scenarios. Are you turning your nose up? Why? Are you surprised?

Stranger: Of course I am surprised, because it's one thing is to put together a scenario for improvised performance, another to write an engaging full-length comedy with beautiful and well-thought-out sentences, rather than hearing words like: "give him the bed warmer," "the *lazzi*," "at which," "stays," and "leaves," as is usual when actors improvise.[6] Because, to be honest, I don't want to be jostled around, which is what usually happens when you are down there with the crowd.[7]

5. The Italian *Zannata* is translated as Buffoon Show to convey its meaning of being comedy made by the servant Zanni, usually described as Buffoonery.

6. The *lazzi* refer to any kind of comic business that could be inserted at suitable points to punctuate the action. *Lazzi* mean "laces" in Italian and were regarded as places where plot strands could be tied together or emphasized. The Stranger is repeating the accusation frequently made that comic business is thrown in randomly to divert the audience and proves that the commedia dell'arte is full of cheap tricks. The other words "at which," "stays," and "leaves" are stage directions which are crucial in improvised comedy since they indicate that someone will do something simultaneously, and/or they will remain in the scene or leave as needed to move the action forward.

7. The Stranger is talking about the public performances in the piazza that were open to everyone to watch and, of course, jostle each other, as they vied for a space to see the action happening on a platform of some kind; where audience members might fight for a seat on the stage itself if they were noble, but could also find themselves in a crush standing up; where women might be present to drum

Let's get out of here for God's sake, since this is going to be a Buffoon Show, as I said.

Actor: Wait, hold on a second! Scala's creations have always been inspiring, and that is what counts in comedies.

Stranger: I've seen some of his things, and they haven't inspired me.

Actor: Apparently, it's not easy to inspire a man like you—by the way you speak it seems you know a lot, or at least you think you do … maybe you have an idea for a script; but now it's only you who criticizes someone who has been universally praised in print. You can't deny that wherever Scala has taken his scenarios, they have always given pleasure, and always been appreciated.[8]

Stranger: True, but you know why? Because he compensated with good performances; good acting companies can improve a scenario with high-quality performances; nonetheless, a composition just sketched out, if it does not have the art of fine writing, remains cold and hollow.

Actor: If you say so, then you'll like this one about to be acted because the actors have chosen their characters.[9]

Stranger: Very well, but even if the script has been memorized, unless the dialogue has been beautifully composed and properly written out, it will amount to nothing.

Actor: That would be the case if you want to celebrate someone with beautiful and dignified speech, or if you want to narrate a sequence of events. But in comedy, as long as the imitation is good and true to nature, and the diction is not poor or crude, it's enough. Actually, a familiar, colloquial, and not too elevated level of diction is more proper, because comedies represent the everyday actions of average men. Indeed, excessive sophistication would be improper.

Stranger: You put it extremely well, but in order to imitate a vast range of parts and to give them the right level of speech, it is necessary to know a lot. Therefore, you can't just use a variation of the dialects from Bergamo, Venice, or Bologna. Your

---

up business if they were prostitutes, or if they were working-class women, along with the men who made up the crowds, escaping from their employers.

8. The Actor praises Scala enough times to identify himself with him or at least as his mouthpiece for comic effect. His comment about being in print is also part of his pitch, since he had become famous with his publication in 1611 of *The Theater of Tales*.

9. Scala is commenting on the fact that since this play has had all the dialogue written out, the actors will know what their characters are going to say in advance. This comment indicates that *The Fake Husband* was probably not being performed by Scala's Confidenti troupe, whose performances were improvisatory in the commedia dell'arte tradition.

imitation must be accompanied by proper diction and the right words; otherwise you will distort the dialogue. For this reason, I will repeat that I don't expect much from this play, because each person should stick to what he's good at.

Actor: The real art of making good plays belongs to those who represent them well, I think. Because if experience teaches us everything, those with the ability to create and perform them well, can be also taught how to write them properly—provided they were not born in the Voltolina where they say "I" for "me." But tell me, if you please, in what does such an art consist?[10]

Stranger: In respecting the rules and imitating reality as much as possible.

Actor: Who can know the rules of art better than the actors themselves? Since they put them into practice by exercising the art every day? And they learn it by doing; and who is better in the art of imitation than they are? They not only imitate emotions and plausible actions, but, by introducing several other languages, they are obliged to give perfect imitations not only in their own dialects but in others than their own. So naturally, if a Venetian actor was able to speak Florentine, and a Florentine actor Bergamask, it wouldn't be considered unusual.

Stranger: Rules are to be drawn from those fine authors who have written on the art of the poetics, because the imitation of dialects has little value if the style and the words do not express joy and sorrow, fear and bravery; orators and philosophers teach such things, not the actors.

Actor: All rules are important and valuable; but putting them into practice is the essence of any art or science.

Stranger: Agreed. But practice must be preceded by rules. Or even better, forms can only be derived from rules.

Actor: Experience produces art, and since the repetition of actions makes the rule, rules in general are drawn from experience. A valid rule derives from actions; for this reason, an actor can give rules to playwrights, not they to him.

Stranger: Since when have you taken up syllogizing?

Actor: I follow natural logic, which is based solely on reason.

10. Falavolti, 231n9, notes that he means Valtellina, a valley in the Lombard region. This may mean that Scala is really talking about the invented dialect that the Academy of the Blenio Valley made so famous in its clever mixture of many regional dialects, mingled with Bergamask. The reference is complex because he is claiming that individual actors were all potentially great artists since they had access to the study of literature and rhetoric and were able to use it with genius in their improvisations.

Stranger: And it is with reason I want to refute you; an artist cannot perfect his art without subject matter, instruments, and an objective he is working towards.

Actor: I grant you that.

Stranger: The subject matter of the art we are discussing is oration, or better, locution. The instruments are concepts and inventions, and the final objective is to imitate and delight, from which utility follows.

Actor: For sure.

Stranger: Right then. In order to achieve the goal of imitating and delighting effectively, it is necessary, beyond inventions, to find proper concepts to express and signify what one wants to imitate, together with oration, and well-organized locution, both representative and expressive; only in this way it is possible to convey what one seeks to imitate, and to achieve delight and utility.

Actor: Who doubts that?

Stranger: It is therefore proven that valid rules, drawn from those who know how to make them, establish good concepts, which appropriately express and signify what one wishes to imitate. These rules also provide inventions, because in distinguishing a rule to be followed from one to be avoided, one can also distinguish the good from the bad. Oration used in performance and expressive words then, nicely linked and used for imitative purposes, cannot be learnt nor used without rules and precepts. Nor can one know them without referring to the proper texts, which constitute the true foundation.

Actor: Your scholastic argument is very ingenious, but in my opinion, too full of sophistry, and will be overturned by my straightforwardness.

Stranger: Go on then!

Actor: What you said would be sound if writers had given us valid rules on oratory, locution, and style for creating comic dialogue, as well as how concepts and inventions must be used in composing dramatic poetry. But remember, since you must have read it, as I've heard it said, that your Aristotle gave us rules only for tragedy.[11] He never gave any particular guidance on comic style; nor can one find anything substantial in Horace.[12] The only rules and precepts that comedy has derive from good practice and good dramatists, and it is from these that today's

11. Aristotle's *Poetics* discusses both tragedy and comedy, but tragedy more extensively. Aristotle had promised to write more on comedy but no separate treatise was ever found. Renaissance theorists such as Robortellus (1516–1567) attempted to reconstruct such a work, publishing *On Comedy* (1547)

12. Horace attacks Plautus while praising Terence in the *Ars poetica (The Art of Poetry)*, but does not provide a theoretical discussion of comedy.

forms come to us, because rules are always taken from practice, and not practice from rules.

For this reason, it happens that many great literary men, including the finest, are able to write plays in a beautiful style, with fine concepts, gracious speeches, and noble inventions; but without the knowledge of stage practice, the plays remain cold, and because they fail to imitate reality, they are remarkably dull and insipid. Instead of being true to nature, they are often unconvincing, even preposterous, and so leave their audiences disgusted; thus, failing in achieving the goal of pleasing, let alone teaching them something. And since audiences don't pay attention to them, they are not only forgotten but have no lasting effect. Good concepts are recognized from their effects, not from preconceived rules. As those in the know say: those without feelings must be made to feel, even if you have to take a stick to them to make them laugh.[13]

For this reason, then, oration or even locution, and words alone, have little to do with imitation, because even the smallest gesture made at the right moment and with the right feeling, will have a greater effect than all the philosophy of Aristotle, and the rhetoric of Demosthenes and Cicero.[14] It's obvious that feelings are aroused more by gestures than words, for intelligent men, and even brute beasts, will always respond better and pay more attention to one who uses a stick, rather than one who relies on words—as the man from Bergamo says "Talk is cheap, actions speak."[15] And this is the case for everything involving the senses. And keep in mind that the power of stones, not words, drove the man down from the fig tree;[16] in regard to actions, they are more imitative than words and proper comedies consist essentially of actions and only incidentally of words. In comedies, therefore, he who wishes to imitate actions will succeed better using

13. Scala goes from eloquent arguments to threats of physical violence in a flash, reminding his readers that commedia dell'arte is full of staged beatings.

14. Demosthenes (fourth century BCE) and Cicero (first century BCE) were the preeminent orators of Greece and Rome.

15. The original is in Bergamask dialect, *dal dech al fach al gh'è un gran trach*, which Falavolti, 234n18, glosses as *dal detto al fatto c'è un gran tratto* (there's a great gap between saying and doing), a Bergamask version of *dal dire a fare c'è di mezzo il mare* (there's an ocean between saying and doing). The translation given here—"talk is cheap, actions speak"—is intended to capture the down-to-earth flavor of the dialect.

16. Scala is referring to the tale of the tax-collector Zacchaeus in Luke 19:1–10. Although his crimes against Jewish law warranted stoning, his on-the-spot repentance when Jesus called him, signified by his climbing down from the tree, may be intended by Scala to refer to the powers of the commedia dell'arte to show bad people the error of their ways. Scala is not reporting the Zacchaeus incident properly, since it was Jesus' words and not having stones thrown at him that brought him out of the tree in repentance. Perhaps Scala is making the point that Jesus's words had the force of stones in this instance.

actions rather than words.[17] And consider how it is with lovers who are moved and drawn to submit more by a beloved's teardrop, gaze, or kiss and suchlike, to go no further, than by the persuasion of any great moral philosopher, who, with well-composed writing, perfect concepts, excellent locution, exquisite words, and finest arguments, praises virtue and urges putting sensuality aside. The senses are more easily moved by the senses than by anything abstract, just as like is drawn to like.[18]

Stranger: Truly, you make a good argument and I'm slowly falling for it. And even if I could say something back, I'll give you the benefit of the doubt for now, because of the harmonious sounds of the music and the delightful work unfolding on this well-appointed stage, and, above all, the presence of such beautiful women stirring my fantasy to do so, causing me to be pulled in so much that I am moved by desire and driven by appetite to the place where I am out of my mind; but however much I yearn for satisfaction, my reason persuades me otherwise.[19]

However, I am sure that this noble crowd is not here to listen to our drawn-out dispute. You, I believe, have to perform the prologue, and I am keeping you here with my endless chitchat. For this reason, I am going to put an end to talking and take a look at the facts; I want to clear it up for myself, if your claims are as impressive as you've indicated. Therefore, I'll listen to the play, and comment on it later.

Actor: I think you'll be pleased. Now, since you are already here, go and sit among the audience, and show an ounce of patience for having taken so long to decide.

Stranger: I don't think I can fight my way through this huge crowd. I hope I don't fall on top of these women![20]

Actor: They'd probably like that! But we need more time to sort out this fight and find agreement, which is so rare in this world. Now go that way, away from the stage; and you, kind gentleman, let this man have a bit of space behind you so that he can watch.

17. Scala is making his defense that actions precede words in embodying felt experience on the stage, as the actors first thought of what they needed to do to move the plot forward before they invented their dialogue.

18. This eloquent passage echoes Quintilian, and shows Scala's knowledge of what great acting entailed and why he put the Theater on a par with Painting and Sculpture. See the discussion of Quintilian in the Introduction, notes 122 and 123.

19. Scala has the Stranger reveal how seeing the beautiful actresses on the stage has aroused his desire, but also makes it clear that it is up to him to control it.

20. The Stranger's admission that he is afraid of landing on the women in the audience with all its double-meanings is picked up by the Actor as not a bad thing, indicating that these women might be prostitutes. Scala is facing the antitheatrical criticisms leveled against the commedia head-on.

Stranger: Whatever, yes, dear sirs, it won't bother me at all to sit behind such a beautiful bunch, and for the sake of politeness I'll mind my manners; since this man here has persuaded me to take a chance. Here I come.

Actor: Gentlemen, I had to do it—I'm speaking the prologue—but this joker, who is unwilling to believe anything unless he can touch it, has made me lose so much time that now I see my actors are ready. I'll let them do the prologue for me, since I don't want to spoil the fantasy by holding it up any longer. But I want to warn you that the author is not presenting a new comedy: all the scenes are old; this play, in fact, has always belonged to him, and will always belong to him.[21] However, having won the favor of a great prince, worthy of immortal fame, who had liked it so much that, exaggerating, he called it "the queen of the comedies"; and only because of this esteem, however ill-deserved, the author has risked writing it out in full to show its merits, under the protection of this most worthy and illustrious personage, and in this way, devotedly to present it to him.[22] But, you know, although he's done a good straightforward job writing it out, he is still an ordinary theater person, not an orator, nor a philosopher, but someone who professes to have no other talent than the power to delight you with this saucy, buffoon-style comedy.[23] But you'll hear what it's about from the actors; because I'm leaving now. Farewell.

Second Prologue: Prologue to be Acted[24]

Actor and Stranger

Actor: For Chrissakes, I don't want to insult you, but move away from here, you're trespassing. Where do you think you're going?

Stranger: Bloody hell! I don't want to swear at you, but you really are insulting me! What's wrong with going this way?

21. When the Actor again speaks on behalf of the author warning that the play is not new, he comes even closer to suggesting that he is the "plainspoken" author. The play he is referring to is the scenario, *The Husband*; see the Introduction for relationship of scenario to play, especially 2–5 and 21–24.

22. Here he praises his patron Don Giovanni de' Medici, explaining that it was on his advice that he had written it out in full for the purpose of showing off its merits. It is probable that Don Giovanni pushed him to do it in the hopes of advancing his own reputation. Ferrone suggests in "Don Giovanni impresario," 180, that Don Giovanni wrote the dedicatory sonnet; see the Introduction, 19.

23. His closing disclaimer that he really is only a theater person out to please protests too much but suggests that he knows that *The Fake Husband* does not shy away from bawdy content. Here *gustosa* is translated as saucy and *ridicolosa* as buffoon-style to indicate that Scala locates himself as belonging to a less refined stage of the commedia dell'arte.

24. The second prologue, designated to be performed, is distinct from the first: whereas the first proves the power of the commedia to entertain, in the second, the Actor, perhaps ironically, sets out to defend its instructional value, in the face of its bawdy content.

Actor: Sir, that's the way to go on stage.

Stranger: To go on stage? Oh, no! Where have I gone? Stop, stop, it's taking me a thousand years to get out of here. Show me the exit.

Actor: My God, you were in such a hurry to force your way through the crowd, so why the big change?

Stranger: If I'd known that this is where comedies are performed, not only would I not have forced my way in, I'd have run away faster than a dog from a beating.

Actor: What do you mean? Why do you say that?

Stranger: Because I don't like these trashy shows of yours.[25]

Actor: Trashy shows of mine? So, this is what you are calling "the mirror of human nature"?[26]

Stranger: This is what I call a show that teaches honest young women to become runaways; instructs young men in how to deceive their parents and live reckless and dissolute lives, encourages servants to play tricks on their masters, and shows maidservants ways to play the bawd. Is that clear enough? For God's sake, let me out of here.

Actor: Hey, hold on a minute, if you please; first you were bothering me just by being here, now you're offending me with what you're saying, and with trying to leave. Do you really think that comedies are this bad?

Stranger: Comedies are not deserving of praise for those who make them, they disgrace those who take an interest in them, and dishonor those who act in them; but are even more detestable for those who listen to them, because enjoying something that corrupts our customs and morals is a vice and a defect. Plus, the wasted time that can never be regained automatically condemns those who consume them as evil from the outset. Moreover, it is true in ancient times that great Republics did not permit actors among them, and everywhere the art was in such disrepute that those who practiced it were not given any honor. Therefore, let me out of here right now.

Actor: Wait, I want to tell my side of the story on my behalf and also that of my fellow actors, because I don't want people to believe that by not responding to you, I agree with what you have said. I know, too, that Sulla, a wise and respected man, loved the actor Roscius so much, that he put him on a par with Cicero.

25. *Cenciaie*, which literally means "rag piles," is translated as "trash," to better convey its meaning of being something of little value.

26. The "mirror of human nature" reflects the classical claim of comedy to portray real people.

And the very same Roscius also wrote a treatise equating the comic art with rhetoric.[27] If what you are saying has any value, it also means that we should flee from medicine, which teaches how to make poisons in order to find antidotes; the same thing for swords, spears, arquebuses,[28] because they all kill men, should be thrown in a well; and yet, fortitude and prudence, the greatest of virtues, are called upon when the above-mentioned weapons are used to protect, defend, and defeat our enemies. But, according to you, even the military, which often provides a chance for men to achieve great victories and gain immortality, should be held in contempt, because it could be—actually, surely is—the cause of homicides? Doctors were also expelled from the Roman Republic; but they were later brought back and greatly honored because they were needed; and furthermore, one flower doesn't mean spring is here, no matter how prized it is; similarly, one example doesn't equal a law.[29] Even if the Republic of Marseilles did not want comedies; Rome, the rest of Italy and the whole of Greece always kept and welcomed actors for their contribution to the well-being of the state; evidence that if they had been thrown out, it would have taken a thousand years to reverse the damage; since comedy is necessary for the entertainment and education of the people. No, sir, no, this is a middle-brow art form, and like all human things, subject to inconsistencies and contradictions, and not blameworthy nor praiseworthy by itself, but valuable for the actions that it leads others to follow after watching it; thus, those who learn their lesson, or those who use it to act abusively or for profit deserve to be praised or blamed accordingly. Indeed, since the goal of comedy is to teach by example, it cannot be blamed for those who use it for wrong ends.[30]

Stranger: True enough, but comedies do stir up strong reactions, and because men in general are more prone to evil than to good, it seems to be more blameworthy than praiseworthy.

Actor: Exactly, you've got it right, you're blaming human nature, not comedies.

Stranger: Yes, but only as a way to point them in the right direction, rather than leading them there.

27. Lucius Cornelius Sulla (138–78 BCE), Roman general, dictator, and man of letters, the protector of the famous actor Quintus Roscius Gallus, whom he raised to equestrian status. See the Introduction, 33, and Falvolti, 238n6.

28. The arquebus is a portable long gun dating from the fifteenth century.

29. According to Pliny the Elder, doctors were banned from Rome from its founding until around 146 BCE. See Falavolti, 239n7.

30. The Actor's eventual response to the Stranger's arguments is to insist on its value as a middle-brow art form providing both entertainment and instruction by portraying human vice in order to encourage virtue. During this era, the commedia dell'arte faced many enemies in the church and the state, which attempted to shut down the professional stage.

Actor: No, no, now what you are saying is that comedy does what it's supposed to do: the well-behaved man understands the good examples from seeing the bad ones, and chooses to not follow the bad ones. And comedy provides the vehicle.

Stranger: Well, then, at least allow me this: what kind of honor can a person have who practices what the law considers dishonorable?

Actor: The same honor that a person receives when he helps others by taking on their failings to show them friendship; not so different from a servant getting dust all over himself from sweeping it off his master, or giving him a lit torch so that he can see and not trip while the servant remains in the dark; but even if I concede that the art is not honorable, you will not deny me that it bestows sufficient honor on those who practice it. So that, for the common good (which you have conceded to me that comedy brings), the actors are happy to submit to having their actions judged by anyone who cares to, whether to consider them to have some worth, or to condemn them out of hand; and since they are intended to teach or reveal matters suitable for instruction, they don't care about the disapproval or injury that these things might cause to their honor.[31]

Stranger: I swear on my life that you are one hell of a salesman! And since I don't want to seem to be the one in the wrong, let me be willing to change my opinion regarding the practice of this middle-brow form, as I will grant you comedy is, and for reason I want (if it pleases you) to throw myself into it willingly, and listen patiently to see what I can get out of it.

Actor: All right then, do it. It'll do you good by showing you a meaningful example. Take a seat here by the musicians. I was supposed to do the Prologue, but since I see my fellow actors are ready to perform, I'll beg them to let me say a few words to avoid further annoyance. Gentlemen, I offer you this capricious comedy that should keep you in greater suspense than usual since you have not been told the Prologue where the story is explained. Instead, accept in its place this unexpected encounter, because I am about to announce the start of *The Fake Husband* by Flaminio Scala, a comedy entirely written by him, even if not a new one. And now I will let my fellow actors put on the play.

Farewell.

31. The Actor supports actors having to accept censure rather than compromise their art to suit their critics' rules.

The Fake Husband

Cast of Characters

Demetrio Aliprandi, old man
Lepido, his son
Scaramuccia, his servant
Ruchetta, his servant
Giulia, his ward
Gervasio Grifone, old man
Flavio, young man
Porzia, daughter of Gervasio
Trapola, his servant
Licinio, husband of Porzia, later Brigida

Act One

SCENE ONE
Lepido and Flavio

Lepido: Lepido at your service, Sir Flavio! And it is really me. Your Lepido in person![32]

Flavio: I don't know whether the pleasure I feel at your return is greater than the desire I have to find out why you've come in such secrecy. And the more compelling the reason, the more it will encourage me to help you. Now, if it isn't too much trouble, tell me everything, I beg you, for that great friendship we share; your presence makes me so happy, imagine how much more happiness I'll feel if you let me in on your secret.[33]

Lepido: Given that you are such a dear and loyal friend, your every wish is my command, and I'll gladly tell you about my problems. Believe me, Sir Flavio, there

32. Lepido has returned home against his father's wishes and is wearing a disguise which he is strips off for the moment to reveal himself to Flavio. The audience has this privileged information which remains concealed from his father until the end of the play, whereby, in accepting the stage's power to deceive, it is made complicit.

33. Flavio was Scala's stage name and his substantial role as the second gentleman lover may have been intended as an inside joke for the pleasure of commedia dell'arte enthusiasts. He and Lepido complement each other as they vie for stage time to express their undying love in overblown Neoplatonic dialogue. Flavio also makes attempts to direct the action, but they are usually brought under control by Scaramuccia.

was never a ship in a stormy sea so battered by such fierce winds and so tossed and torn as my soul is in the sea of my despair.

Flavio: The knot that ties friends together makes them partners in every misfortune. Perhaps I can assure you that, as ever, being part of your troubles makes me want to relieve them. Tell me everything that is causing you grief, so that you can relieve the pain by speaking about it, and what's more, give me a chance to find some remedy for your suffering that I also share.

Lepido: Since you may, dear sir, after my fast-approaching death, tell the world the reason for it, I'll tell you everything; but without hope that any remedy can be found.

Flavio: You're really upsetting me with such a tale of woe, and the more you carry on, the more you'll prolong your agony and with it my desire to find out how I can help you relieve it.

Lepido: All right, here it is: I know that you must remember that it has already been four years since I left the country when I was sent on my father's orders to Lyon in France.

Flavio: I remember, and I also remember how much bad feeling there was when you left.

Lepido: And do you know the reason?

Flavio: Yes, sir—because you were in love with Porzia.

Lepido: And now, you too have begun to realize the reason for my torment. You must remember that my father sent me to Lyon, not for the reason of getting to know my relatives as everyone said, but clearly in order to stop me from marrying the said Lady Porzia, only because her wealth did not match my own.

Flavio: I remember and I know that all your suffering is caused by the love that you have for the Lady Porzia; but tell me please, have you heard any news of her? And whether she is married by now?

Lepido: If I had died when I heard the news that she got married, I wouldn't be afflicted by this torment now.

Flavio: Oh, dear, what are you saying?

Lepido: As I told you, I had to leave to make my father happy, even before I found out how perverse his intentions were. And then, with the help of Brigida, my faithful servant, wife of Scaramuccia, my loyal servant, I spoke to Porzia many times; and she, for the love we shared, when she heard of my suffering at having to leave—suffering that only a man condemned to death feels—she herself almost died from excessive grief. You as my friend and lover can well imagine the terrible pain my heart felt, seeing my love so tormented. Nevertheless, our faithful servant consoled us both, and holding back our tears, we took some comfort, and regained our lost spirits. I begged my Porzia to patiently tolerate my departure, the distance, and my absence for a period of three years, if it was true that she loved me as much as she said; and in that time, to resist her father and other relatives if they wanted her to marry her off. With Brigida as witness, I promised to marry her without fail as soon as I came back. I confirmed it with an oath; and ordered my servant to look after her every day. Thus, I took my leave from her, gave her my promise and my final farewells and with more tears than words, I departed.

Flavio: What a terrible way to part! And after that when you went to France, your life must have been unbelievably sad.

Lepido: It was Love who told me what to do. In this time, I did whatever I could to return home, to keep my promise. But the most cruel of fathers and hostile fortune, always opposing my every desire, never granted me anything; on the contrary, my fate was cursed, revealing itself to me at its cruelest when it unexpectedly stole the life of my Brigida, in whom (alas) all my hope was pinned. On top of this, still not content and sated with this, for my ultimate misfortune, since I was not able to return within the promised time, it brought me news that my Porzia had married. Now judge for yourself how harsh and displeasing that news was for me. My heart understood it well—by divine virtue dying and reviving a thousand times an hour in my chest: dying since it is deprived of any hope of love, and even if it returns and comes back to life, it is only to exonerate itself to Porzia for taking so long and breaking my promise.

Flavio: Your father deserves all the blame, who, as you say, only sent you to Lyon to stop you from marrying Porzia and most likely ordered your relatives to keep you there until she was married. So, don't torture yourself so much—because it's not your fault.

Lepido: Not torture myself? Not suffer and weep? O Sir Flavio, do you think that I value my oath so little or that my promise once given could be broken? I understand the reasons, but the cause of the offence originates with me.

Flavio: The desires of our hearts must be tempered with caution. I want you to show that you are suffering for sure, but at the same time to think about what you have to do to get near to her to justify yourself and explain the true reasons.

Lepido: That's exactly why I'm here in secret. I've found out that her husband Licinio is a bizarre and capricious man who puts his honor above everything and that from the day that he married her, she has never been seen outside the house—not even at the window—so I'm beside myself, despairing of any solution.[34]

Flavio: Watchfulness and constant readiness cut through everything.

Lepido: You're right. And thus, I'm resolved to talk to her and what I want you to do is to keep my plans secret and let me stay with you for a little while. Also, be aware that speaking to Porzia is a matter of life and death for me.

Flavio: I don't know what else to tell you, except that what belongs to you, you shouldn't have to ask others for. I really want you to be careful and since you know me well, give me a free hand in this business as in everything else.

Lepido: For now, I don't need anything other than secrecy. And if when you're going about your business, you run into Scaramuccia, send him to your house; meanwhile, I'm going to walk around here and try to find him myself, since I need his help in this matter.[35]

Flavio: I'll do my very best to do everything you ask. I'm at your service.

SCENE TWO

Lepido and Scaramuccia

Lepido: O sweetest and most merciful Love—for as such you revealed yourself to me in the beautiful eyes of my lovely Porzia: can it be true that I, your faithful servant, am to have such an unusual reward from you? Am I to be so miserably abandoned by you? You, beautiful son of Cytherea, you promised me a happy ending, a glorious victory of my love.[36] You promised, O glorious boy, a happy harbor for my wandering little ship, and as a divine and truthful spirit, you must keep your promises. Will you no longer be sweet and merciful, but rather reveal yourself as full of wormwood and bile? Do you want to be the failed captain, the unjust paymaster of others' hard work? Are you now the cruelest of judges who desires only the death of others? Are you the proud north wind, to sink my weak

34. This is the first of several mentions of the mysterious Licinio, because of whose monstrous jealousy Porzia is kept hidden.

35. At the end of this and most scenes, stage directions will be given to indicate who is leaving and who is staying. When Lepido walks around looking for Scaramuccia, we as spectators will be ready for him to appear. This device also means that we know more than most of the characters and are implicated in making sense of what is going to happen. As the scenes progress, the plot will often unfold with the help of an unseen character's eavesdropping, giving new information which deepens the intrigue and involves the audience in the playmaking.

36. Venus, the goddess of love and mother of Cupid, was sometimes called Cytherea, the name of the Greek island where she was reputedly born.

and tormented vessel? Alas no, alas no, most powerful Archer, have pity on your faithful servant![37]

But wait—who's coming out of my father's house only half-dressed? It's Scaramuccia—I'm in luck.

Scaramuccia: Whoever said that dreams are caused by eating too much was dead wrong—I can prove it because it's happened to me so many times. Last night I went to bed on an empty stomach because my master is so stingy, and the whole night I did nothing but dream; here's a case where the rule's been made by the exception. Anyway, around dawn I dreamt of my young master, that he'd come back from France all sad and hurt, since his beloved Porzia was married, and I said to him, "Sir Lepido, Lepido, here I am, it's Scaramuccia—I've been waiting faithfully for you all this time." But then I woke and found that the sun was up—I sprang out of bed so that my old master wouldn't catch me there.

Lepido: Scaramuccia's been mentioning my name, so he must remember me. I'm going to take a chance and tell him who I am, since I know how much he loves me.

Scaramuccia: These shoes have always been too tight for me. I'll have to do like the song says: "if they hurt at the toe, cut a bit off at the heel."[38] But hang on, who's that all muffled up in the corner over there?

Lepido: And what are you doing, sir?

Scaramuccia: He's not talking to me?

Lepido: Hey, hey there, Scaramuccia.

Scaramuccia: It's true, he is talking to me. What's that you're saying, sir? What do you want with Scaramuccia?

Lepido: Probably more than you think—listen.

Scaramuccia: Who the hell is he to be up so early in the morning? I don't owe anyone any money, as far as I know, and he doesn't look like a cop—though that hat pulled down over his eyes isn't a good sign. Let's be brave: Hey, you, sir—please take that cloak off your face if you want to talk to me.

Lepido: Dear Scaramuccia, I'm not surprised you don't recognize me because I'm not the same Lepido that I once was.

37. Cupid, or Love, was also called the "Archer" since he carried a bow and arrows.

38. The Italian *La mi fa male in punta / di dietro la vo' tagliare*, from a popular Tuscan song, expresses Scaramuccia's philosophy of life, as he shares with the audience how he will react to Lepido's illicit presence.

Scaramuccia: Alas, what's this I hear? What's this I see? O Sir Lepido, is it really you, my master? Is it really Scaramuccia? Am I dreaming, awake, asleep or what? Scaramuccia, come to your senses, open your eyes, it's your master, it's Lepido, it's really him! O, my dear Sir Lepido, what fair wind has wafted you to our city?

Lepido: Sh! Be quiet, speak softly: Yes, it's me, Lepido, but no longer yours, thanks to Love and Fortune who have made me a target and a sacrifice to death.

Scaramuccia: Dear master, don't upset my happiness at seeing you with such sorrowful words and tell me why you want me to speak softly and why you are in disguise. Tell me your news, master. Do you want me to call your father?

Lepido: You speak to me of my mortal enemy! No, I don't want you to call him, nor do I want him to know of my arrival, unless of my death.

Scaramuccia: Of your death? And why is that? What words are these? Is this the price of the happiness your return brings?

Lepido: I am happy, O Scaramuccia, to see that you have not forgotten me altogether, but you have, however, forgotten some things that I was hoping you would always remember. How can you be surprised by my words? And be happy that I am back? Don't you remember how and why I left? What I am back for? What I left with you? And what I am a seeking from you now?

Scaramuccia: Now I remember my dream. My Sir Lepido, I understand perfectly what your words mean, but I thought that the length of time and the distance would have freed you from any thoughts of love.

Lepido: Neither time, nor distance would have been enough (since it didn't happen) to take away my desire for my Porzia. The pain itself will be enough to take quickly my life, but before that happens I want to speak to her, if it's possible, and take away any illusions of wrongdoing that she must have about my long absence, and that is the reason why I have come back here incognito. And because I know you love me with that perfect love with which the departed soul of your wife also loved me, I am happy that you will intercede for me, and using your wiles, make it possible for me to have my rightful wish. You're not answering? What's going on? Take your hands off your face. What does this mean?

Scaramuccia: My master, your words are hurting me as much for the reminder of my dearest wife Brigida, as for your asking for impossible things. What are you basing this expectation on? Perhaps in the love that Porzia had for you? At that time, she was her own mistress, but now she is subject to others and can't do what she wants, and whatever she might have promised you, she can no longer fulfil it, since she waited for you until the time agreed upon, and furthermore, then you could still trust in the departed spirit of my wife who was still alive.

Moreover, since she, being wise, and knowing how weak the flesh is, and remembering the honest pleasures you two had shared in the past, won't want to put her honor in danger, since she knows well enough that even if the flame of your love had gone out, the fire might still be burning.

But what point is there in talking so much and making such strong arguments, since they can't come to anything? All things considered, I tell you that even if she might be willing, it would be extremely difficult and almost impossible to bring it off, because of the very strict watch that her husband keeps over her; a man who, as everyone says, is one of the most jealous men in the world. No one ever sees her.[39]

Lepido: Enough, stop talking, don't even think that these arguments will change the firmness of my resolve. If you care for my well-being, make it happen. Meanwhile let's get away from here in case my father comes by or someone else who might recognize me. We can discuss what to do while we're walking. Let's go.

Scaramuccia: Agreed. Let's get out of here.

SCENE THREE

Demetrio and Gervasio, the old men[40]

Demetrio: Scaramuccia, Scaramuccia!

Gervasio: Trapola, Trapola![41]

Demetrio: Where the hell has the beast gone? His endless meddling drives me crazy.

Gervasio: No, don't get up, you scoundrel—stay in bed, the sun's not up yet! I don't believe that there is a worse sluggard in the whole world.

Demetrio: There's not a servant in the whole city who's more of a go-getter than Scaramuccia, but I don't know if I should praise him for it since it's bad to be so extreme.

Gervasio: Listen, when you manage to get up, join me at the market and watch out you don't go back to sleep, you nasty brute!

39. The leitmotif of Licinio's reputation for jealousy builds suspense.

40. Demetrio and Gervasio's stage appearances have been set up by Scaramuccia, but only the spectators hear of Demetrio's lustful plan to marry off his ward Giulia to Gervasio so he can have access to her.

41. Trapola is first named here, but does not appear on stage until 2.3.

Demetrio: Oh, look here—it's my neighbor, Gervasio. Good morning, Master Gervasio. who are you fighting with, what's upsetting you so much this early in the morning?

Gervasio: A good day, and good year to you, Master Demetrio. I was just shouting at a servant of mine—the slackest, dirtiest, greediest thing in the whole world, and if I don't tip him out of bed in the morning, he'd still be there at night.

Demetrio: And I've got the opposite problem—a servant who's so hyper that no matter how early I get up, he's always ahead of me. But let's not talk about it anymore; what interesting business is getting you out of the house so early this morning?

Gervasio: I have some errands to do for my son-in-law: to invest some of his money and to see if I can find a house nearby to rent because he wants to live on his own, and even if it's an inconvenience for me, I must nonetheless keep him happy.

Demetrio: I truly congratulate you, Master Gervasio, notably for the relationship that you have made for your daughter and this gentleman from Florence. You've done really well to get your daughter off your back, since it was time to marry her off, even more so since I understand that it was very financially advantageous, and also appreciate that there is no more dangerous predicament to be in than this one.

Gervasio: It's true what you say, Master Demetrio. And believe me, for my part, if my daughter had done what I wanted, she'd have been married three years ago, but because of a certain vow she'd made, she was never willing to consent to my wishes. Above all, I thank heaven for it, because with this husband I've given her someone who has some wealth, and some worth. The only thing about him that I really don't like is that he's too jealous—something I would prefer didn't become too well known since he might get a bad name in the city and become a legend with the rabble.[42]

Demetrio: That's disappointing for sure, but don't be too surprised since it's typical for the young to get carried away in the beginning, but then to settle down. It'd make me very happy to have the same luck as you in finding a similar arrangement for my Giulia.

Gervasio: What Giulia of yours?

Demetrio: The daughter of Master Lampredo, my old friend, who was left in my care shortly after his death, so that I could look after her marriage arrangements with what little money was left.

42. This time Licinio is mentioned as a potential danger because the entire community might learn of his excessive jealousy.

Gervasio: Yes, yes, now I understand you, Master Demetrio. But as I am telling you, I thought that you were keeping her for your son to marry.

Demetrio: That's right, but no way. Instead, since I know that he's coming back soon, I want to get her out of the house before he arrives, and my hope is to give her to someone who's mature, who has, in my opinion, already passed through the fury of youth, since she, too, so to speak, is more of a woman than a girl, I'd say, given her age. To put it bluntly, I've thought of you many times, knowing that since Porzia left home, you're in need of some company, and knowing how suitable the young woman is, I've chosen her as someone for you. What do you say to that, Master Gervasio?

Gervasio: Master Demetrio, I'm not sure that you aren't playing a joke on me, since I am not very wealthy, it doesn't seem that I am worthy of such a prize, and as for age, maybe I'm not worthy of such a beautiful young woman. But if my poverty doesn't hold you back, she could do very well to be with me, because I know my nature very well and the kind of appeal I have for young women. And you'd better believe me, that just as the plants turn green each spring, my juices get reinvigorated in the presence of young women.

Demetrio: I believe it already, and because you know that I care more for quality than riches, I assure you that I am speaking the truth, and as such, in fact, is my desire, let's get to the point. Who her father was you know, and that she was raised in my house like a daughter; her dowry is reasonable and with fixed and moveable assets comes to two thousand ducats. Then I, for my love of my Master Gervasio, will offer her such a gift that she will realize how much I love her, and you will taste the fruit.

Gervasio: I am already sure of that and I thank you. Her father was a well-known acquaintance, more of a friend; and as for the dowry that he gave to you for her in trust, I know very well that you don't need it, but that you can give her some of your own. However, for my part, I am content. So, when can we go ahead with this business, Master Demetrio? Because to tell you the truth, I'm very pumped about what you've offered me, and I'm already crazy in love with her—since she is truly a desirable young woman.

Demetrio: I believe it; and maybe everything will be the way heaven wants it, because it's in heaven that marriages are made. Therefore, I am resolved to come to an agreement as soon as possible, according to your wishes. But it seems to me that it's necessary (even if the girl has always done what I've asked) to discuss it with her and explain it all to her first—since she is the main person here and the property belongs to her. However, you could send your servant to me in an hour to get an answer, and in the meantime, I'll do what's required. What do you say? Doesn't this seem like a good arrangement?

Gervasio: Perfectly put, I also wouldn't want to do anything without the consent of the young woman, because a woman who is married against her will becomes a wild beast in the house, as countless examples have shown.[43]

Demetrio: Exactly. Go do your business and I'll do what I've told you.

Gervasio: Agreed then, I am yours, Master Demetrio.

Demetrio: Go and have fun. (*Gervasio leaves.*)
I couldn't wish for smoother sailing! Everything is working out as planned: his stupidity and his poverty suit my purpose. They say that men live off each other, and through him, I hope to be happy in my love. And here, O Giulia, for your love, in my white-haired winter, feeling the passion of the hottest summer, I am burning up. I don't think that any other man of my age can know the sensations of the love that grips me. And the love I have for Giulia has been kept so secret that no one has ever suspected it, mainly because I've been so careful. And who wouldn't have taken advantage of their beloved, having her in their power as I have? No one, I'm sure. But I have, given that I don't love her honor less than I do her noble self and my own health, I have always kept my desire in check. And even those many times when I found myself in danger of losing my life through the pain and insupportable suffering, nonetheless, I didn't take care of myself, so as not to hurt her. And now Love has had pity on my suffering and given me Gervasio; if he takes her as his wife, I'll be able to visit my good neighbor's house. She owes me a debt of gratitude, and because I have money (women can't resist it) it'll be easy for me to get what I want.[44] The only thing I have to do now is to get her to agree to the marriage, and I think that'll be easy. But let me call her. Hey, Giulia, do you hear me? Ruchetta, where are you?

SCENE FOUR

Ruchetta, Demetrio, and Giulia

Ruchetta: Who's that? What's all this noise? Oh, it's you, master. What's up? Do you have to go? Want me to start undoing your breeches?

Demetrio: What the hell do you think I want, you little beast? Call Giulia…

43. Gervasio pays lip service to the new importance being given to women to allow them to choose their partners.

44. Demetrio's monologue gives us a deeper look at his obsession with Giulia and his plan to double-cross both her and Gervasio with impunity.

Ruchetta: Go to hell yourself, I'll call her straight away. Is there some news, master?

Demetrio: Big news and it's really important; call her right now, I'm telling you!

Ruchetta: Giulia, Giulia, come down because the master is calling you! But what's the news? Come on, tell me about it, dear master.

Demetrio: You'll find out if you have ears and the patience. Call her, I say, you beast!

Ruchetta: You! You're in a big hurry! Giulia, Giulia!

Giulia: What do you want, Ruchetta, where are you?

Ruchetta: I'm out on the street, and the master wants you. So, master, you don't want to tell me about it, eh! Maybe you'd like to tell me something that I won't want to hear, yes?

Demetrio: Please, woman, don't fly into a rage! Let me pick up a stick …

Ruchetta: For yourself! I wouldn't do that if I were you, since I'll be deaf then, you know, when you call me in the night as you often do. Oh, here's my lady.[45]

Giulia: What do you want, master? What great news is this that makes you call me out into the street?

Demetrio: Giulia dearest, I have news that is so important and good for you that I couldn't wait to come and tell you inside, because I have to be off again. Now listen, my dear child.

Ruchetta: My lady, I get the feeling this is not going to be good news.[46]

Demetrio: Oh, and why is that, my lady blabbermouth?

Ruchetta: Because you old guys have very little idea of what the young like, and very little about how to make women happy.

Demetrio: Listen here, you hussy, you always talk nonsense.

Ruchetta: Call me what you like, master, a hussy or a hustler—whatever I am, I'll still talk sense.

45. Ruchetta reveals that Demetrio uses her for sex. This kind of exploitation of servants was taken for granted in real society and became a cliché in stage comedy beginning with *Gli ingannati* (*The Deceived*, 1532). See the Introduction, note 107.

46. Ruchetta's running commentary, delivered as asides for the audience to share, responds to Demetrio's proposal with the vulgar truths that Giulia cannot utter.

Giulia: Come on, that's enough now, be quiet. Please, go on, master, and let her babble on.

Demetrio: Ruchetta, if you keep on babbling, one time I'll bang your head in.

Ruchetta: You mean you'll bang … oops, you almost made me say it!

Giulia: Please, master, let her babble on—don't you know what she's like by now?

Ruchetta: I wish he didn't, the dimwit!

Demetrio: Giulia, you know that since your father died I have always looked after you like my own daughter. And if I've taken my time since to find you a husband, it's been because no suitor has come who is to my taste, and worthy of you. Now, with fortune's great blessing, I think I've found just the person—someone whom I'm happy with, and who will bring you the greatest happiness and satisfaction.

Ruchetta: If he's to your taste, he'll be bad at pleasing my lady.

Demetrio: You be quiet, I'm not talking to you, damn it!

Ruchetta: I wasn't talking to you either.

Giulia: Ruchetta, please be quiet for a moment. Well then, master, you've found me a husband?

Demetrio: Yes, my dear Giulia, and he's someone you know well.

Giulia: Tell me who he is, then, if I already know him.

Ruchetta: Who do you think it's going to be?—it'll be some senile old fool like him for sure.

Demetrio: Do you know our neighbor Master Gervasio, Porzia's father?

Ruchetta: Oh, my God! I knew it! What did I tell you? Oh, you poor young thing!

Demetrio: Haven't you anything to say? Don't look down like that, look me in the face—aren't you happy?

Ruchetta: As happy as you are, snot-nosed old man!

Demetrio: Who am I talking to? O Giulia, are you becoming ill perhaps?

Ruchetta: Yes, from her mother, because that father doesn't please her.[47]

47. Ruchetta's comment may refer to Giulia needing to have the protection of a mother since she has no father to rely on.

Demetrio: Come on, answer me.

Giulia: How can I answer you, master, when I see you're giving me a father, not a husband? Are you giving me a second one because of the suffering I endured when I lost my own father? Fortune was kind and gave me you—and you've raised me as your own daughter, and therefore this madness must end, for having already made me suffer so much, without wanting to deliver me now to Master Gervasio, who is more suitable as a father than as a husband.[48]

Demetrio: What do you mean "as a father"? Does Gervasio seem so old to you? Don't you see that his beard is thick and full and not yet white and that he wears it to frame his face and make him look serious and venerable? He's not even forty-eight yet and he still hasn't gone white.

Ruchetta: And if she takes him, she'll cuckold him.

Giulia: Master Demetrio, you know very well how obedient I have been, like a true daughter, and that I have never given you any trouble and have always done everything that you asked me to do.

Demetrio: It's true; I can't deny it. And I hope that you won't let me down this time either.

Ruchetta: It's easy for you to say, you slobbering old man.

Giulia: Now, for the love that I know you have for me and for the friendship you had with my father, I beg you kindly to grant me a favor that I know you can't deny me.

Demetrio: Of course, Lady Giulia—ask for what you want without any hesitation.
Oh, she knows the power she has over me.
Come on, tell me, be quick!

Giulia: The favor is that you give me a little time to think over the marriage proposal, and it will take even less time than you think it will.

Demetrio: How? All right, that's very reasonable, but I would like it if you were quick about it; because I've promised to give Gervasio an answer.

Ruchetta: Master, leave it to me, and joking aside, since now I know how much you care about Giulia, I'll get her to do what you want.

48. Giulia has no illusions about her subservient position as Demetrio's ward whose orphaned state puts her at his mercy in terms of her chances to marry. It's an indictment against young girls being forced into marriage with much older men.

Demetrio: Ruchetta, if you carry out this business according to my wishes, it'll be good for you, and the least you'll get will be to keep doing the same thing again.

Ruchetta: If I don't have you, everything's new for me! Don't worry! Leave it to me.

Demetrio: Come on, Giulia, go in and get this settled right now. Ruchetta, have I made myself clear? Goodbye!

Ruchetta: Play with the devil and he'll break your neck or tear off your limbs![49] O, my poor mistress, I almost wish you'd never been born.

Giulia: Eh, Ruchetta, how much better it would have been, since all the malignant stars were aligned at my birth and only bad things have happened to me. And I can truly say that from the day that I realized what was going on in the world, I became a target for the blows of ill Fortune, which, not satisfied with my endless suffering, added to its arsenal the force and power of Love, making me his subject and making me love someone who proves not so much kind in wounding me as showing cruelty in curing me; neither the copious tears that he sees gushing from my eyes, nor the passionate sighs that issue from my mouth, move him to care for me. And even so, any sign that he shows me only lights a bigger fire in my already inflamed and burning breast. Believe me, Ruchetta, never was a cloud so tossed and torn by raging and unfavorable winds as those that now torture my soul, with the multitude of wounds that puncture it.[50]

Ruchetta: Luck and Love will favor you if you behave wisely. Believe me, Mistress, I know your every secret, and even if I said I wished you'd never been born, I said it, forgive me, because I have known about your love almost from the beginning. And, if you have brought this unhappiness on yourself, it's your own fault. It's nothing but a shame that a big girl like you has delayed for so long to find out about the pleasures of love. Did you think you could live a hundred years in your virginal state? You're fooling yourself—nothing flies by faster than youth. Blessings on the soul of my mother who when she saw that I knew how to eat meat, gave me the strength and the freedom to procure my pleasures! You're complaining about your Luck without any reason, because good and bad luck are in our control. First of all, hasn't Fortune given you a young, handsome, rich, virtuous, well-bred nobleman who loves you as much as life itself? It's Flavio, isn't

49. Falavolti, 260nn4, 5, explains the complicated Italian expression *Va' col trentapara, che ti faccia rompere il collo, o possi tornare a casa come Pasquino!* The term trentapara refers to infernal forces, and Pasquino to a famous Roman statue with missing limbs.

50. Giulia speaks with the same flowery clichés as do Lepido and Flavio, the refinement of their language setting them apart from the servants, with their crude language, and the old men, with their straightforward unvarnished talk.

it? Now why are you feeling so sorry for yourself and complaining about him? Complain about you yourself and your stubbornness! Why did you say: I don't want to give in to him unless he takes me for his wife in public and if Master Demetrio doesn't know about it? And every time the poor man comes around you start to cry and sigh and complain about him. Excuse me for saying it, these are actions that would turn off even a dog who never gives up chasing his lady no matter how much he is beaten!

You need to know that since sir Flavio's a gentleman, he has to behave with you according to his manners and your merit. Ah, ah—you're sighing because it's true, isn't it?[51]

Giulia: I'm not sighing because you're speaking the truth, but because you should be accusing Flavio and excusing me—if it's true that he loves me as you say—for taking so long. Because in saying, "My Giulia, I'm dying for you, I'm in agony, I'll never love another woman but you, you are the only woman in my heart!" he doesn't do it in a way that leaves me happy and fulfilled. My Ruchetta, they say that it's from outer signs that we know the secret wishes of the heart; I don't deny that these sweet words bring me happiness because in these moments I believe everything my Lord Flavio says. But when he's away from me, and I think it over, I find that the words are very far from the truth, because if he feels and suffers for me as he says, he would have given me the sign and the satisfaction by speaking to Master Demetrio; in this way he would have fulfilled his obligation, thus bringing about our desired happiness, and I would not be dying for him the way I am.

Ruchetta: Mistress, you can come up with all the reasons that suit you, but what do you know about a possible scruple that has kept Flavio from revealing his desire to Master Demetrio? Remember that he's smart and sensible.

Giulia: I'm not disagreeing because he's shown it (as he says) in his choice of such a deserving woman who loves him very much and dies a thousand deaths every hour for him. But as for me, I don't know what scruple might be holding him back. My Ruchetta, young men nowadays love to enjoy themselves but even more to talk about it and get the glory for bragging: "that one was enjoyed by that one and that one was destroyed and ruined by that one." But I'm not saying that my Flavio is one of these. All the same, the fickleness and inconstancy of young men naturally makes me frightened. Still, there should be nothing holding Flavio back in asking Master Demetrio for my hand; if he's telling the truth.

51. Ruchetta as the maidservant who understands that she is an item at the sexual mercy of her master, sees the powerless position of Giulia who is about to be exchanged in marriage. She has taken ownership of her sexual pleasure and speaks out against the trap the young gentlewoman Giulia is in by having to safeguard her virginity. Her goal is to encourage Giulia to pledge herself to Flavio by being intimate with him and so prevent being forced to marry Gervasio. Ruchetta is the female version of Scaramuccia in her subversive acts to help the young lovers and in her outspoken social criticism.

Ruchetta: Mistress, I see how your pain is making you hesitate! Now, to bring this to an end, knowing as I do how compelling the force of this love is, I am driven (beyond the service I owe you) to help you out. Don't you worry, leave it in my hands—this old man will not be your husband. And you, on the other hand, be a little nicer to Flavio, and when you're talking to him, try to come to some agreement with him, in a way that you want, remembering always that he is a gentleman who won't do anything against your wishes.

Giulia: Ruchetta, you're right—I'm in your hands and I'm entrusting you with my life and honor. Go now, and find Flavio and speak to him for me, tell him everything, and make him come to me as quickly as possible.

Ruchetta: Leave it to me, go in, and get everything ready for when he arrives.

Giulia: What do you mean—ready for what?

Ruchetta: To put the little bird in the cage, if I bring it to you.[52]

Giulia: In what cage?

Ruchetta: In your natural cage, made by your mother.

Giulia: And where is it?

Ruchetta: Look for it and you'll find it easily.

Giulia: I don't know what you mean. Go and come back fast; and don't forget, I've put my honor in your hands.

Ruchetta: Curse this "honor" and whoever found it! Is it possible that this abuse is so respected and observed as law by everybody and that most women are so afraid to lose this unknown "honor"? I for my part, never had any great pleasure from it, except for the first time when I lost it, because it was a terrible nuisance, and now I could care even less to find it again! But who's coming? By God, it's Flavio, talking to himself as lovers do, coming here. I'll hide and hear what he's saying.

SCENE FIVE

Flavio and Ruchetta

Flavio: In fact, there is nothing, as the ancients noted, that is truer than this. Many like to think that love is nothing but an external contagion that comes into the eyes, and moves to the heart, depriving a man of himself and making him part of the beloved. That this is true, I know not only for myself, but also for Lepido,

52. The Italian phrase *Di rinchiudere il cardellino nella gabbia* is Ruchetta's way of reminding Giulia of the physical action she needs to take, playing on Giulia's naivety.

my dearest friend, who is so beside himself that he doesn't care about obeying his father, his own honor, or even life itself, as he tries to make possible the impossible, despite the odds against him and the risk of losing himself. O Love, these your delights, which you leave us to enjoy at first, how bitterly are they seasoned! I know it very well, now I really feel it, since you have shown yourself to be a lusty youth and now you are a very cruel old man! I believed so much that lured by you, I gathered the sweet fruits that you showed me in flower, but an angry windstorm blew them all away. From whence as I wait in misery for a new spring, I can say for sure: neither the sweetest bitterness of love, nor the spinning of the planet, nor making time pass, makes any difference, since spring is never going to come for me.[53]

Ruchetta: He's talking to himself and about love as always, and if I've heard right, he's mentioned Lepido.

Flavio: I could go on to say that, to heighten the sweetness of my pleasure, you, in the person of my Giulia, have shown yourself to be rather cruel in the past.

Ruchetta: He's still talking, but not about Lepido anymore.

Flavio: And I can already imagine hearing from your sweetest mouth: "Impetuous lover, don't you know that the greater the difficulty, the sweeter the prize?" But who is this I see over there? It looks like Ruchetta; that's her for sure.

Ruchetta: Oh! the hare is caught, and the hound is coming my way![54]

Flavio: Good to see you, Ruchetta, what were you doing standing over there?

Ruchetta: I was waiting to give you some good news.

Flavio: And what good news is this?

Ruchetta: Well, I was wondering if I ought to tell you what I have to say or not.

Flavio: If you have something to tell me, why are you hesitating?

Ruchetta: I was weighing it up because sometimes it's good to alter the plan and the rules depending on whether they could help or hurt others.

Flavio: I don't understand what you're saying. You're keeping me in suspense. Please, tell me what you have to say, and hurry up.

53. The lovers echo each other in stylized Neoplatonic expressions full of classical references and worship of Love.

54. The Italian phrase is *La lepre è scoperta e il bracco viene alla volta mia.* A certain irony is intended as she has also caught him and is about to set him up to get him to propose to Giulia. In 3.6, a similar reference is used to warn us that traps are being set. Hunting metaphors are used throughout.

Ruchetta: Well, Sir Flavio, you may know…

Flavio: May know what?

Ruchetta: Mistress Giulia is to …

Flavio: She is what? Please, tell me! O God, help me now.

Ruchetta: To be married! I'm telling you in good time!

Flavio: Who's to be married?

Ruchetta: Giulia.

Flavio: My Giulia to be married? My beloved? My soul?

Ruchetta: Your Giulia? What! You know that she's yours!

Flavio: Do I know it? And who would be the scoundrel, who so arrogant … who would have the nerve to take away what is rightfully mine?

Ruchetta: Who would it be? It would be Master Gervasio Grifone.

Flavio: Master Gervasio, the father of Porzia?

Ruchetta: Yes, sir, the very same.

Flavio: Alas, I am destroyed! Explain to me, if you please, how is it that this marriage is being arranged in such a hurry? Has Giulia agreed to it? Does Master Demetrio know about it? How is this happening? Tell me, my Ruchetta, please, tell me this instant.

Ruchetta: What do you mean does Master Demetrio know about it? And if he was told everything? Sir, a little while ago, he himself called Giulia and me out of the house and told her to get ready because he wants the wedding to happen tonight without delay.

Flavio: The wedding tonight? What did she say?

Ruchetta: What do you want her to have said? The poor thing (I'm going to give him a bit of rope),[55] like an obedient daughter, not knowing any other father, replied that she would do what he wanted according to his pleasure.

55. Ruchetta's comment is placed in parentheses to show it is an aside to the audience letting them know that she is playing him. These parentheses and many others included in the original 1618 edition help to demarcate different levels of address. They are not noted here in every case because they are too numerous. Characters also often speak to different addressees and even change their addressee on occasion. The reader has to be very aware of the full stage picture to grasp the multiple meanings.

Flavio: His pleasure and his wishes and no mention of me? Of the promises she made to me? Of all that has passed between us? Is this what you heard and saw? And you didn't say anything to her? O ungrateful Heaven, cruel Love, evil Fortune, unfaithful Giulia, what injustices are these? What betrayals of me? Giulia, you are leaving me for Gervasio? For Gervasio, you are abandoning your Flavio? The one you say is your reason for living in the world? On whom your every happiness depends? Alas, why is it that if I now know how false words are, I still don't also know how false hearts are? But Love won't allow me this, because it still doesn't seem to be sufficient cause to kill me! He wants to go slow, the cruel one, so that I have to hear, see, and find out for myself my mistake and betrayal by others, to bring greater suffering to my heart; so that, overcome by rightful indignation (for having been such a gullible lover), I'll kill myself with my own hands!

Ruchetta: The wound is festering too much![56] Hey, hey, Sir Flavio, what's your plan?

Flavio: My plan is to want to die, for the sole reason of depriving that cruel one of the pleasure of remembering how she had tricked me every time she saw me! Now go and tell her about my death and the world about her cruelty!

Ruchetta: I'll tell her what little trust you had in her and the world about how crazy you are! Eh, you worthless man (forgive me), without brains and without sense, what are these words coming out of your mouth? Do you believe that you deserve so little?

Flavio: What are you talking about trust? What are you saying about craziness? About being unworthy? Ruchetta, you're wrong to insult me this way.

Ruchetta: You not only deserve to be insulted, you also deserve even greater punishment, but I'll let Lady Giulia do that.

Flavio: I can't have any greater punishment, or greater pain than what I am experiencing and feeling now. But when you say that I consider myself unworthy, what are you trying to tell me?

Ruchetta: Maybe I'm speaking the truth? Don't you consider yourself to be unworthy for believing that Giulia is leaving you for that filthy snot-nose of a Gervasio?

Flavio: It's not because I don't know that I am worth more than him that I'm saying this, but because it makes me think that it's the nature of you women to

56. This comment, without parentheses, is delivered to the audience as an aside, thereby keeping us aware that Ruchetta is in control.

always bring about your own misery. And this then, which makes me believe it even more, is it being told to me and confirmed by you.[57]

Ruchetta: It's true that I've told you about it and confirmed it all, but for what reason? To see where you were to be found to tell you about it. And remember that you have insulted not only Giulia, but also me with what you've said and I hope above all that she will get her revenge for it. And I promise you that if it weren't for her love, I wouldn't help out anymore at all. So, women always bring their misery on themselves, eh? By God, let Giulia bring a good thing on herself this once, and let me destroy you on the spot.

Flavio: My Ruchetta, I beg you as I have said, don't make my suffering any worse. If I have offended Giulia, if I have offended you, here I am kneeling on the ground begging one and the other for forgiveness and punishment together. Don't you see, my excessive grief has destroyed my reason so much so that I can't speak properly? Come, if you want me to live, tell me everything, tell me what is going on and cheer me up, otherwise, here kneeling before you, I will kill myself with this rapier.

Ruchetta: Get up Sir Flavio, get up, may you not only appease my anger but that of every other furious woman! I forgive you and so Giulia will too. As I am tenderhearted, you young ones also have the sweetest ways with words! Come here, Sir Flavio, be happy, Giulia wants to be yours, in spite of Master Gervasio and the whole world and I have come to find you on purpose to tell you everything you need to know about it.

Flavio: Alas, who returns my heart to me? Who restores my spirits? Who thaws my blood? Who brings me life? My Ruchetta, my loving helper, full of mercy and kindness.

Ruchetta: You young men are all thieves of the hearts of us poor women! At least this life that I give you, you might use it for me another time again, because sometimes even the kitchen fire is good when it's cold, ah, ah, ah.

Flavio: Go on, my Ruchetta, and command your Flavio.

Ruchetta: Then I tell you that just a few minutes ago, Master Demetrio was willing to try anything to make Giulia say "yes," to agree to marry Master Gervasio, spreading his evil talk around. In the end the poor girl asked for the favor of a little time to think it over; yet giving high hopes to the old one who left happy enough but mumbling and grumbling away. Then poor Giulia, with tears in her eyes, threw herself on my mercy and at the same time began to cry over you. And

57. Flavio voices the typical misogynistic accusation that women cause their own misery by making bad choices.

truly, she has good reason, Sir Flavio, since you've had a lot of time, but you've never once resolved to speak to Master Demetrio. I've always made excuses for you and heaven knows how many times I'd have wished I was Giulia to be the first to make you happy! Then seeing her sighing and crying in this way, I promised to come to find you and plan a way that the marriage with Master Gervasio doesn't go ahead and that yours, as you have promised many times, takes place without any delays: and I promised all this to her, trusting only in your word. Now, what do you say, does Giulia love you or not?

Flavio: What can I say, Ruchetta, if not that the lover tormented with thoughts, pierced with jealousy, wasted by passion and conquered by unexpected scorn (brought on by mistrust), doesn't behave like a man but like an animal without reason? I, then, who have been operating without judgment for these reasons, am entitled to some leeway, since where thought isn't operating, it is not possible to punish one's crimes; therefore, I don't believe that I deserve to be punished for any mistakes I've made, neither by you, nor by my most beautiful and charming Giulia, but that they be most generously forgiven.

Ruchetta: Let's not talk any more about forgiveness since, being the law of love, the offended may be the one who asks the offender for forgiveness. But have you thought of a way you might bring this business to a conclusion?

Flavio: Love has taught me in an instant the way to go. Now listen and open your ears to what I am going to tell you, but above all, be silent!

Ruchetta: To give you a taste, I'll open more than my ears! Talk away, but as for being silent, it's hard for me because I'm a woman, still I'll do my best.

Flavio: You'll do fine. Now, know that your Lepido has come back.

Ruchetta: Lepido, the son of Master Demetrio?

Flavio: Lepido, yes, speak softly, so that no one will hear you.

Ruchetta: And why hasn't he come home? Does his father know about it yet?

Flavio: No, and here's why: know that when he left he was in love with Porzia, the daughter of Master Gervasio, and that he is still as much in love with her as he was four years ago.

Ruchetta: I know. But since she's married now, what does he intend to do?

Flavio: I'll explain it to you. In believing that she still loves him as much as she did before and that she was forced to get married by her father, he has decided not to reveal himself to his father until he has spoken to her, and in this way prove his innocence about some promise I don't know about that he made to her before he left. He's confided everything to me. Now, I want nothing more than to help Lepido out and I've thought of something that's good for both of us. Let Giulia pretend to agree to marry Gervasio but ask for a little more time, during which she pays a visit to their house with you and talks to Porzia to find out what she feels about Lepido, because she's more likely to tell her than you. Once you know that, you tell her that Lepido is back and what he's planning to do; and try to get her to agree so that Lepido can get what he wants, and so that I can have what I want as well. Because, to tell you the truth, I have always suspected that Demetrio was holding off marrying Giulia so that he could give her to Lepido on his return. And once we know that Porzia is his, we'll know for sure that any plans of his father are not going to work. And being assured that Lepido is happy, then I'll come forth and tell him everything, including about the love between Giulia and me, and also about what I have arranged with you to help him out. What do you say, Ruchetta? Do you like my plan? Does my reasoning make sense to you?[58]

Ruchetta: Completely! May you succeed! Sir Flavio, you're telling me big things, but I'm not entirely convinced! Now, how to stop this cursed love! As for your plan, it's seems to me to be doable, but you'll have to put it in action as soon as possible. But tell me, if you please, is it really true that the reason you have never asked Master Demetrio for Giulia is because of your suspicion that Lepido might have wanted her?

Flavio: Yes, of course.

Ruchetta: If you had asked me, I would have relieved that suspicion right away, because the old one would never have agreed to such a small dowry; but let's leave this. It seems to me that first you should speak to Giulia to console her, as she's all broken up.

Flavio: You're right. Ask her if she'll come out.

Ruchetta: She'll come out all right. Hide over there. Knock, knock, knock.

SCENE SIX

Giulia, Ruchetta, and Flavio

Giulia: Who's knocking?

Ruchetta: I am, mistress.

Giulia: Why don't you come in? Are you alone?

58. Flavio is trying to take charge over the plot, but he will be forced to fall in line with Scaramuccia's master intrigue.

Ruchetta: No, mistress.

Giulia: Who's with you?

Ruchetta: Your bridegroom, who's come to take your hand.

Giulia: Damn it, what you almost made me say. Come in, to hell with you, don't stay out there any longer.

Ruchetta: Come outside, I say, the master wants you.

Giulia: The master?

Ruchetta: Yes, my lady.

Giulia: I'm coming. O unhappy Giulia!

Ruchetta: It's all good. This time I'm giving you the bad taste first, and then following it with something sweet!

Giulia: Here I am. Where's your master? O Ruchetta, you're trying to upset me (be patient), oh, well, that's the story of my life. So, then, did you see that ungrateful Flavio? The one who is the reason that I am burning up with hopeless passion?

Flavio: O my love, if you are burning up, I am already turned to ashes—only the hope of enjoying you keeps me alive.

Ruchetta: Well, I found him, and I didn't: here he is, half alive and half dead. It's up to you to revive him.

Giulia: Ah, you traitor—is this the love you said you had for me? Is this my reward for trusting you? O miserable creature that I am, I can see that it's another flame that warms your breast, a different fire that inflames your heart. Oh, where, where will I ever find trust, if I now see it dead in the breast of someone who swore he was its true temple?

Flavio: My Giulia, here stands your Flavio, here is the heart which has always been, and still remains the temple of true love, just as your face is the temple of true beauty.

Giulia: Alas, my Flavio, my soul—what betrayals are these? I beg you, forgive this poor wretch, if driven by sorrow she said anything that offended you. Ruchetta, how could you do this to me, eh? Enough!

Flavio: My dearest, don't worry about Ruchetta, or fear that I won't forgive you: how could that beautiful mouth give offence, the mouth where I want to spread love's nectar like a busy bee.

Giulia: My only love, you have already seized my heart like a bird of prey. Then also take from these lips, as they are, that happiness that you desire.

Ruchetta: Come on, what are you waiting for? Accept the invitation, strike while the iron is hot!

Flavio: O happy, fortunate Flavio: what are these words that come to me from the source of all my happiness? When and how, can I repay my Lady Giulia for such a gift as I am now receiving?

Giulia: When, my dear sir? When you keep the promise you have made so often, to be my husband—and we must not delay if you want me to be yours, for you may not know what fortune threatens us with.

Flavio: Ruchetta has told me everything, and we have worked out a solution that she will tell you about—just do as she tells you. You know too well I have promised to be your husband, but here again in the presence of Ruchetta as our witness, I solemnly swear to marry you, calling as witness not only Love, but all the gods who look after marriage. And if Flavio ever falls short of the promise he now makes to his beautiful and dearest bride, may he not only die disgraced, but may his soul suffer forever the fires of hell.

Ruchetta: Well, my stingy lady, what do you say to that? This is how men like to be. Go on, yes, take her hand, we're blushing a little, and we're so overcome with tenderness we don't know what to say—come on, what are you waiting for, aren't you going to kiss her?

Giulia: Hold me, my love, oh, I am afraid that happiness will overpower me in a way suffering never could, my dearest Flavio.

Flavio: My soul, my happiness, what is this my heart is feeling? Hold me, hold me close, my love!

Ruchetta: Hey, wait, you young pups! We're in the street here—hey, you there, don't get carried away, let's at least get inside the house!

Giulia: Alas no, my Ruchetta! Come now, my lord, I leave you feeling utter joy.

Flavio: And I too depart full of bliss.

Giulia: I am so thrilled, my love.

Flavio: And I'm over the moon, my dear heart.

Ruchetta: Liars! From what I see, you're ready to do more than talk. Stop, stop, break it up, now! Giulia, into the house, because if the master or Scaramuccia were to come it would ruin everything.

Giulia: Goodbye, Sir Flavio, take care of my heart.

Flavio: And you my soul, Lady Giulia. Ruchetta, remember to keep Giulia informed of what we've agreed; I'm in your hands.

Ruchetta: It'll be up to you to keep her in line, with a good bang the way shoemakers do with their little hammers.[59]

Act Two

SCENE ONE

Scaramuccia, Licinio, and Porzia

Scaramuccia: I'd rather be trying to keep check on a dozen wild stallions in a pack of mares, than reining in a young man in love—or to put it more clearly, raring to go. I've talked to him for three hours, but nothing has changed: he's possessed, I'm sure, because anyone with sense would listen to reason. But he's as willing to be reasonable as I am to starve myself, and he's resolved that he's going to speak to Porzia or kill himself. Speak to a young lady, only six months married, and, moreover, who is she married to? Only to the most jealous husband ever seen in this city—as rumor has it! A tiny brain and a pair of hands like the devil, and never leaves her side. What the hell have I got myself into? Lepido says "She used to love me," but that's past tense, you've got to see how she feels in the present. In the good old days, when she did, she didn't know what she knows now: you brought joy to her eyes, to her ears, to her mouth—but what about that other mouth she's now discovered down below? That one that gets bigger without feeding it? We've got trouble, I tell you, real trouble. I've promised to help him and if it kills me, I have to do it. Come on, Scaramuccia, smarten up, show some courage! Master Gervasio's not home, what'll I do? I'll knock anyway, and I'll know who it is from their voice. Knock, knock, knock, knock.[60]

Licinio: Who's down below? Who's knocking?

Scaramuccia: Bad beginning! This is the voice of the husband, I'll knock again, whatever happens. Knock, knock, knock, knock.

59. The Italian is *Toccherebbe a voi d'informarla con un buon bussetto, come fanno i valenti calzolai.* Falavolti, 272n1, notes that a *bussetto* is a little steel hammer with a raised part in the head and that there is an obvious obscene double meaning.

60. Scaramuccia's monologue as he approaches Licinio and Porzia's front door serves multiple purposes in setting up the first stage appearance of the fake husband and his wife. Licinio's maniacal jealousy is associated with the devil himself. Scaramuccia, like Ruchetta, refers to the part the body plays in lovemaking in no uncertain terms to make this marriage seem real. The sound of the knocking shows how Scala includes noises and sounds beyond the dialogue.

Licinio: May your hands and tongue shrivel and fall off. Can't you knock more softly and answer the first time? Who's knocking, I say?

Scaramuccia: And may your blood dry up in your veins! Oh, no, Licinio is going to appear when the door opens; I'm going to hide here since I don't want to see him.[61]

Licinio: Hello, who is it? Who was knocking at the door? I don't see anyone, Porzia. Come down.

Porzia: I'm coming, my lord.

Licinio: I don't doubt that there are those who want to do me harm in this city; I don't know what kind of mischief they do to the houses of gentlemen. I'm sure that this must be some knavish ruffian.

Scaramuccia: He's got good judgment; and knew me from my knock.

Porzia: I'm here, sir, what do you want me to do?

Licinio: Did you hear someone knock at the door?

Porzia: No sir, when?

Licinio: Just now, and where were you hiding, in the cellar? (Don't be surprised at the way I'm talking—we're being watched and heard.)[62] Where the devil were you hiding?

Porzia: I was on the veranda, hanging out your collars.

Licinio: Haven't I told you not to go into the veranda where you can be seen and heard from the piazza? Porzia, Porzia, this desire to have your own way, your not wanting to pay attention to what I say is going to lead to a time when I will be permanently displeased by you! Then you won't have a husband anymore but a big devil who will torment you endlessly.

Scaramuccia: If you are the devil, go back to hell then, since you can never conquer your wife—if the novella is telling the truth.[63]

61. Once Scaramuccia is in hiding but known to the audience, the jealousy scene between Licinio and Porzia can be played to the hilt, with Licinio responding to Scaramuccia's suggestions and pushing them even further to include all the spaces in the house where women have to stay locked up—including in the toilet.

62. Licinio's parenthetical remark to Porzia indicates that she knows who is there and wants to play her role as the devil himself as Porzia's captor. The audience has the extra pleasure of being in on the duplicity and seeing who can be the wittiest.

63. The novella in question is a story collected in *A Hundred Popular Tales from Lucca* by Idelfonso Nieri in which the devil loses a sewing contest to a woman because he forgot to tie a knot in his thread,

Porzia: My dear husband, please forgive me: you are always complaining about my shortcomings.

Licinio: I always have a reason to grumble when you will not do what I ask. I'm telling you once again that when I am not at home you must never dare to answer the door to any living person.

Scaramuccia: Then she'll go to the window.

Licinio: Neither show yourself at the window.

Scaramuccia: She'll go to the balcony overlooking the garden.

Licinio: And take care that temptation doesn't lead you to go to the balcony that overlooks the garden.

Scaramuccia: And what will he say about her answering a call of nature?

Licinio: And should it be necessary, I'll have a key made to the door of the bathroom.

Scaramuccia: By God, I hit the nail on the head! May you be circumcised like a Jew!

Licinio: (They'd have very little to throw away!)[64] Go into the house as I want to go to the market and when Master Gervasio gets home, tell him that I want to dine early.

Porzia: Of course. Do you want anything else?

Licinio: Nothing else, do what you've been told. Now go inside, because I want to leave.[65]

Scaramuccia: Go away—the way my father did, and never come back.

Porzia: O heavens, I thank you so much for giving me a husband who you see loves me to perfection and looks out for my honor. And I would be deserving of whatever severe punishment he wished if I the slightest intention of doing him any wrong ever came into my head. O my dear husband, if only you knew how much love I have for you, you wouldn't be so jealous of me.

---

leading to the expression, "a woman knows more than the devil." See Falavolti, 274n1.

64. Licinio's parenthetical remark in response to Scaramuccia's curse gives us privileged information: he is, in fact, a woman.

65. The dialogue indicates that Licinio leaves, but that Porzia remains outside despite being told to go in. Porzia is now able to receive Scaramuccia.

Scaramuccia: Good God, it seems to me that I've already got evidence of the opposite without a fight. Now go Lepido, and trust in those words "she used to love me"! At least you heard these four words spoken! Eh, for his sake, I want to talk to him and let him know his fortune; and then let her do what she wants.
Greetings, Lady Porzia.

Porzia: Greetings, Scaramuccia. And what miracle is this that I am seeing you at this time. What are you up to?

Scaramuccia: My lady, there are many reasons that keep me from coming to pay my respects to your ladyship.

Porzia: And what are they?

Scaramuccia: For one because of the sight of your very jealous husband and me being a coward; the other because when I see you, my blood runs faster thinking of the great love that my poor wife Brigida had for you, so much so that I don't know if she could have loved you more even if she'd carried you in her womb for nine months. Ah, ah, my dear wife taken from me so soon by heaven, ah, ah, ah.

Porzia: Why are you crying, Scaramuccia? Are you crying because Brigida is dead? If that is so then you're different from most husbands who are for the most part delighted when their wives die.

Scaramuccia: Yes, those that don't love them, Mistress Porzia; but I loved Brigida while she was alive and now I love and honor her even more in death.[66]

Porzia: How true, Scaramuccia because, as they say, "when you have loved someone once, you'll never wish them ill, and a true and perfect love is never forgotten."

Scaramuccia: That saying suits my purpose. Do you believe that this is true, mistress?

Porzia: I do believe it and consider it a certainty. But why are you asking me this?

Scaramuccia: Do you want to hear what I have to say?

Porzia: Why, don't you want me to?

Scaramuccia: Tell me, please, have you ever found a greater love in the world than you had for Lepido? And have you completely forgotten it now? O mistress, if you knew what Lepido's life is like now…

66. Scaramuccia's tears would indicate that he recognizes who Licinio really is, adding to the levels of deception that must be maintained in order for the plot to unfold.

Porzia: I couldn't care less, and it is true that I've forgotten him, but he forgot me first, and he showed it, by not keeping the promise he made me. Moreover, he didn't even have a reason to abandon me. But I had reason and cause to abandon him since we all know that one abandons mother and father for the husband; and therefore, it's easy to abandon someone who breaks their promise and betrays you.

Scaramuccia: You're right. But you can't call Lepido either a promise breaker or a traitor.

Porzia: No, why not? You don't know what arrangements we made when we were parted. Your dear departed wife knew it well.

Scaramuccia: Mistress Porzia, I also know something. I only want you to see for yourself what a predicament Lepido is in at this time.

Porzia: You couldn't find anything so bad that he doesn't deserve worse! With this little bit of news, you have offended not only me but all the mighty gods to whom he swore that he'd marry me. But what evil has befallen him? Perhaps some news of him has come?

Scaramuccia: Mistress, according to his thinking, he has always kept his promises to you. But misfortune has unhappily thwarted his plans. It would be enough if you could take his hand and listen to his humble explanation and the reasons for your misunderstanding. But you're asking me if I have any news of him? O mistress, is it possible that your soul hasn't told your heart that your Lepido has come back?

Porzia: Lepido is back?

Scaramuccia: Mistress, yes, he's back. And he's back for you and no one else. And to prove it, he hasn't told anyone except me, so that he could come and see you.

Porzia: And you're bringing him to me for what reason? O Scaramuccia, he's passed the time, not to say the end date that I would have been happy to hear such news, and maybe my heart (as you said) would have felt his return. But now he is no less far from my thoughts than I am from his because of his lack of love and loyalty.

Scaramuccia: Mistress Porzia, forgive me; you are wrong. I'll show you and show you clearly that you have remained forever in Lepido's thoughts. It's very true that fortune, jealous of your happiness, has tried to make it impossible for him to ever carry out the promises he made to you; but if you are willing to hear him out, you could understand better from him, since he has no other purpose (once he was allowed to leave Lyon) but to return home incognito, in order to defend himself to you, and if you do not accept his true and just reasons, to tell the world that he was your true husband before Licinio, and having done so, leave you free to enjoy your happiness, and then kill himself with his own hands.

Porzia: Scaramuccia, what you say is making me laugh; and aware of my mistake, I can't stay here with you any longer, nor respond to what you've told me. So, go away with your great plan as I want to go in so that my husband won't find me talking to you. Your master can console himself with a new love that he must have left behind in Lyon, and that's the reason why he's here incognito, to be able to go back to her. I understand that his conscience is eating away at him, and for this reason he would like to make his lame excuses to me. And so, Scaramuccia, goodbye.

Scaramuccia: Mistress, for the great love you have for Lepido, listen to a few more words.

Porzia: When love is cancelled in the mind, the ear shuts off when it hears about it; thus, I swear to you, my Scaramuccia, your words won't affect me.

Scaramuccia: If you're mine, hear one word and for the love that you have for your husband, make it two.

Porzia: My love for my husband is too great! Come on then, tell me, I'm listening.[67]

Scaramuccia: What luck—here he is, your Lepido!

Porzia: Answer me, what are you looking at? Hurry up, tell me what are you waving at?

SCENE TWO

Lepido, Porzia, and Scaramuccia

Lepido: That's Scaramuccia in the distance over there and he's trying to say something to me. Oh no. What do I see? Isn't that Porzia talking to him? It is—O Love, I beg you, help me in this endeavor.

Porzia: Scaramuccia, are you possessed? Well, if you won't talk, goodbye again.

Scaramuccia: Where are you going? Please listen, Porzia. Lepido, come here, come on, oh hell, what are you waiting for, you wretch? My lady, please listen to this gentleman who wants to speak for me.

Porzia: What gentleman? Ah, traitor, you want me dead, don't you?

67. Here Porzia is having it both ways, professing her loyalty to her husband, but showing she is ready to listen.

Lepido: On the contrary, my death would give you more life, my beloved Porzia.

Porzia: Me, your beloved? Ah, go away, Lepido, and stop trying to sully my honor with your insolence. O misery, I can feel my soul leaving my body! Help me, Scaramuccia, help me! Who is stealing my light! Oh, help me, give me the same hand that once pierced my heart! Hold me, I'm dying![68]

Scaramuccia: Lady, take courage. Hey, what's this? Lepido, what's going on here, Lepido? Porzia? Hey, this is serious! She's gone so cold! Alas!

Lepido: My dear Porzia, what is causing you so much pain? Does my very presence reduce you to this? You don't answer? Answer me, my beloved—O heavens, why did you give me the courage to come here? Maybe so that I might become my own murderer? Because that's what will happen if something stops my Porzia's soul from returning to her most beautiful body. I, with my own hands, will dispatch my suffering soul so that it may go to find the soul of the one that lights it, with God, and thus, in spite of my father's wishes, they shall be joined together, if not in the flesh, at least in the spirit!

Scaramuccia: Master, I'm going to drop her, I can't hold her any longer.

Lepido: And yet here, my dear Porzia, as now my hand touches you with gentle affection, the same hand that will be no less a thief to Lepido than it has been to Porzia; since, as you said, it robbed you of your heart, and will rob me of my soul. And here, unfortunate me, also with those pale and cold cheeks that once showed themselves to me like a blanket of snow making a bed for the purple roses of your beautiful face.[69]

Scaramuccia: I'm telling you, I can't hold her any longer! And we're running a risk being here.

Lepido: O Porzia, my soul, these are those very beautiful loving eyes, from whence shot the arrow that through my eyes pierced my heart, and left it so deeply wounded. O lovely, beautiful eyes, now closed, but no less lovely—cursed be destiny, and the moment that led me to gaze on you! Cursed be Love who gathered up such beauty in you! Cursed be the arrow that wounded me, and—finally—cursed be all the blessings which are in you, tyrant Love, since they are the cause of her death and mine.

68. Porzia faints, allowing Lepido to fall into declaiming on the sorrows of death and its sting.

69. The Neoplatonic theories of bodies and souls being exchanged by lovers is made concrete by Lepido. Scaramuccia counters this exalted thinking by struggling not to drop Porzia.

SCENE THREE

Trapola, Scaramuccia, Lepido, and Porzia

Trapola: O mistress, now where have you got to?

Scaramuccia: Lepido, get out of here, I hear someone, it sounds like Trapola, heaven help us now! Duck in there, the door's open.[70]

Lepido: Oh, woe is me, Scaramuccia, hold her, don't drop her on the ground.

Scaramuccia: Leave it to me, don't worry. Godspeed you on your way, I'm telling you.

Trapola: It's very hard work to keep women locked up in the house, since they're always yearning to be seen! O poor Licinio, if your jealousy doesn't make you into a cuckold, then I'm an idiot! Where in God's name has she gone? This isn't like her.

Scaramuccia: Attention, O neighbors, O people, O good friend, O Trapola, O nasty beast, oh!

Trapola: Who's that calling me?

Scaramuccia: O poor girl, what does this mean? Hallo, who am I talking to? Aren't you her servant? O you scum, come and help me, damn you, can't you see it's your mistress?

Trapola: Alas, what do I see? Isn't this my mistress? You've killed her, you traitor! Justice! Justice! O my poor little mistress, and who'll make the good soups? Who'll bake the cakes in our house? O poor Trapola! How did you kill her, traitor? Show me your weapon.

Scaramuccia: I'll show you the rope that I'll hang you with, you stupid sheep! Can't you see that she's only fainted and if by good luck, I hadn't arrived here to catch her, she would have fallen down and killed herself.

Lepido: O good Scaramuccia! Hear me, my life, wake up!

Trapola: Where did she faint? Then she isn't dead? Her eyes and mouth seem dead to me, where is the life?

Scaramuccia: Hmm, you baboon, take her, hold her, put your arms around her, and let's carry her inside.

70. Lepido leaves the scene and hides nearby where he continues to express his torment over his dead beloved.

Trapola: Put my arms around her? How stupid is that! And what would Master Licinio say?

Scaramuccia: It's only dangerous if Licinio finds out about it: let's carry her inside, I say.

Trapola: Come on then, let's carry her. You take the bottom, and I'll take the top. O poor mistress!

Scaramuccia: Don't kiss her; you traitor.[71]

Trapola: Your loss, my gain; let's go in.

Lepido: Oh! My most unhappy day ever, oh! You cruel tyrant Fortune, to you alone I must complain, you alone are the cause of my misery! Cruel you, you tried everything to put out my loving fire, but you failed, since you don't have any power over our hearts. Unhappy me, now I know so clearly that I was born under an evil star and malignant ascendant, since I see my lady in others' hands and as if dead before my eyes. Now what will you, my sorrowful eyes, do without your beloved object? All you can do is keep on crying a never-ending flood of painful tears. Cry then, eyes, cry and join with my wretched broken heart, until the pain becomes so unbearable that I lose my tormented life, which I so desire to end, since my Porzia (woe is me) no longer cares for me.[72]

SCENE FOUR

Giulia, Lepido, Ruchetta, and Scaramuccia

Giulia: Remember, do for Lepido and me what you would do for yourself.

Lepido: I see the door of my father's house opening and Ruchetta coming out. I'm going to hide and see what she's up to.

Ruchetta: Leave it up to me, mistress, don't worry about it! I thank heaven that I have a sweet nature and that everyone knows it and so everyone is pleased. In fact, I've never wanted to know about the problems in this world and the biggest one that I have had has been to make myself lovable and receive caresses from everyone. And this seems to be the most beautiful and useful thing that an easy-going woman like me can have. My lady is truly in the worst possible situation for a lover to be in, and in the end, she's right, because it's bad for anyone to starve

71. Trapola's role as the uncouth manservant leads him to take extreme liberties with Porzia's unconscious body, since he is holding her top half. The physical comedy is played to the extreme.

72. Lepido's tirade against Love for inflicting such damage sets up a perfect contrast to Porzia's limp body being carried off. His lament is contrasted by the grotesque comedy of playing with her "dead" body. This elastic gag is milked into the next scenes.

and worse for those on whom nature has bestowed the means to enjoy the fruit. I haven't seen that low-life deceiver Trapola for so long that I bet he's found some other oven to fill, while I go wanting.[73] But maybe I can make him agree that if he'll switch ovens, I'll switch pokers! I want to go to Lady Porzia's to do whatever my mistress has asked me to do.[74]

Lepido: I have to leave so that Ruchetta doesn't see me.[75]

Ruchetta: But who's that coming out of Porzia's? My God, it's Scaramuccia! What business does he have there?

Scaramuccia: Come on; goodbye, Trapola, take good care of your mistress. Oh, what a big mess this is! Thank God the poor girl came to, and even better that she said, "My Lepido!" That means she really loves him.

Ruchetta: He's talking about Lepido. I'm sure that he must know that he's back.

Scaramuccia: O, you're here, you hot piece? Where're you going, Ruchetta, my tasty morsel?

Ruchetta: To search for a bit for human seed for my mistress.

Scaramuccia: What, human seed? What are you talking about?

Ruchetta: Roman seed, yes, that I know.[76]

Scaramuccia: Ah, I believe you said it right the first time, no need to repeat yourself. But what does your mistress want to do with this seed?

Ruchetta: Plant it in her garden.

Scaramuccia: The roots are planted, and the little radishes that then make the seed, and are the best for her garden where these noble little plants are spread. But where are you going to find it?[77]

73. Ruchetta uses the Italian phrase *la nature patisce* ("nature can't wait"). This phrase reoccurs several times in the play: Trapola in 2:9; Licino and Porzia in 3.7.

74. Ruchetta's monologue fills us in on her freewheeling sexuality and her disdain for female "honor" which seems to be a typical stance of the maidservant and speaks to the self-reflexive awareness that working-class women have towards their status as outside the middle and upper-class marriage market. Her vivid descriptions of pokers and ovens tells us that she spreads herself around the city. We also appreciate her willingness to settle down with Trapola, even if they have been around the block many times.

75. Lepido introduces the scene as an eavesdropper but has to leave, so that he does not hear what Porzia says when she wakes up.

76. Flavio is Roman, but so is Gervasio.

77. Tasty wild radishes fit the metaphor of Giulia's getting the right man in her garden.

Ruchetta: In her bridegroom's house.

Scaramuccia: Which bridegroom?

Ruchetta: Then you don't know? Hasn't your master told you? Master Gervasio Grifone is the bridegroom and Master Demetrio made the arrangements a little while ago. But Giulia …

Scaramuccia: I didn't know anything about it because I haven't spoken to the old man this morning. But what about Giulia?

Ruchetta: Honestly, she doesn't want any part of it.

Scaramuccia: That's sounds smart to me that she thinks like this! What could she possibly want with a stupid old man like him? But why is she sending you to find him now?

Ruchetta: I'll tell you, Scaramuccia, because with you I can speak freely and share all the details. Giulia is sending me not to talk to the old one, but to Porzia to tell her that Lepido is back and to beg her, on my mistress's behalf, to talk to him.

Scaramuccia: And who told Giulia that Lepido was back?

Ruchetta: Sir Flavio, who, with me as witness, also married her. And he asked her to send me to Porzia as a favor to his friend.

Scaramuccia: Everything's going according to my plan; and if the old man is at home?[78]

Ruchetta: I'll pretend to be visiting him as the bridegroom, because Flavio has asked her to act happy in order to help Lepido.

Scaramuccia: Yes, yes, I get it. They're ahead of me! My Ruchetta, I know all about it: go home and don't do anything else; and tell Giulia to cheer up because I'll make it happen that she'll have Flavio soon enough, and Lepido will also definitely get what he wants.

Ruchetta: Eh, you scoundrel, I heard you talking about Lepido a while ago, and to tell the truth, I know that you've always been his confidant, but in this case, it's my loss.

Scaramuccia: Loss of what, your honor?

78. Scaramuccia gets Ruchetta to fill him in on everything she is doing to help the lovers and then he claims control over the larger plan, possibly indicating his position as *capocomico*, but also showing how the ensemble works together to streamline plot development.

Ruchetta: Don't talk about that, I never had it, nor do I care to. I'm telling you this because if I did go to Porzia's house, I could see something that appeals to me.

Scaramuccia: And what thing, maybe your Trapola, eh? Slut,[79] you think I don't know you and understand what you're up to?

Ruchetta: A slut, why? I've never swallowed anything of yours. And then you, you haven't asked since you've taken an oath of chastity since your wife died. How stupid, what is chastity to the dead, it is a waste of time! You ask what do I want? Yes, you're right, to see my Trapola; what harm am I doing? I'm taking care of myself; don't you know that if you don't have a fire at home, you look for it nearby?

Scaramuccia: Eh, as for fire, you could lend some to all the fireplaces in Rome. Now Ruchetta, go home, and I promise you to make some plan with Trapola that will make you happy; what do you say?

Ruchetta: Yes, oh hear me, my dear Scaramuccia, I'm counting on you! And if you don't want to service the mule yourself, at least find the doctor who will!

Scaramuccia: Oh, drop dead, you good-for-nothing! Still on the one hand, I like her attitude, which isn't like that of most other slutty female servants, who knowing that they have the goodwill and protection of the master, play the mistress of the house and pinch the pennies, acting cocky not only with the other female and male servants, but with their own masters, relatives and the whole neighborhood, and always want to keep the keys in their hands and be the custodians of the bread, wine, oil and everything without any exceptions, nor let anyone else open anything when they aren't present. I wish we could get rid of such useless riffraff! As for me, I would like it if all masters agreed with me, so that they wouldn't allow such rabble into their homes, but would only employ servants suited to the work, so that they can go to the piazza and everywhere, at all hours without any danger.[80] But who is that couple looking so downcast coming this way?

SCENE FIVE

Flavio, Lepido, Scaramuccia, and Gervasio

Flavio: Take it easy, Sir Lepido, I don't want you falling into the same depression as before! You don't know what may come out of this business. Seeing Ruchetta

79. The Italian is *lova* which also means "she-wolf" or "prostitute."

80. Scaramuccia's commentary is cynical and misogynist but at the same time aware of Ruchetta's more generous spirit, including her promiscuity.

coming out of the house isn't bad because, as I told you, she must have gone to Porzia's on your behalf, as I asked her to.[81]

Lepido: Ah, Sir Flavio, it's much easier for you to console me with words than for me to believe that I will ever be happy by way of love.

Flavio: Do you think there is any other way?

Lepido: Yes.

Flavio: What?

Lepido: In despair, the way I will come to the end of all my misery.

Flavio: Hear me, Lepido mine, please put away these troubling thoughts and believe me, my heart tells me that not only will you see Porzia alive today, but that you will find happiness with her.

Scaramuccia: It's time to make an appearance. What's going on, Sir Flavio, perhaps you are talking about Sir Lepido?

Flavio: Yes, my dear Scaramuccia. Well, what news do you have?

Scaramuccia: Lepido, (alas) she is …

Lepido: Scaramuccia? What? Dead?

Scaramuccia: Gone, there's no remedy.

Lepido: What do you say, Sir Flavio? Are these the favors, the pleasure that your heart is preparing for me? You are dead, my life? You, are you thus gone to the celestial home without me? And me, cruel murderer of all that is beautiful in the world, do I remain unpunished? But don't believe, don't ever believe, my most beautiful love, that having promised to find you, I won't come for you now that you are circling with the stars! And here is my right hand, that you called upon for help, already preparing for my death?

Scaramuccia: Slow down, Sir Lepido, I don't know how to tell you this.

Flavio: Stop, Sir Lepido, what craziness is this? You haven't understood properly. Go on, Scaramuccia, what do you have to tell him?

Scaramuccia: That she said this to me in the house, "My Lepido!"

Flavio: Then she isn't dead; listen, Sir Lepido.

81. The fact that Lepido is last to hear about Porzia's return to life spins this gag out to its explosive end, as the words she utters on awakening almost burn off Scaramuccia's beard.

Lepido: What are you saying, Scaramuccia? That my love isn't dead?

Scaramuccia: Sir, yes, she is dead. But…

Lepido: O Sir Flavio, it's clear that you are teasing me.

Flavio: Take it easy, my lord. Scaramuccia, what are you saying? She's dead but, but what?

Scaramuccia: But she's come back to life and is alive.

Flavio: What do you say, Lepido?

Lepido: Alas, I am dying! Scaramuccia, is my Porzia alive or dead?

Scaramuccia: She's dead. That is, dead to you, but alive to Licinio, her husband.

Lepido: Just the fact that she's alive makes me happy, since she will always be alive in my mind, even if I know I am dead in hers. Patience, I'll live with the hope of speaking to her one more time.

Flavio: Sir Lepido, I have hope in my heart that it'll come true what I told you about earlier.

Lepido: May it please heaven, Sir Flavio. But please tell me, Scaramuccia, didn't you say that she said, "My Lepido"?

Scaramuccia: Oh, that's only the beginning.[82] You know that when she woke up, she let out a huge sigh, and then she said, "My Lepido," so passionately that she almost scorched my beard.

Lepido: Sir Flavio, what do you say now?

Flavio: The very best sign, good work, Scaramuccia.

Scaramuccia: From these words, I've concluded that the Lady Porzia still loves you, and that everything she does, is out of fear of her husband. Many ideas are churning around in my head, and amongst them, those of Sir Flavio, as explained to me by Ruchetta, which are nothing if not good. But I've thought of another plan that might be even better.

Flavio: Do you know if Ruchetta has talked to Porzia yet?

Scaramuccia: No sir, she hasn't because I sent her back home. Enough, gentlemen, don't you worry; what more do you want than that I do everything in my power

82. The Italian compares her initial reaction to a small tinkle that turned into the loud clanging of a bell. See Falavolti, 287n1.

to make both of you happy? Sir Flavio, I know about your love and what has happened between you and Giulia.

Lepido: Ah, Scaramuccia, I'm the one who is suffering; Sir Flavio can call himself happy.

Scaramuccia: Take it easy, sir, there's always a way out for everyone.

Flavio: Go ahead and believe it because Scaramuccia is telling the truth.

Scaramuccia: Come now, let's get down to business. There's something that I want us to try: Sir Flavio, I know that Master Gervasio doesn't know you, nor will he recognize Sir Lepido because he's been away so long.

Lepido: He's right that he won't recognize me, but he'll know Sir Flavio who lives right near here.

Flavio: No, he won't, because he's a doddering old fool and he has never paid much attention to me.

Scaramuccia: Now, when you see him, I want you to introduce yourselves and congratulate him on his betrothal to Giulia; and tell him that everyone in Rome is delighted with his marriage and that you, virtuous youths, want to show respect for his wedding and wait on him. Since he's half crazy, he'll accept your offer, and when that happens, tell him that you want to see where the banquet's being held and get into his house. What the hell, here he comes, keep your wits about you, because I want to hide so that I don't spoil our plan.[83]

Lepido: Sure, but what'll we do? What if it doesn't work?

Flavio: Whatever happens, let's try hard to get into his house.

SCENE SIX

Gervasio, Lepido, and Flavio

Gervasio: One hour seems like a thousand waiting to find out if my marriage will happen. When I tell my friends about getting married they all compliment me. I feel my blood surging as if I were twenty-five again. But who's there in front of my house?

83. Gervasio is listed in this scene because he is seen arriving as it ends. Scaramuccia's plan to trick Gervasio into letting them into his house takes place in 2.6, which follows. Here Flavio and Lepido assume false identities to torture Gervasio with veiled insults about his masculinity as they pretend to be musicians wanting to play at his wedding. An interesting comic diversion, this plot strand goes nowhere. See the Introduction, 25–26.

Lepido: Master Belisario, what did you say was the name of the master of this house?

Flavio: Master Cesario, I don't remember very well, but I know that it is a name like Galafrone or Gastone.

Gervasio: Castrone? Who the hell are they talking about? And he's looking at my house, and they'll trap me very quickly, if they're talking about me! But what can they want? They're standing there, what's this all about?

Flavio: Master Belisario, let's ask this gentleman here.

Lepido: Good idea. At the service of your lordship, master, would you know where to find a certain gentleman named Gervasio Galafrone or Gastone?

Flavio: Castrone, castrone, who is the bridegroom?[84]

Gervasio: Do you mean Grifone, young man?

Lepido: My lord, yes, that's it, if you know him, please tell us how to find him.

Gervasio: My young gentlemen, could I know who you are and why you are looking for him?

Flavio: Yes, sir, of course. This is Master Belisario, the ballet master, and I am the musician Cesario, well-known and respected throughout Rome.

Gervasio: Ah, ah, I heard the musician spoken highly of a little while ago, please continue.

Flavio: Yes, sir, now having understood that this Master Castrone …

Gervasio: Grifone.

Flavio: Yes, sir, since he's signed a marriage contract with Master Demetrio, we, as virtuosos, would like to see him happy and have come to honor his nuptials, knowing that Master Demetrio would wish it. Therefore, your lordship, could you please point him out.

Gervasio: To tell you the truth, Master Cesario, I am that so-called Master Gervasio Grifone.

Flavio: Your lordship, is it Sir Gervasio? O, my sir, O my master, I go down on my knees for you.

84. Having Flavio and Lepido mistake his name over and over again so that they can call him Castrone foreshadows that he will be a castrated cuckold if he marries Giulia.

Lepido: O my master, my dear sir, I kiss the hem of your lordship's cape.

Flavio: And I do the same.

Lepido: O Master Gervasio, how happy it makes me to know your lordship.

Flavio: O sir bridegroom, my master, let's go inside and see the room for the festivities.

Lepido: Let's go in, my lord, isn't this your house?

Gervasio: Slow down, gentlemen, your happiness alarms me. I thank you, I praise your goodwill and I promise you that I'll make use of you on the day; however, leave it for now until I tell you when to come.

Lepido: Then you don't want us, your lordship, to come in to see the room where the dancing and the music will be?

Flavio: O Master Castrone, sir bridegroom, your lordship believes that it will be suitable, yes?

Gervasio: No, no, no, sir, forgive me for now, because I have things to do; but come back later. This is my house. I am yours, young men.

Lepido: Sir, as you command, so we will do. I kiss your lordship's hands.

Flavio: And I, my master, I am your slave; I bow and kiss your hands.

Gervasio: I'm yours, Master Cesario; I kiss your hands, Master Belisario.

Lepido: We are always at your command to serve you, my master. What will we do now?

Flavio: Leave and come back.

Gervasio: I've never seen men as polite or better-favored. They almost swept me off my feet. Come now, it's done. I've waited a little too long to go home. I'm convinced that Giulia must be panting for it: I didn't want to spell it out for Master Demetrio, but I'm sure that Giulia will be more than satisfied, because although it's true I'm a bit older, I am also supernaturally endowed which, in itself, is a wonderful attraction. O poor girl, it makes me truly sad that she's already dying for me. I'm not going to wait any longer. Let me call Trapola. Hey, Trapola, are you there![85]

85. Gervasio's monologue confirms his delusional belief in his sexual attraction, making him a target for punishment.

SCENE SEVEN
Trapola and Gervasio

Trapola: Hey, what insolence is this? Who's calling out in such a rage? It must be some lowlife.[86]

Gervasio: No, it's me, it's your master—come out of the house.

Trapola: He can't—he's not in the house.

Gervasio: Oh, what a dumb donkey—he always gets things the wrong way around. Of course, I know that he's not in the house.

Trapola: Well, if you know him, why do you want him to come out? May you rot in hell!

Gervasio: Oh, what a lunatic, what a lunatic! Hey, can't you hear that I am your master?

Trapola: You're lying through your teeth! I have only one master, and that's Master Gervasio Grifone.

Gervasio: O you demon! Come out, I'm telling you, I am Gervasio.

Trapola: What Gervasio? O master, I'm sorry—when I am busy with the housework I don't see who is speaking.

Gervasio: Yes, yes, I get it, everything the wrong way around. Come on, get over here. I want you to go to Master Demetrio's house and ask him what answer he has to give me concerning that business. Understood?

Trapola: Better than a deaf man. Do you want me to go now?

Gervasio: When else, you brute? Now, I say, and come back immediately.

Trapola: I'll go, master, but first I would like …

Gervasio: What would you like?

Trapola: That you'd tell me what this business is about. I see you are more cheerful than usual, master. Come on, please tell me.

Gervasio: So that you'll go more willingly, I'll tell you everything. Do you know that I've taken a wife?

Trapola: Tell me for real, master? And who have you taken?

86. Trapola plays the dim-witted but insolent servant to perfection.

Gervasio: The trouble I've taken! Giulia, Demetrio's ward, and this is why I'm sending you to his house now.

Trapola: Master, you couldn't do better, and I, who has good judgement, see that you have already become (a cuckold wearing the horns of the devil for having annoyed him) a family man. But when is the marriage to take place?[87]

Gervasio: Tonight, for sure. Now go and don't waste time. I'm going to give the order to light the fire.

Trapola: Go on, master, and clean yourself up while you're at it.

Right now, as the saying goes, for me the cheese has landed on the macaroni! If my master marries Giulia, I'll have all the satisfaction I want from Ruchetta, who is dying for what I have to offer, I'm sure.[88]

SCENE EIGHT

Scaramuccia and Trapola

Scaramuccia: What is he babbling on about Ruchetta? I'm going to eavesdrop so I can hear what gossip he's spreading.

Trapola: Now, with this chance to ask Master Demetrio if he's satisfied with the marriage contract, I'll be able to talk to Ruchetta, and when she might want to take away my worldly honor and then maybe I'll decide, I might decide to marry her; however, I want to make my own plan.

Scaramuccia: Oh, he is carrion for the crows, how can someone so idiotic talk about worldly honor? Yes, but only in the belly of a galley ship like that of Admiral Doria and by making him a jailer in command with a bullwhip![89] But wait, this love of his suits my purposes. O my God! Yeah, yeah, I've thought of the way to get him on my side! Let's go for it![90]

87. Trapola's parenthetical aside is obviously intended for the audience.

88. Trapola's final speech echoes Gervasio's in the previous scene.

89. Giovanni Andrea Doria (1539–1606) was a famous admiral who inherited the fleets from his better-known uncle Andrea Doria, who commanded the Genoese navy. Don Giovanni de' Medici was given a mission to prevent Doria's fleet and Savoy troops from seizing Marseilles, where he had built the fortifications to protect its harbor. See Dooley, *A Mattress Maker's Daughter*, 41. Scaramuccia is imagining Trapola's claim to have "honor" as something that could only be credited to him under the lowest of circumstances, for example as the cruelest of jailers wielding a bullwhip on the backs of the rowers in the hold of a ship.

90. As he decides how to get Trapola to go along with his most nefarious plan, he also seems to get so excited that he is covered in liquid and asks for a handkerchief.

(Phew!) I'm soaking wet! God only knows if he's home. Oh, here's Trapola; where are you going? Is your master in? Have you eaten yet? Have you got a handkerchief on you?

Trapola: What's the big hurry, Scaramuccia! I was just off to your house. My master isn't in, we haven't eaten yet, and I don't use a handkerchief. Anyway, what's driving you so crazy?

Scaramuccia: I'm coming to bring you two pieces of news: one for you, and the other for your master.

Trapola: Could it be the news that I'm looking for, the one for my master?

Scaramuccia: Maybe yes; here it is. My master has sent me to Master Gervasio to tell him to put everything in order so that his marriage to Giulia can take place tonight. But then there is the other.

Trapola: As I expected, my master was sending me about this matter. But tell me, what's the other?

Scaramuccia: The other news involves you, but I won't tell you unless you give me a big reward, since it is the best news you could ever want.

Trapola: Ah, I don't know, what can I give you, my friend? I could give you a bit of my appetite.[91]

Scaramuccia: Thanks all the same, I have plenty of that. I need something else, otherwise it's no deal, and I'll go and look for your master.

Trapola: Wait a minute, Scaramuccia—don't go, you won't find him anyway. What can I give you for real? I want to prove I'm serious about this, watch this.

Scaramuccia: What are you doing?

Trapola: Stripping off, to give you my shirt.

Scaramuccia: Hang on, I'll accept the loss, if you're prepared to do me a favor, I'll give you the good news—and what's more I'll give you a hand with it so you'll end up happy. Here's a hint: it involves Ruchetta.

Trapola: She's part of the good news, eh?

Scaramuccia: Yes sirree.

91. Their hunger is an ongoing theme, as is their poverty. Here it could also be sexual appetite but there is no doubt he is poor as wants to sell him his fingernails.

Trapola: Your wish is my command, my brother. I'll sell my fingernails to help you—and they are the most valuable things I own when my scabs are itchy.

Scaramuccia: I believe you. Here's the news: Ruchetta is to be your wife, and I'm the one to give her to you.

Trapola: Ruchetta to be my wife? Scaramuccia, I'm so happy I'm going to give you two of my teeth. Go on, speed it up.

Scaramuccia: Now the favor I want from you is this: call Porzia outside now so that I can talk to her; and urge her to do what I am asking her to do. And so that you'll know what is going on, it's to help Lepido, my master's son.

Trapola: Has he come back from France?

Scaramuccia: Yes, he's back, what about it?

Trapola: Look at it like this: you scratch my back, I'll scratch yours. All I want is to see my master Licinio cuckolded, because he's the most annoying person in creation and his bizarre jealousy makes the whole household miserable.[92] Now when do we want to talk to her? Now? Get to the point, will Ruchetta be mine?

Scaramuccia: Yes, as a matter of fact, and there's no time to lose in this important matter.

Trapola: Hide over there, please, and leave this to me.

Scaramuccia: It's up to you, I'll hide over there.

Trapola: Leave it to me. Knock, knock, O mistress.

SCENE NINE

Porzia, Trapola, and Scaramuccia

Porzia: Who is it? Is it you, Trapola?

Trapola: Yes, mistress.

Porzia: Why don't you come inside?

Trapola: Scaramuccia wants to ask you something.

Scaramuccia: What the devil are you saying, you brute?

Porzia: What are you saying?

92. Licinio's jealousy and unpopularity remain an issue.

Trapola: To come outside for a very important reason. Did I say it right?

Scaramuccia: Right? You couldn't say it worse. Watch out, she's coming.

Porzia: Why'd you call me into the street? Do you want me to get into a fight with my husband?

Trapola: Why not? Your husband, with your permission, is a beast, mistress.

Porzia: And what does that make me, if my husband is a beast? You ignoramus, you'll always be a cretin! So, what is this news? And why did you make me come into the street?

Trapola: Mistress, I can't explain it on my own; here's Scaramuccia to help me.

Porzia: Oh, oh, I am surprised, not so much at you, but at you, Scaramuccia! What do you want from me? What are you doing hanging around my house? Alas! I'm well aware that you want to ruin me completely! Maybe you have made some sort of agreement with him?

Trapola: What do you mean by him? O mistress, you're hurting me a little too much![93] Scaramuccia, does she know that I have become a bridegroom?[94]

Porzia: What is this rascal talking about? What's he saying?

Scaramuccia: Nothing, nothing, mistress, pay attention to me if you want to know why I am hanging around here? Lady Porzia, is it really true that you have completely, absolutely, forgotten Lepido?

Porzia: That's why you're back again to torment me! I'm telling you clearly that I do not love Lepido, and that what you saw a little while ago happened because my soul was so offended by him that it separated from my body as long as he was there.[95]

Scaramuccia: And I believe the opposite, my lady.

Trapola: We're going to sleep together tonight, Ruchetta and me, aren't we?

Scaramuccia: Yes, if you please, shush up!

93. Porzia must be hitting or restraining him in some painful way.

94. Trapola will keep throwing out comments about getting to sleep with Ruchetta as a counterpoint to Porzia playing coy. Porzia's apparent obliviousness to Trapola's naked desire underscores her fake reluctance.

95. Porzia and Scaramuccia parry back and forth about Neoplatonic issues concerning the body as containing the souls of the beloveds. Scaramuccia's unexpected expertise in such exalted matters increases the humor.

Porzia: How is it opposite?

Scaramuccia: It's not that your soul hates Lepido, rather it loves him and it was so upset on seeing your body refuse to recognize him properly that it left your body so as not to be separated from him, nor was it willing to return to you as long as Lepido was nearby. And I also believe that being divine, it knew very well that Lepido is not guilty of what you are accusing him of and didn't want to be considered ungrateful.

Trapola: Strike me dead, you speak so well! You must have studied Launcelot and Guinevere! I not so sure I'll know how to assist you here!

Scaramuccia: Shut up, you, it's not time yet!

Porzia: The body moves in accordance with the soul, Scaramuccia. If my soul knew what you say, it wouldn't have left my body. But if Lepido had known how to stay loyal as you say he did, we wouldn't have to ask all these questions that are better left alone, and you can go and serve your master in other ways. Trapola, let's go in.

Trapola: Have you convinced Scaramuccia?

Porzia: Who cares whether Scaramuccia is convinced, idiot! Let's go in.

Scaramuccia: Lady Porzia, I have a favor to ask which will benefit you.

Trapola: Yes, dear mistress, do him this favor, because it's for my benefit too, and "nature can't wait."[96]

Porzia: I'm not a princess who can grant favors.

Trapola: Take notice that the moon is growing and pretend to be one![97]

Scaramuccia: Listen, my lady, for the love you have for Lepido, and for your dear honor's sake, grant this favor to Scaramuccia.

Trapola: Scaramuccia, good God, maybe I could do this for you, without having to ask her?

Scaramuccia: I beg you, my lady! (and you, stop bothering me!) But what are you thinking?

Porzia: Come now, Scaramuccia, out with it, what is this favor?

96. The expression in Italian is *la natura patisce* (nature can't wait) when sexual desire is aroused; first said by Ruchetta, it is later repeated by Licinio and Porzia in 3.7

97. An unidentified allusion.

Scaramuccia: O my sweet lady, that you might agree to hear twenty-five words from Lepido.

Trapola: That's all? Yes sirree, we're willing, where is Sir Lepido?

Porzia: Yes, where is Sir Lepido, you rogue? And what if my husband comes back?

Trapola: Poor excuses, and besides, Sir Licinio doesn't know him! O mistress, why do you want to commit this sin against nature, when it gave you such beautiful ears to hear with? And who should you listen to, if not your friends? Would you rather listen to your enemies who want to hurt you?

Scaramuccia: That's great, Trapola! Great work, you're getting through, you're saying the right thing! Come on, my lady, you don't want to be responsible for the death of this unhappy young man!

Trapola: If you want it to turn out right, act now, because women can be easily swayed!

Porzia: O my aching heart, what can Lepido want from me? Does he think he can get water from a rock, ice from fire, sweetness from the salty ocean waves? Oh, how his heart errs!

Scaramuccia: Now, my lady, this is such a small thing to ask and may be enough to restore his health and give you some peace.

Porzia: Trapola.

Trapola: Mistress, what are you saying? What do you want me to do?

Porzia: What do you think I should do?

Trapola: Don't only listen to him; give him everything that he wants. Do you want to be thought of as an ingrate? Heaven is watching you because this sin is too big! Scaramuccia, go and call him!

Scaramuccia: What do you say, my lady, are you willing?

Porzia: Come on then, Scaramuccia, go away, I'm willing to talk to Lepido, as much for love of Trapola, as for love of you, and in order to relieve my inner torment.

Trapola: O, bless you, my lady, yes, yes, for your love and no one else's, I thank you on my behalf, considering myself forever in your debt.

Scaramuccia: The same for me, mistress. So, I'm going to find Lepido now. Trapola, I'm yours, keep it together.

Trapola: Comrade, don't you forget either. Mistress, it makes me very happy when you do what I want and every time you do, you'll see it's the right choice.

SCENE TEN

Porzia, Trapola, and Licinio

Porzia: Ah, Trapola, believe me, I'm doing this against my will!

Trapola: I know, I know; this is how women usually are: they do it against their will the first time.

Licinio: What are they doing in the street? I'll stay and listen in for a while.[98]

Porzia: I don't deny having loved him, Trapola, but now I must take care of my husband.

Trapola: It's good if you can take care of your husband and make yourself happy at the same time, mistress. Do you think that you're the first married woman to take on a lover? You're fooling yourself! And how many are there of you? May they likewise be blessed, women worthy of enjoying a life of eternal youth out in the world.[99]

Porzia: Eh, really, you don't want to give me the impression that such things are acceptable.

Trapola: On the contrary, I do, because they're all nature-made, and you only need to put them in practice. O mistress, you make me laugh! Why is it that men have more freedom than women? Why is it legal for a man to go out with a hundred sluts and an honorable woman not to have the right to make one gentleman happy and steal some pleasure for herself?[100]

Licinio: O Trapola, my good man, by God, I'm going to give you a raise for this!

98. The "lesbian husband" will listen in on the subterfuge. "His" commentary underlines the predicament women are in as pawns of their husbands. For purposes of plot development, Licinio's words portray the jealous husband, but also suggest that there is more to him than meets the eye, as we already know.

99. Trapola here urges Porzia to commit adultery. Her name, Porzia, is ironic, given that the name Porzia is usually associated with upstanding women such as the steadfast Portia, the daughter of Cato the Younger, and second wife of Brutus is first century BCE. Here Trapola makes a strong case that women should also be able to enjoy their lives. Possibly Scala is making a point that the great actresses profited from their close comparison to the great courtesans who often flourished as cultured refined artists. Isabella Andreini who invented the Porzia role for the stage was known for her literary and poetic achievements.

100. Trapola states the liberating truth: women should be free to enjoy their sexuality.

Porzia: Many things are legal for men that aren't permitted to women; but then only beautiful women run these dangers, and I'm not one of them.[101]

Trapola: Then heaven help me and take your husband away as soon as possible, and as for your beauty there are countless gentlemen who have spoken about you to me many times. And if in the past, I've always said no, in the future, I'll act differently because it seems to me that you are just a meal to your husband, who is so jealous and so miserable. One flower in bloom doesn't make it spring.[102]

Licinio: You rascal, oh, no, not this! If I don't beat you for this, too bad for me.

Porzia: O Trapola! You're going too far, is this really what you think?

Trapola: Forgive me, mistress. My regard for you makes me talk too freely.

Porzia: Enough said, speak up, if not, I'll get angry with you. And believe me that if I ever (unless heaven wills it) cheat on my husband, I'd always be afraid that he might catch me in the act (Alas!) What if he found me in the house with another man? O woe is me !

Licinio: Eeh, my lady shows a bit of disgust, you're getting the knack, for sure.

Trapola: No need to ever worry about this, mistress, because there is never any shortage of excuses, and when something good like this comes along, it's even better to have a faithful servant like me! As for being caught in the act, it's impossible, because nature, compassionate towards you women, takes care of this as part of human procreation. However, it's necessary to back up a little and for everyone to return to his place, because men are not dogs.[103]

Licinio: Ah, you criminal, Trapola, are you leaving because I've found her out?[104]

Porzia: *Porzia*: You have a great talent for making a good woman bad; I don't know if you would be as skilled at turning a bad woman good.

Trapola: O mistress, no.

Porzia: Why?

101. Porzia speaks about female desire and the prohibitions against it.

102. Trapola mentions the many potential clients she could have. He is also repurposing the line from the Actor's speech in the Second Prologue: Prologue to be Acted about the fallacy of making rules from isolated examples; see 49.

103. Trapola's last sentence retracting everything indicates that he has glimpsed Licinio.

104. Licinio hasn't yet revealed himself; this line is spoken to the audience.

Trapola: Because nature is more easily inclined to evil than to good, and so, whether what I have told you can be called evil, is not up to me to say![105] O mistress, here comes Master Licinio, we need to find out how much he's heard.

Licinio: Trapola, what's going on?

Trapola: The sea is rough! O master, I have to tell you many things, send your wife inside. Oh, my spine is tingling.

Licinio: Porzia, what are you doing here in the street?

Porzia: Nothing, sir. I was talking with Trapola about something concerning my father.

Licinio: About your father, eh? Do you think that I didn't hear everything? Get inside.

Porzia: I'm going. Sir, I pay you my respects.

Trapola: Oh, the poor girl.

Licinio: What do you have to say for yourself?

Trapola: That you have an honest young woman.

Licinio: And how do you know?

Trapola: You know that a short while ago, seeing her here in the street, I was suspicious, only because of my great concern for your honor, and so I began to question her to see if she was up to anything, and if she might be in love with someone else.

Licinio: He's a smart one! And what did she say?

Trapola: Sir, she turned to me in anger and said, "You viper, you scoundrel, what drives you to say these things to me? I'll break both your arms with a stick!" And then she went on to accuse me of the kind of villainy that would make a prosecutor lose his case.

Licinio: And how did you save yourself?

Trapola: Listen, I didn't lose on this account, no; rather, I said to her that I was only asking her these questions because many gentlemen were in love with her and were asking about her every day. And again, she started in on me, telling me

105. Trapola is echoing the Stranger's response to the Actor when he insists that showing human behavior on stage is dangerous because it stirs up strong reactions and encourages the natural propensity to do evil; see 48.

to be quiet, that no respectable women in the world would ever have thought about, or listened to a single word, and that I was jeopardizing your honor and your person as well. On these grounds, I insist on telling you that you are married to the most prudent young woman in the world.

Licinio: Ah, you rascal, you know very well that you're the most vicious trickster who has ever lived! So, she seems prudent to you, eh?

Trapola: In the extreme, sir, believe me, I swear it as a good and honorable man, in short, your faithful servant.

Licinio: Why my faithful servant?

Trapola: Because the faithful servant takes his qualities from his master, I draw qualities from you and I can swear as a good and honorable man, something most servants can't do, nor attorneys, notaries, or courtiers.

Licinio: I don't know if that's you. I know that from the day I married Porzia and found you in the house, I've always had a bad feeling about you. Still, if you are claiming to be my faithful servant now, maybe my opinion has been wrong and you don't deserve to be disciplined as much as rewarded by your actions. I believe this is to your liking, yes?

Trapola: I don't understand, master, speak more plainly, please.

Licinio: You will understand, all the more so because what I'm planning isn't to your liking. Let's go in, you'll find out soon enough what I'm planning to do.

Trapola: Go in, master, I'm coming. He's being vague, but I bet he's going to beat me! Come on, whatever will be, bring it on! I've tried to flip the cake over but I don't think I did it in time, and now it's burned a little on one side. If he's going to put marks on my back, I'll do what Scaramuccia wants and put marks on his forehead and he'll sprout horns like a billy goat. Baa! Baa! Baa! I need to find Master Demetrio.

Act Three

SCENE ONE
Demetrio and Ruchetta

Demetrio: The business at the marketplace always goes on for too long; it kills me. I've wasted time without getting anything done. And then there are still lots of annoying detail that trouble me, the biggest being my insatiable longing for my dear

Giulia. It's pretty clear that where Love rules, we can't see any faults! O Heaven, o Fortune, who would have said that at my age I would become enslaved to Love, eh? Come then, in fact there's nothing left to say: where it will go; even less: what it is. I know that it's really wrong, but really, what more can I do? Whoever is driving me has driven other men besides me; there is nothing more to say other than that Giulia goes along with it and that that beastly Ruchetta has done what she was supposed to. I'm going to call her to come here before I go home. Hello, Ruchetta, knock, knock, knock, knock.[106]

Ruchetta: O sir, it's you, eh?

Demetrio: Yes, come down, I want to talk to you a bit.

Ruchetta: I'm here, sir, have you got the tip ready?

Demetrio: Come on tell me, what news do you have?

Ruchetta: The mistress is resolved to …

Demetrio: Marry Gervasio.

Ruchetta: Master, no.

Demetrio: How so?

Ruchetta: Bloody shit, master, I know how eager you are to get the poor thing out of the house! Be happy then, because she has agreed to do what you want. Do I deserve a tip or not?

Demetrio: You're very greedy.

Ruchetta: Yes, so it seems to you, because you have done so little to fill me up! Master, everyone says so! Come on, the tip, the tip, you miser.

Demetrio: Come on, shut up, I'll give you what I promised, and, in addition, I want to give you a husband! But who's coming here singing?

SCENE TWO

Trapola. Demetrio, and Ruchetta

Trapola: "The unmarried woman, if she's good,
spreads herself around the 'hood.
She says it whets her appetite,

106. Demetrio's monologue confessing that his obsession to have Giulia is wrong deepens his psychological profile and shows the human underneath the facade.

When she eats whatever she likes."[107]
Oh, look here, it's that gentleman, Master Demetrio.

Demetrio: Isn't that Gervasio's servant. I like his temperament; he's always happy.

Ruchetta: I don't know, master. You see, I'm not acquainted with him.
Hey you, my darling!

Trapola: She's staring blindly at me, the traitor! Good day, Master Demetrio. My Master Gervasio Grifone greets you, as I do the tramp Ruchetta.[108]

Ruchetta: Oh, and where do you know me from, you ruffian?

Demetrio: Look at what that little schemer is up to! Take no notice of her, Trapola. So, what does your master say?

Trapola: She's a smart one! He wants to know what decision has been reached. But, my lord it seems to me that I'm being insulted by this housekeeper of yours.

Ruchetta: What do you mean housekeeper? If I'm the housekeeper it's because I have to look after all my master's business, so what do you mean? Master, you know, a little respect is owed to me here.[109]

Trapola: Oh, what a cheat, she pretends not to know me, and the old man is grumbling away.

Demetrio: You be quiet, you imbecile, you're talking like an idiot, as usual! Trapola, come here, and ignore her.

Trapola: Master, she's threatening me—can't you see? You're lying through your teeth! Get out of the way, master.

Ruchetta: You devil—talk like that to someone like me, eh? Here, take this slipper![110]

Demetrio: Stop it, you bitch—don't push me like that.

Trapola: Throwing slippers at someone like me, eh? Take that, you tramp! Look out, master!

107. The Italian verse uses local Tuscan phrases: *La bona donna che non ha marito / confida ne la bona vicinanza / e dice gli si aguzza l'appetito/quando la mangia della mescolanza.*

108. Ruchetta and Trapola pretend not to be acquainted and hurl insults back and forth.

109. The Italian word *massara*, meaning housekeeper, leads to her angry response, which also highlights her role as keeper of more than his house.

110. The insults exchanged between Ruchetta and Trapola become physical blows with a slipper, and Demetrio is deliberately caught in the crossfire. Such reverse master-servant punishment scenes feed our subversive desires to even the playing field and increase our pleasure watching violent actions.

Demetrio: Ouch! My head! Stop it, the two of you!

Ruchetta: Ouch, master, I'm hurt!

Demetrio: Damn it all—stop right there! Trapola, stop it now! You, Ruchetta, put your slipper back on; and tell him you're sorry. And Trapola, hitting me on the head, eh?

Trapola: I'm sorry, master, I didn't mean to.

Demetrio: Did you hear me, tell him you're sorry, I said.

Ruchetta: I'll do it for love of you, master. I beg your pardon, sir.

Trapola: For the master's love I forgive you, and I apologize to you again, master, because I didn't mean to hit you.

Demetrio: I forgive you: try and be friends from now on. Trapola, tell your master that the matter is all arranged, then, and that my Giulia has agreed; she was talking about it with Ruchetta just now for the express purpose of sending her to tell him all about it.

Ruchetta: Master, remember that you promised me that Master Gervasio will give me a reward; he's a lot more likely to if I take him the news.

Demetrio: If you want to go, go with him. So, to be clear, Trapola, act as my emissary, and I'll return home. Go with him if you want, Ruchetta.

Trapola: Come on, master, I'm your servant forever. I'll go and give the message to my master. This young lady, if she wants, can keep me company.

Ruchetta: Since the master commands, I'll come, but I warn you to respect my honor, young man! Master, I'm going with your protection.

Demetrio: Yes, yes, get going and come back quickly.

Trapola: Go and be damned! I was about to burst out laughing! I know what a good liar you are, you slut, but you're a female after all! Let's go; how are you, my darling?

Ruchetta: Your darling, eh? Whew, if I wasn't already laughing! I know what you want, my gentleman. You're leaving when we've just met again?

Trapola: Sister, God knows you are always in my heart, but I have so many worries at home that I don't even have time to eat; but believe me, my Ruchetta, no man ever loved a woman as much as I love you.

Ruchetta: Eh, really. I'm fed up with words, brother, how are you going to make sure it happens?

SCENE THREE

Scamaruccia, Ruchetta, and Trapola

Scaramuccia: I swear to it, Ruchetta.

Ruchetta: A plague on you, you scared me to death! Where'd you come from?

Trapola: O my dear Scaramuccia, you're here just in time.

Scaramuccia: Now, guys, there is no time to waste; I understand everything that's happened. Ruchetta, you know that I've always loved you like a sister, and that being true: here's Trapola, who knows what I've told him about you.

Trapola: All the good in the world, Ruchetta.

Ruchetta: And what else could he say about poor little me?

Scaramuccia: All right, I know that you two love each other, so it seems a good thing that you get married and I'll help you do it in a way that the old guy will give you a lot, so that you can put a little aside and find a way to get by like the rest of us. What do you say?

Trapola: Great, it's perfect. And Ruchetta, what do you say?

Ruchetta: It couldn't be better! What about it, Trapola?

Trapola: I'm happy.

Ruchetta: I'm the happiest of all, for being able to have you for my husband helps me to be "a good woman" who knows that time is passing.[111]

Scaramuccia: That's right. Give me your hand, Trapola—and you give me yours, Ruchetta.

Ruchetta: There. O God, marriage is such a big thing—I'm blushing all over, I'm so embarrassed!

Trapola: There's my hand, Scaramuccia.

Scaramuccia: And so, by taking each other's hands, you promise to be husband and wife, right? And I am here as your witness.

111. The wedding ceremony performed by Scaramuccia travesties the solemn exchange of vows that rest on an assumption of female virginity. Ruchetta and Trapola play at being bride and groom.

Trapola: I promise; and swear.

Ruchetta: And I do too. O Lord, I'm so overwhelmed!

Trapola: Isn't this where we kiss?

Scaramuccia: Of course, it is—what are you waiting for, you idiot?

Ruchetta: Hey, not so fast, husband dear—can't you see you're making me blush. Scaramuccia, when will the marriage be consummated?

Scaramuccia: Not blushing about this are you? What a "piece of ass" you are!

Ruchetta: I'm not saying anything bad about anyone, heaven help me, but why not hurry it up.

Trapola: What's my lady bride saying, Scaramuccia?

Scaramuccia: As for the consummation of your marriage, I want you to enjoy each other tonight since I've already figured out how you can. That's enough for now; I want you to help with something else.

Trapola: O Scaramuccia, we owe you so much! And now, let's get to it; what do you want us to do? I'm asking about Lepido. My dear bride, be happy!

Ruchetta: O God, when will night come? I'm more excited about what's going to happen than what already has.

Scaramuccia: Come here, both of you, and go, as you've been instructed, to give the news to the old one and try to get him out of the house with Licinio, if possible; so that it will be easy for Lepido to talk to Porzia. But how to get him out of the house? We need to figure out now.

Trapola: That's easy.

Ruchetta: But how?

Trapola: He can go visit the bride.

Ruchetta: What do we do with Licinio?

Scaramuccia: Wait a minute, I've got it! I want you to put it into their heads to buy something for the bride: like necklaces, jewels and so on.

Ruchetta: By God, that's good; and tell him to take Licinio with him since he knows about such things.

Trapola: You're right, because Licinio has sold a lot of jewelry since he arrived here.

Scaramuccia: It's a great plan. Start knocking; I'm going to hide over here. Get knocking.

SCENE FOUR

Ruchetta, Trapola, Licinio, and Gervasio

Ruchetta: Come on, let's knock, my sweet husband; or bang, as we like to say.

Trapola: You're right, because I have my stick here to help. Bang, bang, bang.[112]

Licinio: Who's down there? Who's knocking?[113]

Trapola: It's Licinio's voice. It's me, sir, and someone else, we want to talk.

Licinio: And who is this person? I'm coming now.

Trapola: I'm sure the master's not home. Here's Licinio now.

Licinio: Where've you been, Trapola? What have you to say that you can't say inside? Who's this?

Trapola: I didn't come in because I've got an idea to offer some advice to Master Gervasio. This is our neighbor Master Demetrio's servant, who'd like to speak with the master.

Licinio: So, you are in Master Demetrio's service, you beautiful young thing!

Ruchetta: At your lordship's service, my handsome sir.

Trapola: Ah, you good-for-nothing, what are you saying? He is thanking you because he has a beautiful wife nearby.

Licinio: Who are you to answer me, you brute? Perhaps you think you can refuse my requests?

Trapola: Or if not, that I will become a cuckold? O Scaramuccia, what a crazy mess you've got me into! It would be really great if you'd help me now!

Licinio: You, young thing, thanks, we'll talk again at a more convenient time. What is your name?

Ruchetta: Ruchetta Campana, to serve you always, my lord.

112. The words "bang, bang, bang" signal the performance of a lazzi.

113. Licinio gets to reprise the earlier scene of the jealous husband. Here "he" keeps up his imposture by flirting with Ruchetta for several of the following lines.

Trapola: And I'm Trapola Battocchio, to start over from the beginning.

Licinio: My pleasure. The master isn't home. If I can be of service, ask away.

Ruchetta: I thank you, my lord; I would like to speak to him on my master's behalf.

Licinio: I know that she is very smart, and whoever marries her will become a cuckold.

Trapola: They say that children and crazies can predict the future, and who is crazier than a jealous husband!

Licinio: What are you saying?

Trapola: I'm saying that I'll never be jealous! But, what good luck, here's the master.

Gervasio: That butcher shop was a bit hard to take; it looked to me as if everything had been flayed! But what are they doing? Licinio, my son-in-law, what are you doing here? Ruchetta, what's the good news? Trapola, did you go there?

Licinio: Sir, this maidservant has something to tell you, together with Trapola.

Trapola: Sir, I've been there and Ruchetta here will give you all the answers.

Ruchetta: Master Gervasio, please hand over my tip! My Mistress Giulia has agreed to marry you and you're to be married as soon as possible.

Gervasio: I've no more need to deceive myself. I knew that Giulia would instantly fall head over heels in love with me! O my sweetest love!

Licinio: Hey, Master Gervasio, my father-in-law, what wedding is this? So, this is how things are done, all in secret, eh?

Gervasio: My dear soul! I'll tell you everything in good time. And when does Master Demetrio want me to take her hand and have the wedding?

Ruchetta: As soon as possible; it's up to you when to take her hand.

Trapola: Master Licinio, please, hear this.

Licinio: I'm here.

Gervasio: What're you saying, Trapola?

Trapola: Master, please forgive me if I'm taking liberties: you know that this young woman is well-born, has a good dowry, and therefore it looks to me as if you should treat her properly. It seems to me that, if it pleases you, you should go right away with Sir Licinio to the jewelers and buy some beautiful jewels there, and then take them to her and ask for her hand. What do you say, Licinio?

Licinio: If she's a very sweet and deserving person as you say, it seems like a good idea.

Gervasio: What do you mean, "if" she's deserving? I bow to your advice. Let's go, let's go, Licinio, and I'll tell you all about it on the way. Ruchetta, come with us too, because afterwards we'll be going altogether to Demetrio's house.

Ruchetta: I'm coming, sir, go, and I'll catch up.

Gervasio: Keep her company, Trapola. Let's go, Licinio.

Ruchetta: What do you think, Trapola, things couldn't be going better!

Trapola: Yes, but …

Ruchetta: But, what …

Trapola: Go on, you go first, because I'm a little angry with you.

Ruchetta: If you're angry you'd better go first—I don't want you to stab me in the back.

Trapola: Eh, unfaithful bitch, if only I could get anywhere near you … Come on, move, the master's looking back at us.

Ruchetta: Even if you couldn't, it wouldn't stop you from trying. Go away, you dirty rascal!

SCENE FIVE

Scaramuccia and Lepido

Scaramuccia: That plan of yours and Flavio pretending to be virtuosi to get into Gervasio's house is taking too long. And since what you want is a chance to talk to Porzia, it seems to me that right now is a good opportunity because you'll have time to fully explain yourself, since those who live there have gone out, as you see, and won't be back soon, as I know what I told Ruchetta and Trapola to get them to do.[114]

Lepido: And is Porzia willing to listen to me? What did she tell you?

114. Scaramuccia plays the *capocomico* by putting an end to further developing the action from 2.6, where Lepido and Flavio try to get into Gervasio's house as musicians. In citing the time frame as not viable, he draws attention to the exigencies of plotmaking the actors had to operate under as well as having some fun with the audience. See the Introduction, 26, and above, 89–91.

Scaramuccia: And how many times do you want me to tell you? If you want, I'll draw up a contract for you.

Lepido: Don't get upset, I beg you, and don't wish me ill because too much happiness is almost enough to make me go crazy and believe nothing.

Scaramuccia: I'm not ignorant of this fact, so I'm surprised, since not only do I wish you no will, but I want only the best for you. Come now, follow the plan, I'm going to knock.

Lepido: So, knock, my Scaramuccia, because this is the moment when we'll see which is stronger, life or death. And you, winged god, who by your power and your will subjugate men and gods, see that I too am yours and see also the danger I am in. O most beautiful son of Venus, I pray you, give such power to my speech that it will move her to be kind, she who was once your chosen![115]

Scaramuccia: Ah yes, don't talk too much now, I say. Save it for when you're talking to her. Go hide now. Hey, here we are, knock, knock, knock, knock.

SCENE SIX

Porzia, Scaramuccia, and Lepido

Porzia: Who is it? Who's knocking?

Scaramuccia: I am, my lady, Scaramuccia.[116]

Porzia: Is it you, Scaramuccia? Is there anyone in the street?

Scaramuccia: No, my lady, don't worry, you can come down.

Porzia: All right, I'm coming.

Scaramuccia: Lepido, your turn! Now I'm turning the hare over to the hunter, be ready.[117]

Lepido: Whew, my heart's pounding.

Porzia: Here I am. Well, what's new?

115. That is, Cupid, the son of Venus. See also notes 36 and 37, above.

116. Scaramuccia's knocking reminds us of his similar action in 2.1. Repeating the knocking scene many times over to get Porzia to reunite with Lepido gets funnier every time as we are more familiar with the circumstances.

117. An echo of Ruchetta's line in 1.5 where she refers to herself as a hare about to be caught but where she will in fact trap Flavio into confessing to love Giulia.

Scaramuccia: As you know every promise has to be kept, now remember what you promised me.

Porzia: Against my will and only because you forced me, I remember that I promised to speak to Lepido.

Scaramuccia: All right then, my lady, Lepido is here. I won't say anything other than that you at least have the patience to listen to his explanation; meanwhile, I will stand guard in case someone comes.[118]

Porzia: Ah, Scaramuccia, what sin are you making me commit? Come now, bide your time, keep an eye out, please.

Scaramuccia: Leave it to me. Come closer, Sir Lepido.

Porzia: O dear and beloved vision, if you show yourself to me such as you are, what happiness can it bring me?

Lepido: Alas, how agitated I am? What fearful thoughts, harbingers of death assault me now?

Porzia: Your betrayal, your bad conscience, Sir Lepido, takes away your courage to come near me.

Lepido: Neither my betrayal, nor my bad conscience, my Lady Porzia, can prohibit me from coming near to you! But so great is the pain that I feel in my soul, seeing you in the power of another and knowing that I did not break my promise or betray you but that what happened was caused only by my father's cruelty, and the will of my evil fortune which, jealous of our happiness, worked against us, and your failure to believe in me has brought me to my death.

Porzia: Slow down, Sir Lepido, I'll answer you about this death in short order. You're accusing me of being cruel and of not believing you while I know that you're wrong because I've always believed firmly in everything that I could possibly find to be entirely true; but for all those things that are impossible to believe, do you want me to believe them? No, my lord, because I would be making a very serious mistake and acting in a way that is totally opposite to who I am.

Lepido: My lady, I beg you to listen; aren't we talking about our love?

Porzia: Yes, of things past and still present.

118. Scaramuccia's known presence allows him to turn into a side coach and stage manager, as he hears their overheated lovers' scene of betrayal and forgiveness. Their back and forth dialogue becomes a virtuosic set piece.

Lepido: As you wish. Of the past (O my heart, why aren't you dead?),[119] tell me please, what are the things that you think worthy to be believed?

Porzia: I'll tell you, Sir Lepido, and I'll show you that I'm a smart woman and not the foolish girl I once was. The first thing I believed was that because of your burning desire for me, you would not have gone to France, would not have obeyed your father, if I had not given you my word that, because of my same burning desire for you, that I would wait for three years. You, consoled by my pledge, left. That pledge (as you well know) remained inviolate all that time. I believed, moreover, that during that long time when you were in France, you were drowning in the tears, sighs, pains, and the feelings that lovers suffer, and I still believed that during that time you would have come back home if it hadn't been for fear of your father. What do you say, Lepido, was it true what I believed?[120]

Lepido: Up to now, you've got it right, my Lady Porzia, but I'm not sure if you aren't trying to draw me in, so that you can strike me dead in the end. But tell me more about the things that aren't believable. Speak, speak, speak, loving mouth, speak, most beautiful flame that burns me up so deliciously, what are they?

Porzia: What are they? They are the ones on which you would like to build your defense. But because you know that your defense is neither just, nor true: be afraid and don't dare (as you did a little while ago) to approach me. Don't you realize that you are like a guilty person who shakes and trembles in front of a tribunal because he realizes that the judge sees his guilt in his face?

Lepido: There are two things above all that I yearn for and desire, my Lady Porzia: one is that heaven grant me the blessing to tell you what punishment to give me for my sin, if I am guilty; the other, that it might give me as much power to my speech as I need to describe to you the anguish that my soul has suffered during our lengthy separation; and at the same time explain to you the unassailable reasons why I could not return at the promised time.

Porzia: Heaven, by putting me into another's power, has already granted one part of what you desire; as for your punishment, I'll tell you what to say. Now listen: you're going to tell me that not only did you suffer continuously for three years, but that you are still suffering now, and that you will suffer unto death; and you will say that you have done everything in your power to return to keep your promise, but that your relatives in Lyon wouldn't let you leave on your father's orders, isn't that true? Isn't this what you wanted to say, am I right?

119. The parenthetical phrase reminds the spectator of Lepido's early speeches about his heart. A similar parenthesis in a later speech also shows him quoting himself.

120. Porzia's parenthetical phrases serve a similar purpose to Lepido's, revealing their self-reflexive acting.

Lepido: Ah, Love, as you let Porzia read in my mind everything I wanted to say to prove that I hadn't broken my promise (which is in fact the truth), then why can't you show her in the mirror of my eyes what internal pain my soul suffers from her lack of faith in me? What do you want me to say, my lady, if not that it's true that I wanted to say exactly this, because it really is the absolute truth?

Porzia: Is it really, eh, Lepido?

Lepido: Really, lady, if you believe it; and if not, you'll see it soon enough or else will hear such news of me that you'll be forced to believe it.

Porzia: So, you want me to believe that you have never stopped loving me?

Lepido: Yes, my lady, and I will as long as I'm alive. And until the stars fall out of the skies, I will never stop loving you.

Porzia: And you want me to believe this? The impossible? Ah, Lepido, let's leave the impossible out of it for now. What proof have you given me that you love me? A false promise? Returning in disguise? And for what? Maybe to take away my honor? How are you going to make me change my opinion that as the son of a very rich man, you are willing to lower yourself to marry a poor woman like me? Why? For my noble birth which doesn't count for much today since there's no money to go with it? Admit it, admit it, Lepido, admit that you have such evil intentions! I am poor, and I want to die poor with my honor intact.

Scaramuccia: O you two, aren't you finished yet? You've already been chatting for quite a while. Lepido, what's going on? It seems that you're crying out for death.[121]

Lepido: Ah, Scaramuccia, don't bother me, I'm begging you.

Scaramuccia: There, I'm going back into hiding.

Porzia: If I remember right, you said you would kill yourself if I didn't believe you; this doesn't bother me at all now, since there are reasons for it.

Lepido: Not to bother you, my lady, but, to make you happy, I am willing to die.

Porzia: Ah, yes, you still don't get it! You know why it won't bother me? Because you've already been dead to me for a long time.

Lepido: Look here, O most cruel of women; you are confessing that you haven't loved me for a long time, and that I had already been dead in your heart! And who knows if this didn't happen on the first day that I left you?

Porzia: And who knows this better than you?

121. A reality check from Scaramuccio indicates that they are dragging out the scene unnecessarily.

Lepido: What do you mean, better than me?

Porzia: Better than you, yes, because when you left you took my heart with you and you said that you'd left yours with me, isn't that true? If you deny it, you'll be contradicting yourself.

Lepido: I can't deny it, Lady Porzia, just as I can't deny having left mine with you.

Porzia: Not being able to deny it, will you then not deny that, almost immediately you forgot that you had it since it never occurred to you to give it back, nor to respect the conditions under which you had promised to keep it? For this, I say, that it's been a long time since you've been dead to me in my heart and that a new heart rules over you now.

Lepido: Ahh, most cruel Porzia, is it possible that with these twisted arguments you are trying to bring down the truest and most faithful lover that lives? That you believe, I am ruled by another love? That I am living in another heart than yours, my Porzia? Ah, don't say it, because it won't ever be true! Rather, not having you to live for in this world, I don't want to live for anyone else. And this is the resolution that I'd already made when my estranged father wouldn't let me return home. And it was confirmed even more when I found out that you were getting married to someone other than your Lepido, who more than any other deserved you for his devotion and constancy; when since you rightly belong to him, you couldn't be with another.

Porzia: Hold on, Lepido, answer me this, I beg you. Don't get so frenzied, who can you blame for this?

Lepido: Who? My most cruel of fathers, spiteful fortune, and you, cruelest woman!

Porzia: Shhh!

Scaramuccia: Shhh! What the hell! I can hear you and I'm a mile away.

Porzia: Hold on, Scaramuccia. Do you know who to blame for this, not me, no, but your own heart.

Lepido: How, my own heart? Perhaps because it was in your breast?

Porzia: No, sir. But because, being in my breast it might have protested that it belongs to someone else now.

Scaramuccia: Wrap it up, Lepido! This woman has a devil on her back!

Lepido: It's not surprising, Lady Porzia, my heart is so happy to be inside such a beautiful case that it no longer cares to return to its original home; rather it is happy here with you; and doesn't care if the rest of me that was born with it, dies. Such being the case, it asks for one favor only: that on seeing or hearing of my death it will bring tears of love to your eyes, as a little sign of sorrow and devotion.

Porzia: Be quiet, Lepido, because your heart has convinced me and proved that you love me; and now, I, reassured of your love, pray that you may live, and even more that you may leave now quietly with your servant, and I'll do everything for our happiness. Now do this without fail, and without question. And be happy, no more bowing. Scaramuccia, go away now too. And you, Lepido, don't look at me, I beg you, and leave here, if you love me.

Scaramuccia: And me, Porzia?

Porzia: Yes, I say, you too, go away, Scaramuccia!

Most powerful Love, it is from you that I find my strength: what other woman, in love as I am, could have resisted so firmly the sweetest entreaties of my dearest Lepido? No one else could have, I am sure. O unlucky me, I felt myself dissolving little by little like a snowflake, exposed to the hottest rays of the sun while he was trying so hard to defend himself. Now I know his excuses are completely true, and I am finally completely sure that my Lepido yearns for me with a love that is real and never-ending. Now the time is fast approaching for me to find my happiness and I want to go after it as quickly as possible without waiting any longer. But here comes Brigida.[122]

SCENE SEVEN
Licinio and Porzia

Licinio: And here you are, out again? Haven't I told you not to come out into the street? Porzia, Porzia, you're looking to harm yourself and ruin me; you'll make me do things and commit such follies that I would never have imagined! Remember that the husband has power over the wife and with his blood washes the stain of her lost honor.[123]

Porzia: O poor little me, what are you saying? Ah, the time has passed to keep hidden the fire and passion that's bursting forth on its own. My house is on fire now and burns everything with its amorous flame, and already through the windows of my soul, you see the sparks of this uncontrollable blaze. I am telling you

122. Porzia gives it away that Licinio is really Brigida. The audience is now in on Brigida's male impersonation, but it is not until the end of Act Five that the deception is revealed to the other characters. The emphasis is on the deceptive powers of theatrical illusion. The comedy deepens and the social commentary continues.

123. Licinio's angry husband speech resonates differently now.

that Lepido's love is constant and unshakeable and my own infinite love for him became so clear that I almost fell down dead listening to him.

Licinio: Now heaven be praised since for you, doubt and sorrow have been lifted, and for me, the long wait is over. How many widowed nights, and how much fasting we have endured; in the end, nature can't wait any longer having learned of love's sweetest pleasures. I'm not speaking for you, Porzia, since you have not yet tasted the delights of the garden of love.[124]

Porzia: If I haven't tasted them as yet, I have already felt their power, since, I'm telling you now that my nature has gone out of control![125]

Licinio: Porzia, the longer we wait and the more we desire it, the sweeter and more sublime it will be. Come in; come inside, it's time to end all this.

Porzia: Yes, let's go in; an hour seems like a thousand years until I can embrace my dearest Lepido.[126]

Act Four

SCENE ONE

Demetrio and Scaramuccia

Demetrio: I sent that greedy little schemer Ruchetta with Trapola to speak to Master Gervasio, and neither of them has come back. Actually, giving servants too much freedom is sometimes more harmful than not, because it makes them so bold that they become arrogant, insolent, and lazy.

Scaramuccia: What in the name of God was that woman implying?[127] But I've glimpsed Demetrio in the distance talking to himself and he's still at it; I'm going to find out what he's saying, if I can; I'll just stay in this corner to hear what's going on.

Demetrio: Oh, how thrilled Master Gervasio must have been to find out for sure that Giulia has agreed to marry him; I, on the other hand, feel the opposite at the

124. Licinio admits to their sexual deprivation. He uses the Italian phrase "*la natura patisce*" (nature can't wait), repeating the words of Ruchetta in 2.4 and Trapola in 2.9.

125. Porzia makes the phrase her own, saying "la natura mia patisce ormai in extremo."

126. This well-wrought play brings about the reconciliation of the lovers at the midpoint. The reveal of the fake husband imposture is still only known to the audience, and possibly Scaramuccia, who has to play somewhat dumb to move the action forward. Now, the plot will turn on getting the lovers into bed with each other.

127. Scaramuccia is puzzling over Porzia's intentions from the last scene.

thought of her leaving my house! O woe is me, my heart feels as if she is smashing it with a hammer and my soul is shattering into a thousand pieces! O my beautiful Giulia, my dearest Giulia, what will I do without you?

Scaramuccia: Oh, so that's it, I hadn't realized that the old polecat is in heat. You deserve to be eaten by wolves in a rocky cave! Demetrio in love with Giulia, eh? Well, I didn't know this but it's all good for me and fits right into my plan. I'm going to let him see me and learn more about this new love. Good day, Master Demetrio, good day, master, you look very upset, more than you did before, what's wrong, perhaps you are not feeling well?[128]

Demetrio: Sick and with a bad sickness, as you see.

Scaramuccia: Would you like me to call the doctor?

Demetrio: For this sickness neither a doctor nor medicine would help.

Scaramuccia: What the hell is it? Would you have the bad luck to have a cancer that eats you? If so, that's a very bad illness because there is no other remedy than to set it on fire?

Demetrio: Yes, set fire to a load of sticks, burn me up and turn me into ash! Eh, Scaramuccia, you don't get me.

Scaramuccia: The police would get you better than I would.[129]

Demetrio: I'm trying to say that you don't understand what my sickness is.

Scaramuccia: Master, for every ill, there is a remedy. Tell me, if you please what sickness this is, because maybe I could offer you some medicine that works better than an explanation would do.

Demetrio: I'll tell you what I'm feeling, because speaking will relieve my heart: but I'm warning you to keep quiet about it, because this sickness loves to be concealed, secret and hidden.

Scaramuccia: What the hell kind of sickness is this? Speak up, master, I'll be your faithful secret keeper.

Demetrio: I believe you, however, my Scaramuccia, know that I, know that I, know that I … I don't know if I ought to tell you or not.

128. Scaramuccia enlists the audience to share in his entrapment of Demetrio. His dialogue now will often be asides to the audience but some of them are heard by Demetrio and then Scaramuccia will have to cover his tracks. For the reader it means watching for layered meanings.

129. The Italian *bargello* refers to a magistrate who has the powers of the police.

Scaramuccia: If you don't want to tell me, it's your funeral. Master, remember that the more the sickness is secret and hidden, the stronger it gets.

Demetrio: You're right, and I feel like I'm going to burst if I don't tell you.

Scaramuccia: The sooner the better.

Demetrio: Now hear this. When I think of Giulia leaving home and going to her husband, it breaks my heart.

Scaramuccia: And when does she have to go?

Demetrio: Tonight, to become Master Gervasio's.

Scaramuccia: And this is why you're so unhappy? And this is your sickness? O master, now I get it, now I understand your reasons: you are, without doubt, in love with Giulia.

Demetrio: On the blood of a cuckold …

Scaramuccia: Don't swear, master.

Demetrio: You've guessed it. I'm dying, I'm spasming, I'm perishing for her beauty, and I regret never having tried to assault her after her father's death.[130]

Scaramuccia: Really, so now you deserve to have me call you an "old imbecile, old fool, old sloth, old wretch, old deceiver, old disgrace, old criminal."[131]

Demetrio: Hold on, hold on, you're piling on too much, slow down with the insults what the devil are you saying, you wretch, what are these words?

Scaramuccia: I'm not saying that you are these things, I'm saying that you deserve every shameful insult because you have kept the calf at the table and eaten the cow.[132]

Demetrio: You've always been suspicious of Ruchetta.

Scaramuccia: Suspicion is borne out by the evidence, but now, if I were you, I wouldn't want to hold off any longer, and I'd like to be the first to taste this tasty dish.

Demetrio: And how, Scaramuccia?

130. Demetrio incriminates himself by regretting not having assaulted her.

131. Scaramuccia is speaking to us as much as he is to Demetrio when he speaks in asides about how horrible Demetrio is.

132. Scaramuccia conceals the intended insult by mentioning that Demetrio resisted Giulia and had sex with Ruchetta instead.

Scaramuccia: Leave the details to me, and if I don't succeed, say that I am the son of a cuckold! You, master, in the meanwhile, enjoy yourself, and I'll see that you have her first, for sure.

Demetrio: If you do this for me, I'll make you a beneficiary of my will.

Scaramuccia: Into the breach, horse, the fodder awaits. But here are Master Gervasio and Ruchetta talking about something. Leave this to me.

SCENE TWO

Gervasio, Demetrio, Scaramuccia, and Ruchetta

Gervasio: Good day, Master Demetrio.

Demetrio: Good day, Master Gervasio: I see my servant Ruchetta with you, so I expect you already know that my Giulia has agreed to marry you—Oh, I wish I'd never said that, I wish my tongue had fallen out. Aah, it hurts so much!

Gervasio: Goodness, what's happening? What's the matter, Master Demetrio?

Demetrio: To tell you the truth, I suffer from a hernia, and wear a truss, but every so often the pain gets me.[133]

Scaramuccia: You cursed old man, you deserve what you get.

Gervasio: Has the pain gone?

Demetrio: It's getting better.

Scaramuccia: It'll take you to the gallows.

Ruchetta: Master, do you want me to get the small chamber pot? If you try pissing even a little bit it'll help. Or should I bring the big pot?

Scaramuccia: Yes, and stink up the whole neighborhood.

Demetrio: No, I don't need either of them. Scaramuccia knows what's wrong with me, and what the cure is.

Scaramuccia: A good beating. Don't worry, master, I'll cure you in no time.

Demetrio: Ah, that's a bit better. Schemer, gas pains are very bad! O God be praised, the pain's gone. Now, where were we: I think Ruchetta has told you that Giulia has agreed to take you as her—Aah, aah, here they come again, it's swelling up, O alas, help, save me, who can help me?

133. Demetrio's lust becomes manifest when he sees Gervasio, leading to this scene of crude physical comedy as he tries to hide his sexual frustration by blaming it on gas.

Scaramuccia: The executioner.

Gervasio: My sir, this illness of yours is very serious, and very dangerous.

Ruchetta: Master, try to blow a fart to make a bit of wind! Ah, sir, remember good health is a great treasure.

Gervasio: Since the pain comes on so often, why not go into your house, and then in an hour or so, once you're better, we can touch hands for the betrothal.

Demetrio: No, wait a minute—the pain's going, thanks to Ruchetta's suggestion. Oh, it's marvelous what a little bit of wind will do.

Scaramuccia: Yeah, we know—we can smell it from here.

Demetrio: If I hadn't managed that fart I'd have been in great pain, but now I feel new again. So, to get back to what we were talking about, she accepts you as her husband.

Gervasio: O, thank heavens for that! And since it is customary for the groom to send jewelry to his bride, I went one better, and have brought some with me. Here they are, what do you think of this diamond? What do you say this this ruby? These earrings? This necklace? And these expensive pearls? Have I done well?

Demetrio: Extremely well, and they will be the reason why the bride will give you more caresses in the long run rather than the beginning.

Gervasio: It seems that brides like jewels more than husbands, perhaps because husbands die and jewels always stay with them.

Ruchetta: Yes, women have always been greedy, but those who love their husbands would give up all the jewels in the world for one good night.

Demetrio: Scaramuccia, go into the house and tell Giulia to get herself ready and come outside with you.

Scaramuccia: I have you, master.

Demetrio: Where?

Scaramuccia: In… I was speaking in reverence! In the house, as you asked.

Demetrio: The time has come to exchange vows with Giulia, Master Gervasio, and give her the jewels; when do you want the wedding to take place?

Gervasio: Tonight at the very latest.

Demetrio: Damn it, that's too soon! It seems to me that you need to wait longer and put it off to another evening when it's more convenient.

Ruchetta: When the bread is rising, it's necessary to put it in the oven and not wait until it falls and goes sour.[134]

Demetrio: It's impossible to have the wedding tonight because there's only a little left of today and we haven't got the feast ready or invited the guests. It would be so much better to postpone it at least until tomorrow evening.

Gervasio: I'll do what you want; but remember that tonight I can be making a son, and if I wait until tomorrow, it could be a girl.

Demetrio: No, no, let's leave it like this: that tomorrow night the wedding takes place without fail and we'll follow this arrangement for the honor of both houses. Ruchetta, call them. What can they be doing, why don't they come?

Ruchetta: Now, master, but there they are, coming out of the house.

SCENE THREE

Scaramuccia, Demetrio, Gervasio, Ruchetta , and Giulia

Scaramuccia: Leave it up to me and don't worry about finding another solution. Master, we're all happy, all joyful, and the Lady Giulia, most of all. For her each hour seems a thousand years until she takes Gervasio for her husband.

Demetrio: What do you say, Master Gervasio? Isn't she a fine young mare good for two or three stages without a bridle?

Gervasio: Certainly, but I won't do anything that wild, of course.

Ruchetta: Of course, even if you hadn't said it, I sadly already know it.

Giulia: What are your orders, master?

Demetrio: It's not up to me to give you orders anymore, that's for your husband to do.

Giulia: What husband?

Demetrio: You seem not to know about it.

Giulia: This is the first I've heard of it.

Gervasio: O Master Demetrio, what about the promises you made?

134. Another of Ruchetta's sexually-charged references to rising bread and ovens.

Demetrio: Just a moment, excuse me. Giulia, come here for a minute. Didn't I tell you that I had promised you in marriage to Master Gervasio Grifone, and you said that you wanted to think about it, and then you sent a reply with the servant, that you had agreed?

Giulia: These are the first warning signs from the realm of the unhappy brides. Sir, there is no need to find me a husband, because I don't want any other husband but you, or more exactly, another father: I don't want to leave your house, because I love you too much.

Demetrio: And I love you too, my little darling.

Gervasio: Hey, Master Demetrio, it looks to me as if you two are making love together! O crap, this thing is starting to stink! But what's he up to?[135]

Demetrio: Just a moment.

Gervasio: A moment? It seems to me that she doesn't want me, and she says openly that she knows nothing about it.

Demetrio: Don't be surprised—she's not used to getting married, and that's why she's playing hard to get.

Scaramuccia: Giulia, you'll ruin everything I've cooked up! Tell him you are willing, and leave everything up to me, like I told you.[136]

Gervasio: Just be quiet, if you please. Giulia, do you agree to marry me, or not?

Giulia: Master Gervasio, forgive me if when Master Demetrio first mentioned it I said no, but it is because I had heard nothing about it. I said it out of the love I have for him (I love and honor him like a father). So, let me say that my will is the same as his, and as yours, and I willingly accept you as my husband.

Gervasio: Now, that's the way to fix a problem—don't you agree, Scaramuccia?

Scaramuccia: It seem that you've fixed it. But I'm going to fix you even better, you dirty old man.

Gervasio: Master Demetrio, I am here, come forward; come forward, Ruchetta, and you, Scaramuccia, because I want you all to be witnesses to the exchanging of vows and my offering her the gifts.[137]

135. Gervasio speaks more truthfully than he knows on Demetrio's behalf.

136. Giulia's exchanging of vows with Gervasio unrolls as a farce that only proceeds when Scaramuccia intervenes to get her to stick to the plot.

137. Everyone participating in the scene has a different agenda and we as spectators know more than the individual characters.

Demetrio: Here I am.

Ruchetta: Me too.

Scaramuccia: And I appear to be the third; don't know if I'm witnessing or what.

Demetrio: Now, Giulia, hold out your hand to Master Gervasio, and you, Master Gervasio, hold out yours as a sign of your betrothal.

Giulia: Make him be the first to put his out, because I don't want to be first.

Gervasio: She's right, she wants to be first to be on top.

Ruchetta: She won't be on top of you, or under you either, you silly old fool!

Gervasio: Here is my hand, my beautiful Lady Giulia, my sugar-sweet bride.

Giulia: And I give you mine as a sign of our betrothal.

Scaramuccia: Good luck to you, Master *Gervasio*: may good fortune be yours, along with a bouncing baby boy for the new year.

Ruchetta: Good luck, Lady Giulia, I want to see you like an onion, twice as big and round in breadth.

Giulia: It will turn out as heaven wills, won't it Scaramuccia?

Scaramuccia: Certainly, my lady, without any doubt.

Demetrio: Giulia, I'll do my part of the ceremonies with you inside, where it's more comfortable. Master Gervasio, give the jewels and finery to the bride.

Gervasio: Here I am, my dear wife. Give me your delicate hand, take this diamond and ruby for your fingers, put this golden necklace around your neck, this string of pearls on your throat, and hang these earrings in your ears, I'll keep these moss and amber ones for later.

Ruchetta: More like mildew and rot![138]

Giulia: My husband and dear sir, I thank you for such beautiful presents, given because of your nobility and not my worth.

Gervasio: You deserve so much that not all the gold in the world could do justice to your great worth! And with this, I kiss your hands, even if I'd rather kiss your lips.

138. Ruchetta's comment, *Più tosto de muffa and di lezzo*, plays with the sounds of Gervasio's description of the earrings he will later give her, *che sanno di musco e d'ambra*, which are meant to be delightful objects and odors, while *muffa* means moldy and *lezzo* smelling of sweat.

Giulia: Save that for a better opportunity! Master, with your permission, and that of my husband, I'm going in now.

Demetrio: Go, I'm coming too.

Ruchetta: Scaramuccia, do you remember the favor you promised me?

Scaramuccia: I do remember. Now that we're alone, I have something good to tell you, Master Gervasio.

Gervasio: What good thing is this?

Scaramuccia: Something that is sweeter than sugar or manna from heaven.

Gervasio: And where is it coming from?

Scaramuccia: From hairy valley.[139]

Gervasio: And who is sending it to me?

Scaramuccia: Master Not-too-bright!

Gervasio: Who is he?

Scaramuccia: A dealer in horns.

Gervasio: And what does he want from me on my wedding day? Wait a minute.

Scaramuccia: He wants to trade merchandise with you.

Gervasio: He can't trade with me because I don't want his merchandise.

Scaramuccia: How so? Doesn't similar merchandise make a lot of people rich without having to work for it.

Gervasio: I'm not interested in this traffic.

Scaramuccia: Eh, Master Gervasio, higher up there's a lady moon.[140]

Gervasio: What's the moon got to do with my wedding?

Scaramuccia: It's got to do with giving you a chaste and honest bride.

Gervasio: I don't want her chaste, but the way wives usually are.

Scaramuccia: You're making good sense, and your wish coincides with Lady Giulia's, who also doesn't care so much about chastity and would like to spend

139. The Italian is *val pelosa* and refers to female genitalia.

140. Diana, the moon goddess, is known for her chastity.

tonight with you, even if she was too modest to say it in front of Master Demetrio. But when we went inside she begged me to do everything in my power to make it possible for her to sleep with you tonight.

Gervasio: O my dear love, I got it right when I said she was dying for me! As for me, do it, I'm all for it. But what way, what route, what plan is needed to bring us together without getting caught?[141]

Scaramuccia: This is what I want you to do: two hours after dark you're to be here at the door of the house. When you're ready, you're to cough loudly three times, and I'll hear the signal and come down and open up for you, and sneak you into the house, into the ground floor room and after everyone goes in bed and falls asleep, I'll take you to your darling Giulia who'll be there waiting for you. What do you say to that? In any case, she'll be yours.

Gervasio: That's wonderful, wonderful, so wonderful! Couldn't be better, because in any case, she's mine, as you say, and there is always a risk in delaying. Who knows what tonight may bring, let alone tomorrow.

Scaramuccia: Exactly, well said, go home now and send your servant Trapola to me, right away, to help out with this plan.

Gervasio: I'll do it gladly. To my happy and delightful night of pleasure! I'm going.

Scaramuccia: May you go straight to hell, you old bag of guts. How well these two old idiots think they've worked this out. But it's going to turn out differently from what they expect, because I've decided to make the young ones happy and let the old men go hang. They're about to die anyway, and the young ones have a whole life of good times to look forward to. Hey, who am I talking to? O Trapola, hey, come on out![142]

SCENE FOUR

Trapola and Scaramuccia

Trapola: I'm here, what's with the shouting? You've got the whole neighborhood buzzing with so much yelling.

Scaramuccia: I thought maybe you were deaf.

141. Gervasio gets trapped by his own vanity.

142. When Scaramuccia tells us that he is on the side of the young, speaking as *capocomico* and Scala's mouthpiece, he indicates the new direction toward which the commedia dell'arte is moving. See the discussion in the Introduction, 21 and 27.

Trapola: I'm a fava bean. I hear with my eyes and see with my ears, since one seems like the other to me.[143]

Scaramuccia: So, you're speaking figuratively. Tell the truth, Trapola, did you go to grammar school when you were a boy?

Trapola: No, master, but I'm naturally smart. What do you want from me?

Scaramuccia: My Trapola, you know that Ruchetta, soon to be your wife, is so hot for you that she can barely contain herself

Trapola: Oh, the poor thing, it seems wrong to me.

Scaramuccia: And she told me to find you and tell you that she would like to find herself sleeping with you tonight by any means.

Trapola: To sleep with me? No, master, I want her to stay awake all night when she comes to me to see if I can make a beautiful little Trapolino! But how can this be done to satisfy Ruchetta? How do you want to guide this ship so that it doesn't sink or break up on the rocks?

Scaramuccia: I'll tell you: I have planned that two hours after dark, you dress up as a woman and, in disguise, you come under our windows and then, hit two stones together three times to let me know you are there. Then, I'll come out and very, very, quietly, take you into the house and in due course put you with Ruchetta. What do you say about that?

Trapola: What do you want me to say? If I dress as a woman, then maybe I'll turn into a woman and if you put me with Ruchetta like this, I won't be able to do anything, because grater against grater doesn't make cheese.[144]

Scaramuccia: Whew, idiot, oh, listen to what he's saying! Really, you think that perhaps dressing yourself as a woman will turn you into one, eh? O you cretin, the

143. Trapola likes to distort reality whenever he can by reversing positions or just going with the flow. The reference to the fava bean is not identified.

144. The Italian phrase *perché grattugia con grattugia non fa cascio* appears in the episode dealing with the love between Fiordispina and Bradamante in Matteo Maria Boiardo's *Orlando innamorato*, 3.9.11. Apparently, it was a popular proverb at the time and turned up in other plays. Its meaning refers to the fact that two graters cannot make cheese and the implication is that sex between women can't make offspring. However, it also suggests that the act of grating was similar to the rubbing together that was regarded as pleasurable in the female same-sex act known as tribadism. See Laura Giannetti, *Lelia's Kiss: Imagining Gender, Sex, and Marriage in Italian Renaissance Comedy* (Toronto: University of Toronto Press, 2009), 257n80.

time we believed in transforming sexes has passed, moreover it's not up to you to transform yourself, that's Ruchetta's job, as you will find out over time.[145]

Trapola: What are you talking about, turn me into what?

Scaramuccia: Into a castrone, a gelding, a deer—I'm sure of it!

Trapola: Oh, she can do what she wants, in any case, I won't be the first or the last, because when women want something, they know how to get it, so that even if the husband had eyes everywhere, he wouldn't see anything; and then the disgrace is his and also the shame, because he who tries fails.

Scaramuccia: I couldn't agree more! Let's not talk about this anymore because you don't have this problem: Ruchetta is a good girl, smart, honest and decent.

Trapola: You have to believe this when you take a wife, and then pray it'll work out.

Scaramuccia: This is a good way to go, because with women you never know the truth. Now then, there is no time to lose because night is falling. Go home and tell mistress Porzia that I absolutely must talk to her, and for her to come here where I'll be waiting at the door.

Trapola: I'm going inside to do everything that you have asked for. Oh, if I get Ruchetta into my hands as I am hoping, Scaramuccia, I want you to taste her, because I hear she is delicious!

Scaramuccia: Like herring or tuna, without even trying her. Whew, you filthy beast, are these things to talk about?

Trapola: No sir, but so good to do! I'm going.

Scaramuccia: Go to hell!

SCENE FIVE

Demetrio and Scaramuccia

Demetrio: Scaramuccia, O Scaramuccia, where are you?

145. Falavolti, 329n1, suggests that he is referring to an earlier theatrical period when all the women's parts were taken by men, before women were allowed on the professional stage. He is also recalling an earlier time period when hermaphroditism was regarded as a condition which allowed hermaphrodites to appear as either male or female at will. In any case, Trapola is addressing the power of the stage to trick us into believing that the clothes make the man or woman, as Licinio is doing. Later, in 5.6, Scaramuccia himself worries that he will become a woman when he puts on the nightshirt and cap to get in bed with Licinio.

Scaramuccia: Oh, my master's calling; I want to shake him up a bit.[146]

Demetrio: You're not listening are you? Scaramuccia? Where the hell are you hiding? Scaramuccia, are you getting drunk in the cellar as usual?

Scaramuccia: Master, what do you want?

Demetrio: Where are you?

Scaramuccia: I don't know where.

Demetrio: And who does?

Scaramuccia: You do.

Demetrio: If I'm in the house, how can I know?

Scaramuccia: Because, if I'm not in the house, you know that I'm outside.

Demetrio: Good answer, you savage! Wait there, I'm coming!

Scaramuccia: Come and make it quick.

Demetrio: I'm here. What's new, gallant Scaramuccia? Don't you remember what you promised me?

Scaramuccia: And do you think I'm forgetful? Master, yes, I remember.

Demetrio: If you remember why haven't you started to make it happen?

Scaramuccia: If you'll be patient, you'll be eating tail for a quarter the price.

Demetrio: I know how to hunt and trap tail on my own.

Scaramuccia: If you're so good at trapping tail, why don't you pluck that Giulia bird by yourself?

Demetrio: Because this one needs to be plucked with your birdlime, Scaramuccia.[147]

Scaramuccia: Ah, ah, say it one more time!

Demetrio: Scaramuccia, I'm warning you that we can't let this night pass because then we won't be able to do anything for the love of Master Gervasio, whom, however, I have given time to let matters run their course.

Scaramuccia: I know it as well as you do; what do you think, that I'm sleeping? Now, listen up to what I'm saying.

146. Scaramuccia invites the audience to watch him wind up Demetrio.

147. Birdlime is a sticky substance smeared on branches to catch small birds.

Demetrio: I'm starting to swim in a sea of milk and honey and sugar and of ...

Scaramuccia: And of ... I 'll tell you! I want you to go in the house and once you've finished supper, about two and a half hours after dark, wait for me over there until I give you the sign.

Demetrio: And where?

Scaramuccia: Where? On your face! What sign? I'll have to tell you.

Demetrio: You're right. Love's robbed me of my mind and my memory.

Scaramuccia: So, from the three powers of the soul, you only have one left—your appetite.[148] The sign will be that I will whistle three times, when you hear it come to the door and I'll bring you Giulia.

Demetrio: How will you bring me Giulia, if she's in my house?

Scaramuccia: You don't know the rest of the story, so I'll fill you in: Master Gervasio has begged and begged me to put him to bed with Giulia tonight in her room, because he can't wait any longer, and I've promised to do it for sure.

Demetrio: It's me who's supposed to put them together! Hey, Scaramuccia, why did you promise this on the night that is owed to me?

Scaramuccia: Hold on! You don't know how many roads lead to Rome. I'm planning to take Ruchetta to Master Gervasio at the appointed hour, convince him that it's Giulia and say that she didn't want to have him in her room in order not to disrespect you.

Demetrio: Slow down a bit. And how is it that Ruchetta will agree to sleep with Gervasio?

Scaramuccia: Listen to this: Ruchetta is in love with Trapola and I've promised to take her to sleep with him and make him her husband.

Demetrio: You've promised everyone in the neighborhood, heaven help you!

Scaramuccia: You'll see in the end. When it's time, I'll come with Mistress Giulia, pretending to take her to Master Gervasio, and after we've walked around for a while, I'll turn around in some side street and bring her back home, and then, in the dark, put her in the ground-floor room, without a light, where you'll be waiting to enjoy her, pretending to be Master Gervasio.

148. The three parts of the soul according to Plato were: reason, spirit (emotions) and appetite. In the just soul, the first two are aligned to resist falling into appetite, as the unjust soul would do.

Demetrio: Excellent, excellent! But who will you take in Giulia's place to Master Gervasio?

Scaramuccia: I'm planning to take Ruchetta, haven't I already told you? And to make it all happen smoothly, I've told Master Gervasio that Lady Giulia is ashamed to be enjoyed with the light on and that is why I've got the ground-floor room ready, so that no lights are needed; moreover, I've told him she'll be wearing different clothes in order not to be recognized if anyone sees her.

Demetrio: You spin this web of intrigue very well! I hope it makes the cloth that you want!

Scaramuccia: Leave it to one who knows how to spin, scheme, and weave![149]

Demetrio: I hope that, unlike the weaving of Arachne, who was punished in the end, everything will go well.[150]

Scaramuccia: Master, you amaze me, hearing you speak so poetically.

Demetrio: I remember reading about this when I went to the school of grammar, logic, and rhetoric, and so on.

Scaramuccia: Very good, it's enough at your advancing decrepit age to remember the works of Virgil and the other poets.

Demetrio: What decrepit age? You make me laugh calling me decrepit! How old do you think I am?

Scaramuccia: I think you're around sixty, seventy, eighty, or ninety-five years; and with that truss attached to your ass, you could be a hundred.[151]

Demetrio: Go to hell, scoundrel! I've reached forty-five, I'm in my forties: do I look decrepit to you?

149. Scaramuccia is bragging about his powers of invention in creating this master plan, which is so intricate and complicated that it requires perfect organization, precise staging, and accurate timing to deliver. He also is telling the audience what will be taking place behind the scenes to add credibility to such a farfetched set of events.

150. In Greek mythology, Arachne was a maiden famous for her weaving, whom the goddess Athena turned into a spider for having challenged her.

151. Scaramuccia often utters such brutal insults to Demetrio that they must have been spoken more as asides to the audience, although of course Demetrio hears and pretends to ignore him. The truss he refers to seems to be connected to the large piece of cloth attached to his belt and used as a handkerchief for various purposes.

Scaramuccia: Not like a shit, but like dog's shit.[152]

Demetrio: Eh, Scaramuccia, those who are old and decrepit have poor health and bad complexions: while I'm lusty, muscular and made of steel.

Scaramuccia: As you say, you're an iron man and more.

Demetrio: You know it well, and so will Giulia, that beautiful little mare, when she is under me, how many miles per hour I'll make her go.

Scaramuccia: Yeah, brag about it, you do have a nice handle on your basket.

Demetrio: Giulia will feel it! But tell me, Scaramuccia, given that you'll have both Giulia and Ruchetta in that ground-floor room (as you say), how will you get them out, if they don't know what tricks you are playing?

Scaramuccia: I'll tell you, master, I won't wait until morning, but at the hour before dawn, I'll go for the women and take both of them home.

Demetrio: You're a good man, and very practical. Tell me the truth, Scaramuccia, were your father and mother procurers?

Scaramuccia: Both of them went to the public school of procuring in Rotten Garden and Frying Pan Piazza.[153]

Demetrio: I got it right when I said that the wolf doesn't give birth to the lamb! Now everything's in order, as long as it works.

Scaramuccia: I'm not worried about anything.

Demetrio: Now then, night's coming and it's better for me to go inside and start arming myself for my love tryst.

Scaramuccia: And what kinds of arms?

Demetrio: Marzipan, wafers, pistachios, bonbons, and good wine from Candia or Ischia.

Scaramuccia: Oh, if they armed soldiers like this today, how many more would go to war? But, master, remember not to be too forceful with her, so that her beautiful new clothes aren't shredded into gypsy rags.

Demetrio: Leave it to me, this is not the first saddle mare I've broken in.

152. Obviously, this particular insult must be delivered as an aside, as are several others. Demetrio listens selectively.

153. Rotten Garden (*Ortaccio*) and Frying Pan Piazza (*Piazza Padella*) are slang names for poorer parts of the city where prostitution flourishes.

Scaramuccia: I know that you're a horse tamer; so, go now.

Demetrio: Scaramuccia, I'm going to get ready now.

Scaramuccia: Go in alive and come out dead as soon as possible! I've got to get away from this annoying fly—this disgusting giant insect who is turning my stomach.[154] Well, if my eyes aren't deceiving me, that's Lady Porzia peeping out of the window.

SCENE SIX

Porzia and Scaramuccia

Porzia: I sent away my Lepido and Scaramuccia in a way that makes me think neither of them will ever want to come near me, and I've blown Lepido off like a piece of dust that gets in your eyes.

Scaramuccia: That's her and she's talking to herself, I'll say hello. Lady Porzia, at your ladyship's service.

Porzia: Oh, what are you doing? And what about your friend? I'm talking about the one who lives and dies a thousand times an hour?

Scaramuccia: Eh, Lady Porzia, how much better it would be if you stopped deluding yourself for once and recognized how unhappy Lepido is!

Porzia: Scaramuccia, don't leave, wait for me, I want to come a little closer to talk to you.

Scaramuccia: The mule has taken the bridle and is starting to foam at the mouth.[155]

Porzia: Here I am, Scaramuccia. What do you have to say about Lepido?

Scaramuccia: What I have to say is that maybe it's about time to listen to what he has to say; and prevent the awful thing that's going to happen.

Porzia: What awful thing?

Scaramuccia: What awful thing? Death!

Porzia: Whose death?

Scaramuccia: Lepido's death; or your husband Licinio's death because he can't live knowing that what belongs to him had ended up in someone else's hands.

154. Scaramuccia is expressing his overwhelming disgust at having to deal with Demetrio.

155. Scaramuccia is describing Porzia's excitement at reuniting with Lepido.

Porzia: But is sir Lepido really that desperate?

Scaramuccia: Really, really desperate—and if you don't do something, maybe you, too, will die.

Porzia: Me, as well?

Scaramuccia: Because he's your desperate lover, blind with passion. He'll kill the first thing he lays a hand on without thinking twice. So, you'd better be careful, and find a solution because it can't go on the way it is.

Porzia: How do you mean, me find a solution? heaven help me!

Scaramuccia: Well, maybe I can—because I've got a solution, if you'll only listen, and do what I say.

Porzia: What's your solution; do you have a cure for this awful thing?

Scaramuccia: Yes, I have—it's the cure you get under the sheets when you purge the lover's wound.

Porzia: O, come on, Scaramuccia, stop joking—this is serious.

Scaramuccia: I am serious! My cure heals all, believe me.

Porzia: And then …

Scaramuccia: And then he'll leave and be fine.

Porzia: You seem to be like a giant cicada buzzing nonsense.

Scaramuccia: And you seem like a little cicada who wants to die buzzing.

Porzia: Come on, get to the point. What about Sir Lepido? I know that he was very unhappy when he left me.

Scaramuccia: Very, very unhappy.

Porzia: And where did he go?

Scaramuccia: Where do you think? To work off his frustration at the house of a beautiful courtesan newly arrived in Rome, the most beautiful young woman you've ever seen—good, virtuous, sings, dances, and behaves like a princess.[156]

Porzia: Oh, dear, what's this? Now Lepido is making a copy of himself with another woman? With a prostitute? Ahh, unlucky me, I wish that I had never been born rather than hear such news!

156. This "honest courtesan," a high-class prostitute, is given the attributes of a gentlewoman.

Scaramuccia: Don't despair, Lady Porzia.

Porzia: You don't want me to despair, when just as I was on the verge of giving in to him (unhappy me), you've taken away all my hopes.[157]

Scaramuccia: Why have your hopes fallen? Perhaps you believe that Lepido went to enjoy her? Eh, my lady, no. Lepido went as many other gentlemen do, to the waiting room to relieve his torments with companionship, since in that house they play cards, music, and other honest entertainments. Lepido, touching another woman? And do wrong to Lady Porzia? These are all things that are utterly impossible to imagine happening.[158]

Porzia: You've given back my life and soul.

Scaramuccia: It would be better if Lepido gave them back to you.

Porzia: For sure.

Scaramuccia: Come on, recognize that your soul is shaken up, follow my plan and send for your Lepido, so that you can put an end to this once and for all.

Porzia: Woe is me! I find myself between a rock and a hard place, between Scylla and Charybdis, a hammer and an anvil, so I don't know what I should do.[159]

Scaramuccia: Take the handle in your hand and knock on your anvil and let the ship sink along with the rudder and all the rest, and hurry up for once, and cut the chitchat! Lepido can't wait to be with you and from what I can see, you really want it too, even if you don't want to say it, am I right?

Porzia: Oh, dear, it's all too true, and I have to work even harder to curb my desire which until now has been kept under the tightest bonds. My dear Scaramuccia, won by your pleas and my Lord Lepido's great worth, my mind is made up and I want only to make him happy.

Scaramuccia: Thanks to the handle of the dipper. I take note that you have behaved exactly like a straw dog who barks and barks and at the end puts his tail between his legs.

157. The parenthetical phrase (*lassa me*) may be thrown to the audience to foreshadow that Porzia's cunning will soon be revealed.

158. These waiting rooms were also offered to the men of the town by visiting actresses. The Italian *ridotto* refers not only to waiting rooms but to the public entrances to the theater.

159. Scylla and Charybdis are legendary monsters from Greek mythology who trapped ships passing through the straits of Messina.

Porzia: I'm a woman, Scaramuccia, and women don't know how to act differently. Now that I see the necessity, I want to act wisely as a smart woman would. I see no other way to fulfill these desires of ours, but to have you hear my plan, which without your help and risk-taking can't happen.[160]

Scaramuccia: By all means spell out what I have to do, because I'm not afraid to take risks and I'm ready to serve.

Porzia: Tell me what you are willing to do?

Scaramuccia: What? For Lepido? I'm ready to die! Go on, tell me about it.

Porzia: All right, then, listen. I want you at two hours after nightfall, or even later, to bring Lepido to my house, making some sign to let me know that it's you, so that once I've heard, I'll come very quietly to open the door, and let Lepido in and lead him to the apartment near the garden, where he'll wait for me to arrive.

Scaramuccia: Excellent, I like it. I know that smart women make sons.

Porzia: I'll go to bed with my husband and when he's deeply asleep; I'll get up and go find my Lepido.

Scaramuccia: Great, brilliant, it couldn't be better.

Porzia: And, if my husband at that very moment (as he often does when sleeping) by chance reaches out an arm or a leg to touch me and doesn't find me, I've thought of a way that I can be safe.

Scaramuccia: Oh, excellent, excellent, this will be the icing on the cake! How will you do it?

Porzia: Listen, I've thought about it and you're the only one who can make all this work.

Scaramuccia: Tell me about it, please, because I still don't see what I have to do, and I want above all to help you two with all my heart.

Porzia: Without your help we can't do anything—but let's get to the problem that I told you about. When Lepido comes into the house I want you to come with him and wait in the room with him till I arrive. I'll be there as soon as my husband drops off to sleep, and when I get to the room where you are I want you to strip to your nightshirt, put a lady's nightcap on your head and follow me: I'll take you to my bedroom and put you in bed with my husband.

160. Porzia speaks with some authority on the position of women here. She reinforces the real strength of the female characters when she turns the tables on Scaramuccia and forces him to listen to her plan, just as all the other characters had listened to his.

Scaramuccia: What the hell? In bed with your husband?

Porzia: Yes, in bed with my husband. Then as he dozes he'll believe for sure that you're his wife, and so I'll have a clear field, and can stay with my Lepido for the whole night. What's up? You're scratching your head.

Scaramuccia: Well, it's a good plan, a nice plan, but it's a bit dangerous; no, it's not, it's very dangerous. Let's see: I strip to my nightshirt, I put a lady's nightcap on my head, and I bed down for the whole night with your husband? You're not going to make me do this sort of homework—I never learnt this sort of conjugation from my Latin teachers. Porzia, are you joking or is this for real?[161]

Porzia: You'll see if I'm joking. If you aren't prepared to do what I've said, all our efforts are useless. We've been building sandcastles in the air and sowing our seeds in a dry land, and there is no point in thinking about it anymore. Are you listening, Scaramuccia?

Scaramuccia: Just hang on for a bit. You, my lady, have had all the time in the world to think it over, you're the one that's going to enjoy yourself, and to talk you into it took a thousand persuasions. I'm the one who's getting the short end of the stick, so just give me a chance to think it over. Now, I climb into the bed, Licinio hears me, and reaches out his hand, I poke out my head, his hand starts to move lower down, I turn my back, he thinks he's touching my breasts—uh, oh, it's too big for breasts.

Porzia: You're worrying too much about the details.

Scaramuccia: It's okay for you to talk, but I'm the one who's up against it!

Porzia: Well then, that's it—it's off.

Scaramuccia: Just wait a moment! He reaches out his hand again, looking for the rose and finds a thorn. He shouts, he raises the cry, and it's daggers at dawn. Forget it, my lady, I don't see a solution.

Porzia: Well, you can go to the devil then.

Scaramuccia: Hold on, if you please. I lie on my side, with my back to him. He comes looking for my breasts and finds my shoulders. He tries again and finds my hairy chest. He goes lower and finds something he can grab onto—it's bad news one way, and worse the other! Forget it, forget it, there's no way out.

161. Scaramuccia becomes completely entrapped in his own plot, showing perhaps that the *capocomico* is also subjected to the aesthetic vision the play must fulfill. The detail by detail description of how a bed trick works with all the possible variations and combinations plays with the power of the stage to stimulate the imagination to believe what is heard.

Porzia: Well, even if it did happen like that, so what? If it were me I wouldn't be so scared.

Scaramuccia: Well of course, it'd be no problem for you—you young ladies have a way of wriggling out of any tight corner, with arguments that would convince the whole city, let alone just one man! But someone like me, that hasn't got your extra parts, and has one part that you haven't got—qua pars est?[162] Joking aside, but what if your husband is tempted by lustful desires (half-drunk with sleep) and in a frenzy, wants to take it out on me? My lady, old things break easily: if he found out that I was a man like him, and got his hands on the bed-warmer's handle, what would I be supposed to do then? What would you do if you were me, Lady Porzia?[163]

Porzia: Thinking about the problems stops you from doing anything—but in the thick of things it's not a problem, and you end up doing things you wouldn't expect.

Scaramuccia: Lady Porzia, you certainly have a way with words, but I'm the one who's risking my life here, and I can just see myself hanged, drawn, quartered, and slaughtered like a pig.[164]

Porzia: Look, don't worry—once my husband drops off to sleep, he sleeps right through till morning. And any way he never touches me, apart from once a month.

Scaramuccia: When's the start of the month?

Porzia: It's just started and he's already had his share, so that's it for this month.

Scaramuccia: Well, if it's like that it should be okay.

Porzia: Don't worry; it's a certainty.

Scaramuccia: Sure, a certainty. Taking the place of a woman, climbing in bed beside your husband in your nightshirt, and not being scared? To tell you the truth,

162. *Qua pars est?* translates as "What part is that?" Obviously, the missing penis which assumes phallic proportions.

163. Scaramuccia brings up questions of how different anatomical parts fit together to make it clear that women have an easier time "passing" in the dark, if they are part of a bed trick.

164. The punishment of being tortured and killed in the public square for being caught in a sodomitical act may possibly have been on the Florentine books. Such brutal displays were not usually carried out, as fines and prison terms were generally imposed instead. See Michael Rocke, *Forbidden Friendships: Homosexuality and Male Culture in Renaissance Florence* (New York: Oxford University Press, 1996). Although he is dealing with an earlier century, Rocke discusses the severity of the penalties for sodomy especially between two consenting adults, if the participants were caught. See also Laura Ikins Stern, *The Criminal Law System of Medieval and Renaissance Florence* (Baltimore: Johns Hopkins, 1994), 224–26. She posits that sodomy continued to be criminalized throughout the sixteenth century.

that's a bit hard to believe. But hang on, excuse me a minute—wouldn't it be better if Lepido stripped to his nightshirt and came to your bedroom and hopped into bed on your side, so you're in the middle? Then if your husband suddenly got tempted you could fix him up and once he's gone off to sleep you could work the other side of the mattress without making a sound.

Porzia: Lover's passion is worthless in the dark: I want to be able to look at, and gaze upon my Lepido, and for him to be able to see the face and breasts of his beloved lady. I want our lovemaking to be without care, and for any inconvenience to be borne by others, not me. So, look here, Scaramuccia, if you aren't prepared to go and lie beside my husband, the whole plan goes up in smoke. And I must say I'm losing patience with all the objections you're raising.[165]

Scaramuccia: Just hang on a second.

Porzia: I'm not going anywhere.

Scaramuccia: Curse the day I got into this scheme—the devil's found a great way to finish me off! But couldn't we find a woman of easy virtue to put in bed with him, and pay her for her services?

Porzia: Sure, with the whole of Rome talking about our affairs!

Scaramuccia: You're right. But wouldn't there be some way of getting your husband to stay out for the night, and sleep somewhere else?

Porzia: My husband, sleep somewhere else? If only he would! There's no chance, he's so jealous of me he'd never do it. Look, you can think it over as much as you like, but there's only one solution, and it's this: you go and get in bed with my husband for five or six hours. There's no other choice.

Scaramuccia: But wait a minute. What if we tried something else: we put Lepido with your husband, and you come and sleep with me—O Scaramuccia, don't be an idiot! I'm sorry, I'm so scared I'm saying stupid things.[166]

Porzia: As Rodomonte says to Orlando, "This bridge is for gentlemen and knights to pass—not for you, foul beast!"[167]

165. The chastity of the prima donna comes under question with Porzia's open expression of desire and her knowledge of what shared sexual pleasure means.

166. In Scaramuccia's most outrageous counterproposal, he dares to put himself, the master servant, on a par with his theatrical equal, the leading lady Porzia.

167. The Italian verse *Sol per signori e cavalieri è fatto il ponte, e non per te, bestia balorda*, a reminder of unbridgeable class divides, is from Ariosto's epic *Orlando furioso* (29:42–43). As Porzia knows her classics, so does Scaramuccia, since they both know that Orlando was in peasant disguise.

Scaramuccia: I guessed as much—I was only joking with your ladyship. Well then, it's decided. You go inside now, and I'll come at the appointed time with Lepido, we'll make the sign, come into the house, I'll strip to my nightshirt, put the bonnet on my head, go and lie down beside your husband, so you'll have all the time to shoot as many loving arrows as you want, so that you'll be satisfied. Is that good enough? What do you say? Anything else?

Porzia: O my dear Scaramuccia, what else is there to ask me? So, then go and find Lepido, give him my love; and fill him in on everything.

Scaramuccia: This much I'll do, your ladyship's servant. Eh, poor Scaramuccia, I see clearly that taking care of others puts you on a slippery slope. Heaven help me!

Porzia: Goodbye, goodbye, Scaramuccia, don't worry.

Scaramuccia: No, no, don't worry: be happy!

The danger is great, but I don't see any other remedy, I'm resolved to help the young ones, and do what's wanted, whatever that is. But what won't a heart do under the spell of that traitor and tyrant Love? He's taught Porzia to cuckold her husband in such a cunning way. Ahh, go on, go, go take a wife, then? What idiot would take her back! But I want to find Lepido before it's dark and get away from this mess.[168]

SCENE SEVEN

Giulia, at the window; Flavio, in the street

Giulia: If things could happen twice, I don't know if I'd say yes to marrying Master Gervasio again. That wicked Scaramuccia told me: "Do it, do it, trust me. And I, taken off guard, said yes, and now I regret that I did it. Second thoughts are always better than the first, but what good is there thinking about it now? It's happened and it's impossible to turn back and retract it now. O Fortune, how many ways can you hurt my aching soul! But if I'm not mistaken, I see Sir Flavio, my husband, coming now. I want to go down and talk things over with him.

Flavio: I don't know what's going on between Master Demetrio and Master Gervasio in their wedding plans for my Lady Giulia. I can't find Scaramuccia. Ruchetta's not around. I bet something bad is happening.

Giulia: Flavio, Flavio, psst, psst, look at me.

168. Scaramuccia mentions his submission to the demands of the plot in order to serve the young again here; see above, note 142. He also lets the audience in on his knowledge of who Licinio might really be, although he has to play out the bed scene with the deception still in place.

Flavio: O Lady Giulia, my love, now daylight has returned. My life, I was walking in the darkest night of my thoughts, and if you, my beautiful dawn hadn't appeared, I would have stayed in the shadows and the horror.

Giulia: Alas, what has happened to put you there?

Flavio: Not having news of you, my heart, not seeing Ruchetta, and not finding Scaramuccia.

Giulia: Sir Flavio, my sweetest love, I don't trust that rascal not to make a mess of this.

Flavio: If that's true, he can consider himself dead, because I'll kill him even if he's under the protection of the greatest ruler in the world. But what is it that makes you doubt him?[169]

Giulia: I'll explain, my lord: some hours ago he came with Master Gervasio and Ruchetta, loaded with presents for the bride, as is the custom. He met Master Demetrio, who was waiting at the door for him, and they sent Scaramuccia inside to get me. As soon as he was inside he started persuading me to accept the old man's offer of marriage. When I heard him talking in this crazy way I started objecting to the betrayal he was proposing and disagreeing with what he was saying. Finally, after arguing for a long time, he said, "Lady Giulia, just trust me, I know what I'm doing." And there I was, overpowered by his words and pressured for time, and even as we went outside he kept trying to convince me, and there waiting to take my hand in marriage was that hateful old idiot. Master Demetrio forced me to exchange vows with Master Gervasio; and take the jewels he had brought for me. So here I am, neither wife nor widow—well, actually married twice over, married by force to that dirty old man, and married by desire to you, my true husband. And now Scaramuccia's nowhere to be seen.

Flavio: Fortune, aren't you satisfied yet? What do you think you're doing? Perhaps you'll let your fickle wheel turn and crush me? If that's what you intend, reckless as you are, you'll be sorry, because wherever Prudence rules, Fortune has no power—I can resist your ups and downs. Lady Giulia, we can't tell why Scaramuccia said to you, "Do it, trust me." This way of speaking reveals assurance and wisdom, diligence and the desire to find a solution to this messy predicament.

Giulia: Be careful, because this way of speaking is deceptive, lots of people have a habit of saying, "I know what I'm saying, I know what I'm doing, don't doubt me,

169. Scaramuccio's disappearance in this scene creates such high anxiety in the characters under his direction that they badmouth him in increasingly sharp ways, expressing doubt in his abilities to make the complicated plot work; but at the same time, they also show how dependent they are on him. The reference to a powerful ruler may be directed at the Grand Duke Cosimo II himself who liked to see the commedia dell'arte troupes perform; see the Introduction, 19.

trust in me," and then at the end, you find out you've been betrayed. So, I don't trust this rascal Scaramuccia! Besides he may be fooling himself by believing too much in himself.

Flavio: We always need to think of the good.

Giulia: Rather we need to look at the bad, because while the good never hurts, the bad always does.

Flavio: Do what he wants: otherwise I'll never be your husband.

Giulia: Sure, but meanwhile I've taken the hand of the old man, accepted his jewels, and even if I can always give them back, how can the oath and all these commitments be reversed?

Flavio: O Heaven, why couldn't he have put off this business for a few days at least? You, my love, should have said that you needed a least a month, and not accepted the deadline of a day, so this entire situation could be considered your fault.

Giulia: You're right, but I didn't think that everything would close in so fast: the evil is done, so I need to see a way out, and if not, I'll find one myself in desperation.

Flavio: And what might you be planning, my heart?

Giulia: To run away from home, leave the presents to the old man, and come to find you no matter what. My dowry can't be taken from me or kept by Master Demetrio.

Flavio: This has to be the last resort, let's think about other solutions if we can, to save your reputation, so that you don't become the neighborhood gossip. Scaramuccia has told me you'll be mine, no matter what.

Giulia: Yes, and he told me the same, and, moreover, when he was talking to me in the house, he said that above all he wants us to be together, and this is what bothers me.

Flavio: So, we must believe that it'll happen no matter what; that it's necessary to leave it up to him; but if we see that he can't bring it off, that it's going badly, then we admit our relationship and get him to reveal it to Master Demetrio.

Giulia: That conniving Ruchetta, knows exactly what Scaramuccia has in mind but all she says is "Leave it to him." And, from what I can tell, she's in love with Trapola, the servant of Master Gervasio, and wants me to marry him so that she can come with me and marry Trapola. O Lord Flavio, how many crooked paths do we have to travel sometimes to get to market, eh?

Flavio: What you've told me seems like a fantasy and I think that there's some trick hiding here! And if I find out what it is, I know that I'll do it.

Giulia: My Sir Flavio, don't lose time making meaningless conversation. It'd be better for your lordship to find Scaramuccia before night to find out what he wants us to do.

Flavio: You speak wisely, my lady, like a young woman with a lot of sense, so go in while I look for him and find out what's going on. Go inside, my love.

Giulia: I'm going, my only refuge. Remember me, as the one who lives and breathes only for you.

Flavio: I will, and you, wait for me tonight, without fail.

Giulia: I will, my love, because now it's time! Goodbye, my life!

Flavio: I don't know what to say about this Scaramuccia. He's a servant and hired servants these days come in many varieties: there are those who are only stomachs, those who are stomachs and tongues; others who know how to flatter and deceive; and, there are also many who are cruel and perfidious.[170] But here is Sir Lepido, maybe he can tell me something.

SCENE EIGHT

Lepido, Flavio, and Scaramuccia

Lepido: Look here, look there, for that cursed Scaramuccia to find out what to do next! In the end, not even a navigator's map could find him! O Flavio, forgive me, I didn't see you. Any news of that rascal Scaramuccia?

Flavio: Lepido, I came to ask you the same thing. This trickster has put us into a deep labyrinth: he promises big and delivers small.

Lepido: This is typical of him, he's like this and shouldn't be blamed for it.

Flavio: All the same, it seems like a bad thing to me to promise so much and not deliver anything.

Lepido: He'll make some kind of mess; I know that from experience, but I'm convinced he's doing this to play a trick on our old men, and that's good.[171]

170. Flavio considers Scaramuccia's low social status to be a sign that he cannot be trustworthy, drawing attention to the class hierarchy the commedia dell'arte often criticizes.

171. Speaking about his own situation, Lepido also refers to the changes in the commedia dell'arte where the old men were losing their dominance to the young lovers. See note 142, above.

Flavio: I share your opinion and believe we owe it to him to do what he wants: since he hasn't asked anything more of us, other than to keep being his second masters and take care of him as long as he lives.

Lepido: Absolutely, and that's my particular obligation since he's been a servant in my house for many years; but I'd like to clear up any ambiguity. Oh, here he is, right on cue.

Scaramuccia: I don't know if it's sounded twenty-four hours yet, but night is falling, the lovers are poised, the fools are set up, such that there is nothing left to do but set off the fireworks for this knavish trick to make a big explosion as the guns go off one by one.[172]

Lepido: Scaramuccia, O Scaramuccia, where are you going? Tell us what's going on?

Scaramuccia: O Sir Lepido, is that you? Are you there? Big things for sure! Oh, Sir Flavio is with you, eh? Will the time ever come when you aren't attached together?

Flavio: True friends are always together even when far apart because when their bodies are separated from each other, their minds come closer.[173]

Scaramuccia: It's obvious that you have studied, Sir Flavio.

Flavio: Studied? Well, I only studied *belle lettere* a little.[174]

Scaramuccia: *Belle lettere* are the ones that say: "Magnificent Sirs, for this first bank note: you will pay a thousand scudi, and settle our accounts with a valued customer."[175]

Flavio: You don't understand, *belle lettere* refers to literature about human culture.

172. As hours were measured, the twenty-fourth hour, at sunset, marked the ending of the day. The action in Act Five has to happen under the cover of darkness, ending at sunrise.

173. The Neoplatonic doctrine which argues that the souls of lovers became united in one body is a reccurring topic of discourse between Lepido and Porzia, with commentary thrown in by Scaramuccia. Francesco Andreini also described his friendship with Scala as one where they were in two bodies but shared one soul; see Marotti, "Introduzione" to *Teatro delle favole*, xliv.

174. *Belle lettere* refers to the study of literature for its aesthetic purity and beauty. Flavio as a gentleman lover would have been expected to study high literature, another way to separate him from the supposedly uneducated servant Scaramuccio.

175. Scaramuccia plays with the meanings of the word "letter," used to denote individual letters of the alphabet and also a bank letter presenting a bill for funds owed. A *scudo* is a coin struck in silver and gold whose value fluctuated with the value set on it by the state. Estimates vary from around a dollar for silver to fifteen for gold.

Scaramuccia: I don't know any more beautiful about human culture than paying a thousand scudi the first time, and two thousand the next.

Flavio: Not exactly, literature about human culture means: Grammar, Logic, Rhetoric, Poetry and Philosophy.

Scaramuccia: Oh, something else altogether! You should have said so from the beginning so I could have understood.

Flavio: Eh, Scaramucchia, you're always joking, isn't that so? Now, leaving our digression aside, explain to me what you meant when you said to Lady Giulia, "Do it, do it, trust me," when she took Master Gervasio's hand, for what reason?

Lepido: And what's the big news for me?

Scaramuccia: That Porzia loves you, Lepido! And you, Sir Flavio, know that I meant that the outcome will be everything that you and Lady Giulia desire.

Flavio: To say this much and no more is not enough.

Scaramuccia: I don't know enough from not enough.

Flavio: With you there's no winning or losing because you twist the meaning of every word you say.

Scaramuccia: Meaning that the only thing that makes sense to me is trying to stay alive! But joking aside. What time do we want it to be now? It's already around one isn't it? But not by much. What do you think, Lepido, has it been an hour?

Lepido: I don't think so, only a bit more than half an hour.

Scaramuccia: Okay, then. But slow down a little, my lords, what has your Scaramuccia earned for his great pains?

Flavio: Whatever you know to ask for.

Scaramuccia: Asking is easy, receiving is more difficult.

Lepido: In your opinion, what do you think you deserve?

Scaramuccia: We're not talking about deserving, but about courtesy and good manners.

Lepido: Is one hundred scudi enough? Fifty from Flavio and fifty from me?

Scaramuccia: I'm more than happy, I'm thrilled. But could you give me half for a deposit? Because to tell you the truth, I've never liked to work on credit, I'd rather enjoy the present than wait for the future.

Lepido: I don't have any money with me.

Flavio: Neither do I.

Scaramuccia: Oh, what lovers you are, without even a cent to buy a bag of roast chestnuts. But for all that, I want to be a gentleman against my nature and take care of you on credit. So, let's go. The time draws near when you'll find the happiness you desire. In the meantime, I'll fill you in on everything.[176]

Lepido: Let's get out of here.

Flavio: Let's go, the time has come.

Act Five

SCENE ONE

Scaramuccia and Trapola, dressed as a woman; Flavio and Lepido separately and unseen

Scaramuccia: You're all set and it's almost two hours after dark. Stand away from each other, Sir Lepido and Sir Flavio; let me set up the decoy so that the birds will fall when it's time.

Trapola: It's two hours after dark, and here I am, just as Scaramuccia ordered, dressed as a woman, and I have two nice big rocks in my hands for the signal I'm supposed to send—and I could use them to crack anyone's head that gets in my way. I'll just creep slowly up to the door. O Love, the things you make lovers do! Who knows how many lovers are out and about now, disguised as porters, or maidservants, or peddlers—and how many women are waiting for their lovers? And how many cuckolds are there sleeping comfortably, and how many others are making it easy for their wives to crown them king of the cuckolds? Oh, I could be next! But anyway, let's give the signal: tap, tap, tap.

Scaramuccia: If I'm not deceived, this one, according to the signal is Trapola, dressed as a woman. By God, it is. Shush, shush, shush, Trapola, Trapola, don't you know me, it's Scaramuccia.

Trapola: What Trapola? I'm the girl from Piazza Frying-pan who wants to make some money, so leave me alone and mind your own business.[177]

176. Scaramuccia's dig at not being able to get any money out of his patrons may also be intended for the ears of his real-life patrons, in this case Cardinal Carlo and possibly his brother, Grand Duke Cosimo II.

177. Trapola has fallen into believing in his own stage illusion of being a woman because of his costume.

Scaramuccia: Hey, you rascal, a girl from Piazza Frying-pan, eh? Trapola, don't you recognize me, you filthy beast?

Trapola: Watch out, watch out, I'll call my pimp and he'll break your arm! Scoundrel, go to hell.

Scaramuccia: This animal here is pretending to be a woman; and doesn't recognize my voice. Trapola, who am I talking to? Is it possible, idiot, that you don't know my voice in the dark?[178]

Trapola: O, it's you, Scaramuccia, eh?

Scaramuccia: Yes, it's me; you're a real pain in the ass!

Trapola: Forgive me, brother, for not recognizing you. I'm dressed as a woman like this, the best that I know, and I've put on some of my mistress Porzia's old clothes; and now I can't think about anything except getting out of here and spending the night with my Ruchetta.

Scaramuccia: That'll do: go and hide in there for a bit, and don't come out before I can come to get you.

Trapola: See, I'm hiding now.

Scaramuccia: That'll work: stay in there for a bit and don't come out until I can find you. Now I'm going to whistle three times under my master's windows so that he can come as promised to take that untamed Giulia into his house. Fis, fis, fis.

SCENE TWO

Scaramuccia, Demetrio, and Trapola

Scaramuccia: The old one must be sleeping since he is isn't coming.

Demetrio: Oh, how dark it is! Psst, psst, Scaramuccia, is that you?

Scaramuccia: Yes, it's me, master. Great, what've you done?

Demetrio: I've been in the ground-floor room 'til now, waiting for your whistle.

Scaramuccia: And in the meantime, I've taken Giulia out of the house, telling her that I was taking her to Master Gervasio's and she went along with it; I wandered around for a bit, finally coming back and making her believe that she's in Gervasio's house, and right now, I'll lead her into your arms.

178. Scaramuccia addresses the audience over the difficulties of making such a complicated plan work on the stage in a night scene.

Demetrio: O Giulia, my soul, who would ever have believed that I might enjoy you this night, and that I might be the first to put a foot into your garden of love. Hah! Hah! To your beard, Gervasio! It's me who'll pluck the flower that hasn't been picked by anyone before.

Scaramuccia: Speak softly, so that she won't hear you since she's not very far from us. O master, remember to show some restraint with the young girl.

Demetrio: What restraint? In an amorous assault, restraint doesn't work; instead it's necessary to take note that even if she's young, she'll be a tiger in bed.

Scaramuccia: True, but do you want to wipe her out on the first round?

Demetrio: Eh, please, cut the comments! Do I need you to tell me what to do?

Scaramuccia: Go now, do what you want, it matters little to me. Go there now, eh, eh! Remember above all not to talk.[179]

Demetrio: No more advice, take her there early because an hour seems like a thousand years to wait to put a kiss on that sweet mouth from which all blessings flow.

Scaramuccia: Great, perfect, you're a poet of love. Shh, shh, shh. Trapola, where are you?

Trapola: I'm here.

Scaramuccia: Come on, be silent, don't speak. Shh, shh, shh.

Demetrio: Shh, shh, shh.

Scaramuccia: Embrace her and take her into the ground-floor room in the dark as I told you.

Demetrio: Yes, yes, goodbye, goodbye.

Scaramuccia: One down! Bring on the next, said he.

SCENE THREE

Gervasio and Scaramuccia

Gervasio: It's nearly two and a half hours after dark, and according to Scaramuccia's plan, I need to go to his house and cough loudly three times, so that he'll understand that it's our signal. I had no idea it would be so dark and cloudy! But

179. Scaramuccia takes the audience into the darkened world of the senses where sight and speech have been prohibited and the imagination gets full range so that unbelievable events can take place.

it doesn't matter, it will make it safer, if I'm not mistaken. I think I'm close to Demetrio's door, time to cough: cough, cough, cough.

Scaramuccia: My God, the cat's come scratching! You old dolt, what are the young to do, if the old act like such crazies? Psst, psst, psst, Master Gervasio, is that you?

Gervasio: Yes, it is and I've stubbed my toe on a rock so hard that I must have broken it! Curse all rocks to hell!

Scaramuccia: Be patient!

Gervasio: The important thing is that my desire is shrinking after rising up in hopes of the good things to come.

Scaramuccia: Oh, we'll see what we can do then! Wait for me to go into the house and get Giulia and bring her to you.

Gervasio: Yes, yes, go and return fast because my appetite is back. O my dear Giulia, is this what we call love? Are women passionate? Or are they truly in love? As far as that goes I ravished them all in any case! I wasted quite a few of them with my vigor! Think what I must have been like as a young man of forty![180]

SCENE FOUR

Scaramuccia, Ruchetta, and Gervasio

Scaramuccia: Come, Ruchetta, your husband's waiting for you! And to be safe, he's put on his master's clothes so that you when you see him, you'll say it's him.

Ruchetta: O Scaramuccia when will I ever be able to pay you back for the great kindness you're doing for me? A little while ago when I was having to wait to consummate the marriage, I was self-destructing like a candle made of cow fat.

Scaramuccia: I believe that not only do you really want it, but you really need it! However, I'm warning you that I want us to play a beautiful trick on your husband, you'll see, it's this: that you don't say anything until after he makes the assault on your female fortress.[181]

Ruchetta: Why this?

180. Gervasio echoes Demetrio's lustful boasting in a slightly less convincing way, making his claim all the more pathetic.

181. The bed tricks involving Ruchetta and Trapola can only work if they are done in silence. Sly proof that dialogue is not essential for meaningful action to take place.

Scaramuccia: For a trick or a joke, as I told you, and to hear what he will say to you for starters and what he will do next and with what skill he'll scale the wall of your honor.

Ruchetta: And what honor? Haven't I already told you that I lost it once and in good time, so that I have no idea what it might be?

Scaramuccia: So much that Trapola won't have any trouble winding the bobbin! Come on: good, good, walk with me and, above all don't talk, please.

Ruchetta: I'll do it, because it's not that big a deal.

Scaramuccia: Swear, because I don't believe you.

Ruchetta: What oath do you want me to swear?

Scaramuccia: Swear as a woman of virtue.

Ruchetta: I can't.

Scaramuccia: Why?

Ruchetta: Because I've always been a little slut and I can't abstain. That's enough, I won't say anything more.

Scaramuccia: So, that's it, it happens, say it from the start, clearly, without expecting punishment! Come here, give me your hand.

Ruchetta: Here it is. Don't squeeze, you pervert, you think that I don't know about you, eh?

Scaramuccia: Do you want me to tell you that in the dark here I have a huge desire to cuckold your husband?

Ruchetta: What do you mean? Eh, you wouldn't do it!

Scaramuccia: I'm about to grab a piece for myself, and if Master Gervasio wasn't waiting, I'd like to jump her in the dark. Psst, psst, psst.

Gervasio: Psst, psst, psst, shush, is that you, Scaramuccia? Is she with you?

Scaramuccia: I have her disguised as a servant, be silent, don't talk, and take her into your house to the ground-floor room, and don't use any lights as you promised.

Gervasio: Leave it to me! Here, from what I can make out, we're working as if we're blind and dumb.

Scaramuccia: That's it, up to a certain point and then talking would be impolite. Come now, her she is, take her and lead her away. Psst. Psst.

Ruchetta: Psst, psst.

Gervasio: Psst, psst, O my lover, come.

Scaramuccia: I'm going to die laughing! The old rodents are in the trap, now it's time to look after the young ones. Hallo, Sir Flavio.

SCENE FIVE

Flavio, Scaramuccia, and Giulia

Flavio: I'm here, Scaramuccia, what do you want? Remember that time's passing.

Scaramuccia: Then let it pass, in any case no one will be able to stop you. Now, I'll signal Giulia to come to you. Shush, shush.

Giulia: Shush, shush, is it you, Scaramuccia?

Scaramuccia: Yes, it's me.

Giulia: Have you brought Lord Flavio?

Scaramuccia: No, my lady.

Giulia: Why?

Scaramuccia: Because the poor thing was struck with a sudden illness.

Giulia: Oh, no, what illness is it?

Scaramuccia: He's been stricken.

Giulia: And where was he stricken?

Scaramuccia: Where? Here, by you. O you deceiver, one hour seems like a thousand when waiting to taste the sugar cane, yes?[182]

Giulia: But where is he? Let me see him and hold him.

Scaramuccia: Slow down, here he is, Sir Flavio come here.

Flavio: Here I am, my soul, where are you that I can't see you?

Giulia: I'm here, give me your hand.

182. The sugar from the sugar cane has an obvious sexual meaning, as Flavio and Giulia show strong mutual desire.

Flavio: Here it is, with which I again promise to be faithful.

Giulia: Let's go, my heart, there's no time to lose! Hold me.

Flavio: Here you are in my arms, my love, let's go.

Scaramuccia: Solder the bed frame, solder the bed boards for this furious charge! Hey, Sir Lepido, where are you?

SCENE SIX

Lepido, Scaramuccia and Porzia

Lepido: I'm here, where you put me, what do you want?

Scaramuccia: Right now, I want to call Mistress Porzia who is at the lookout. Pssst, pssst, pssst.

Porzia: Pssst pssst, is that you, Scaramuccia?

Scaramuccia: Yes, mistress, and with me is your lover, Sir Lepido.

Porzia: Good, good, oh, how wonderful!

Scaramuccia: You hear, my gentleman? Stay alert! Armed and ready to go, as necessary.

Porzia: But where is the faithless one?

Lepido: I'm here but I'm not faithless.

Porzia: Come, come and take the test: and if you're armed now, I want to fight you in your nightshirt.[183]

Lepido: You'll do what you can and so will I, but know that you'll end up underneath, without the victory you're thinking of.

Porzia: Let's go then, I've prepared by defenses against you.

Lepido: And I, my arms.

Porzia: I'll easily repel them! Come ahead.

Scaramuccia: Go there, so that you can fight or get stuck together like dogs! What a ferocious devil she is! When a woman's hot, she's like a wild beast! Oh, oh, they're all taken care of now, and very, very soon I'd better be ready for the terrible uproar that is going to break loose between Master Demetrio and Trapola

183. Porzia and Lepido's much longed for encounter is presented as a battle of equal armed combatants.

and Master Gervasio and Ruchetta. But Lady Porzia will be waiting for me to go and bed down with her husband Licinio, and I said I would—so I'd better get to it. Ah, my buttocks are tingling—I hope that's not a bad sign! I'm off—no, I'm not. One part of my heart says to go, the other says to stay: What are you doing, Scaramuccia, are you going to jeopardize your honor, your chastity and your virginity? Look at what you're doing—once a woman has lost her honor, she's nothing else to lose. What kind of man, do you think is going to marry you afterwards? You'll live a widow's life full of trouble and tribulations. Hold on, what an idiot, was I thinking I was a woman? Who says that imagining something won't make it real? Well it never works for me, imagining a beautiful woman… Come on, it's time to go, what could possibly happen? I have to do what I said: I'm off. Don't go, Scaramuccia, let sleeping dogs lie, don't tempt the devil, don't go looking for the cause of the disease, the way doctors do! You'll end up dead—and remember that dead men can't fight, and they say it's better to flee than die, and we're supposed to stay alive as long as we can and not go looking for death. But poor Porzia, she must be melting like burning wax, waiting for me. I'd better be off. I'm off, I'm going, going—see, I'm gone.[184]

SCENE SEVEN

Demetrio, and Trapola, dressed as a woman

Demetrio: Ah, traitor, where are you running to? I want to kill you, I see you, I see you with my lantern, stop there.

Trapola: Ah, Master Demetrio, don't kill me! Let me say a few words first, then you can do what you want.

Demetrio: Okay, but I want to know who's behind this crime.

Trapola: I'll tell you, sir. Either your servant Scaramuccia or your ward Mistress Giulia.

Demetrio: Ah, villain, archvillain, what's this got to do with them, eh?

Trapola: Listen please, master, I too am betrayed and destroyed by this thief Scaramuccia.

Demetrio: How so?

Trapola: Believe me, sir, Ruchetta your servant is my wife since Scaramuccia gave her to me in a betrothal ceremony; and because she wanted us to be together tonight, this traitor commands me to dress as a woman in order to be put into bed

184. Scaramuccia's hesitant monologue where he debates joining Licinio in bed captures this pivotal moment demanded by the plot, no matter how far-fetched.

with her, ordering me at the same time, not ever to speak, and telling me that he wanted to play at trick.

Demetrio: Oh, the villain, he said the same to me, promising me Giulia! But I should have known better to believe the word of a lowlife servant who has no morals or decency! Don't go anywhere for a bit, please, since I need to fix this injury while it's still fresh. I heard some strange noise in the house and I want to see what's going on.

Trapola: I know that Fortune has chosen to help me. Ah, traitor Scaramuccia, do I kill you or leave you alive?

SCENE EIGHT

Demetrio, Flavio, and Giulia

Demetrio: To arms, to arms, run neighbors, run!

Flavio: Master Demetrio don't shout, don't raise your voice, because if I'm in your house it's as an honorable gentleman. And even if I'm in my nightshirt, I'm not afraid of you, or your weapons.

Giulia: Listen, master, control your anger, because this gentleman is my husband, given to me by Scaramuccia.

Demetrio: Ah, Scaramuccia, thief and assassin! He's gone and married everyone in the neighborhood according to his wishes! But come here you cunning little monkey: what will Master Gervasio say when he sees he's been tricked by me, by you, by Scaramuccia, and that he's thrown away those presents.

Giulia: Tell him what you want, he can't complain about me since I promised nothing and he can take back the presents since I want nothing of his.

Demetrio: So, this is how Giulia behaves, eh? Do you have so little respect for my honor?

Giulia: The same respect that you'd have shown to me, I've shown to you, if not more. Do you think that Scaramuccia hasn't told me that you're in love with me and that you were planning to enjoy me first and then send me to Master Gervasio? What does that look like? Please, don't expect any further explanation other than that to flee from dishonor, I found a way to take care of myself honorably.

Demetrio: Okay, now be quiet, I believe you've said everything there is to say! But what's that noise I hear coming from Gervasio's house?

SCENE NINE

Ruchetta, Gervasio, Trapola, Demetrio, Giulia, and Flavio[185]

Ruchetta: Stop, I say, I'm not Giulia!

Gervasio: I know that you are Giulia, my bride, my soul! What, you're not her? With this light I can see that I know you very well! Oh! Ruchetta, Ruchetta, who put you in the house?

Ruchetta: That vile Scaramuccia.

Gervasio: How?

Ruchetta: He told me he was taking me to Trapola, my husband and your servant.

Trapola: Ah, good-for-nothing, you went out catting!

Ruchetta: I went to the whorehouse, you lowlife! I came to the house for you because I believed Scaramuccia.

Demetrio: Oh, what a vicious scoundrel he is; he deserves a thousand blows! But where is he? Who knows? Who can tell me?

Trapola: Good luck finding him, he must be hiding underground like a mole.

Gervasio: Wait a minute! Oh, here's my bride, and what does it mean that you are in your nightgown?

Giulia: If I'm in my nightgown, it's not for you.

Gervasio: What do you mean that it's not for me? You took my hand and accepted the diamond, the ruby, the earrings and the pearl necklace!

Giulia: If I took your hand and accepted your presents, it was for Scaramuccia's plan and to play a trick on you.

Gervasio: And what are you planning to do?

Giulia: To be someone else's, not yours.

Gervasio: Whose?

Giulia: Flavio's. My first husband.

Gervasio: Why the first? Who gave you to him?

Scaramuccia: Scaramuccia.

185. Flavio does not speak in this scene but he is by Giulia's side as she explains that they are married.

Gervasio: Let him die, this Scaramuccia! Master Demetrio, what do you say about your gallant servant?

Demetrio: What do you want me to say? He's pulled a fast one on me! Oh, why don't I have him in my hands?

Gervasio: Wait a minute, I hear noises coming from my house.

SCENE TEN: FINAL

Scaramuccia, Licinio, Porzia, Lepido, Gervasio Demetrio, Trapola, Ruchetta, Flavio, and Giulia

Scaramuccia: O God, have mercy on me don't kill me!

Licinio: Ah, traitor, this is how men of honor are killed, eh?

Porzia: O God, dear husband, don't do it![186]

Lepido: Ah, Master Licinio, were you in bed with a vile servant?

Scaramuccia: Oh, my God, who's that I see in his nightshirt? My God, Licinio has braids like a woman, and he looks just like the ghost of my poor dead wife come to kill me!

Gervasio: Caught in the net too, eh, thief? Pull it tight. Alas, alas, my son-in-law?

Demetrio: You, too, are trapped like a fox.

Trapola: Ah, you traitor, you got me, eh?

Ruchetta: Ah, dead man, you sure got me, eh?

Scaramuccia: You're all right, I admit to doing a thousand wrong things and I deserve whatever punishment; and now you can all go, because I forgive you all.

Demetrio: You don't say! Good, good.

Scaramuccia: Ah, please don't bother me now! Let me take another look or two at sir Licinio, who looks a lot like my Brigida. Bri, Bri.

Licinio: Scara, Scara.

Scaramuccia: Bri, Bri, Brigida?

Licinio: Scara, Scara, Scaramuccia?

186. Porzia and Lepido's entrance together is not highlighted, since all eyes now are directed to Scaramuccia and Licinio, whose disguises are exposed.

Scaramuccia: Brigida, my wife?

Licinio: Scaramuccia, my husband?

Scaramuccia: O my wife, are you dead or alive?

Licinio: Eh, my husband, I'm very much alive, but dead in your memory; since you never think about me.

Scaramuccia: O dear wife, take me in your arms, now what's going on? Is this a dream or an illusion?

Licinio: It's not a dream, or an illusion. I am Brigida, your wife. Yes, Master Gervasio, I'm no other than your son-in-law Licinio.

Demetrio: Go on, look at her braid! While, if that's the case, then Porzia is still not claimed?

Lepido: No, no, Master Demetrio, because I'll never let her go.

Gervasio: Oh, who's this? What do you have to do with this, Sir Sprung-up-from-Nowhere?

Demetrio: Wait a minute. But what are you doing here? Lepido, what's going on?

Lepido: Listen and you'll find out.

Licinio: Listen, thank you! Now, at last that you're all here, gathered around together, I'll tell you. I think everyone remembers very well that four years have passed since Master Demetrio sent his son Sir Lepido to Lyon.[187]

Demetrio: Of course, but what are you doing here now, Lepido? As I said.

Lepido: You'll find out by listening.

Licinio: He, before leaving, since he was in love with Lady Porzia, secretly pledged to marry her, promising to return after three years to keep his promise, praying that during that time she would resist the wishes of her father to marry her to someone else—but with the agreement that if he didn't return in three years, she might have to obey her father and get married.

Gervasio: Porzia, is it true what "he's' saying, or what "she's" saying, or whatever "she" is?

Porzia: Yes, sir.

187. The attention now passes to Licinio, who gradually over the next several speeches fills in the tale of her faked death as Brigida, and her return as an impressive and rich young gentleman.

Gervasio: Then, keep going.

Licinio: The first year passed, then the second, and the prescribed time limit was starting to run out when one day, Lady Porzia, sighing and sobbing, came to me and told me everything, saying that she couldn't stop her father from marrying her off, as every day he was putting her under great pressure.

Gervasio: True enough, go on.

Licinio: Seeing that the poor girl was in such trouble, I felt sorry for her and encouraged her to endure everything with patience and forbearance. And after a while, I left Master Demetrio's house and went to a relative skilled in making potions, who gave me a sleeping powder that made me appear to be dead, and so you all thought that I was, and duly mourned and buried me.

Scaramuccia: I know this so well, my dear wife, because I cried so bitterly over you.

Gervasio: Go on, tell me more! What do you say, Master Demetrio?

Demetrio: I remember everything, and I'm astonished at what happened; but I'm waiting to hear the ending of this strange love story. So, let her tell it, please.

Licinio: I was buried, then a few hours later, taken out of the tomb by my relative who gave me the remedy and restored me to my original self. Afterwards, recovering at his house, I shared my plan with him and got my men's clothing from him. I had brought large sums of money and jewels taken from your house with ease, Master Demetrio; since your mother, Lepido, had put them in my care, as you well know. Thus, I prepared to do what I had decided.

Demetrio: Bloody hell, it's true! But this is too much, I remember when I thought I'd been robbed of so much money and noticing that so many other things were missing.

Scaramuccia: My God, my God, what am I hearing? O, my smart and savvy wife, you deserve a crown!

Demetrio: What? For having robbed me? Not true, you piece of crap? But go on.

Licinio: And so, following the plan, I went to Florence loaded with money, at your expense.

Demetrio: What a swindle!

Licinio: And wanting to create a younger look and to resemble a man as much as possible, I stayed there for some time and did everything I could to change myself, so that I wouldn't be recognized as a woman, and then, as a man, I returned to Rome.

Gervasio: I never noticed, not even once. Please go on.

Licinio: Then, I sent an envoy with information about how much I was worth to ask Master Gervasio for the Lady Porzia's hand. After having courted her for some weeks, I offered to take her despite her very small dowry and promised to give her one myself. I succeeded with the greatest of ease because Master Gervasio, driven by greed, accepted my terms immediately and promised her to me without fail. Does this sound right?

Gervasio: Close enough, but I wasn't only driven by greed as you say, O Brigida.

Licinio: Whatever, have it your way, the master here saw me and was pleased that I was very rich and alone in the world (as I've always said), so he took me into the house and accepted me as a son and dearest son-in-law.

Gervasio: Was I wrong?

Licinio: We had the wedding ceremony, which was splendid, thanks to my lavish spending, and then we went to bed as a married couple, and only the poor Lady Porzia suffered for it. Don't be ashamed.

Porzia: Go on, go on.

Licinio: I say this because, instead of suffering that night, she remained a virgin and pure; but the happiness of having succeeded so well with our plan was sufficient enough that we enjoyed ourselves anyway, and the caresses that she gave to me, she herself, can tell you about as she is here. And then we followed our plan to wait for the desired return of Sir Lepido, since Lady Porzia was never anyone's but his. Finally, once we knew that he had returned because of his passionate love for her, we decided to relieve ourselves of the heavy burden of not being able to satisfy our natural desires. Once Lady Porzia was assured of Sir Lepido's love, which she had greatly mistrusted, and on finding him steadfast and constant, she decided that Lepido could sleep with her as her husband, but without him knowing the truth, and Scaramuccia would go to bed with me, thinking I was Licinio, her husband. All this was done to keep the promise between Lady Porzia and Sir Lepido. What do you say now, gentlemen?

Gervasio: I, for my part, have nothing to say other than it is heaven's wish that my daughter Porzia be his wife.

Demetrio: Then, let heaven be praised! I wouldn't even know how to oppose what has come down from up there, nor least of all, the happiness of my son. I repent having been so rigid, because it is in heaven that marriages are arranged. Hm, hm, hm!

Lepido: And I don't know how to reward you, Brigida, for your good deed. And you, my father, I remain obligated to you for my well-being, as well as for my being at all.

Gervasio: Dear Brigida, you deserve some chronicler to write about you, and some actor to put together a lovely comedy about this beautiful event. O now, Master Demetrio, what's happened, happened, right? Renounce your miserliness so that these young men can have these beautiful women as wives—since they are not food for our stomachs.

Demetrio: You have certainly spoken well, and I apologize to you, O Giulia, for the excessive love I had for you—which was so strong it overpowered my reason. As I praise and approve your desire to be united with Sir Flavio (which I am happy about), I also reprimand myself for any dishonest thoughts I might have had.

Flavio: I remain, my lord, eternally obligated.

Giulia: And I, as a dutiful daughter, won't act like an ungrateful ward of your house, but show you the thanks owed for your paternal love.

Demetrio: To show that I'm content: Lepido take Lady Porzia's hand, since Master Gervasio has agreed; and you, Sir Flavio, take Giulia's.

Trapola: Yes, take hands in public now, because the rest has to be handled in private.

Gervasio: Silence, dirty beast!

Demetrio: On the contrary, Master Gervasio, he's done right to speak, because to show myself as loving and joyful and full of goodwill, I want him to be happy to—if that's okay with you—so that everyone gets their wishes! Come here, Ruchetta, take Trapola's hand; and to recompense you for your service to me, I want to give him to you as a husband.

Ruchetta: May heaven reward you.

Demetrio: Only, however, if Master Gervasio, who was with you in secret, is in agreement.

Gervasio: Trapola, come here, so I can give you away.

Trapola: Thank you so much, and much good may it do you!

Licinio: Master Demetrio, as pardons go, since everything comes around, I'm begging you to forgive my Scaramuccia, since he's already being somewhat punished by having to take on the burden of a wife again.

Demetrio: You're right, therefore I forgive him for every sin committed for your love; not only because it's good to forgive, but because it brings good things. This then is a good place to bring everything to an end, and for everyone to go to their houses for the rest of the night, and tomorrow we'll hold the public weddings as agreed. You, in the meanwhile, Scaramuccia have done such a brilliant job of "Scaramucching" that you've come out clean!

Scaramuccia: More like covered in filth.[188]

Demetrio: Say goodbye to our audience, who've watched and listened to these beautiful and wonderful events.

EPILOGUE

Scaramuccia: Ladies and gentlemen, as you see, the punishment comes to rest on me alone, since I thought I was free from the impediment of having a wife, and now I have to take her back; but happy people enjoy themselves, and therefore, I want to follow their good example and accept what heaven sends without complaint. If there are those among you, ladies and gentlemen, who want to come to the weddings, you'll have to wait until tomorrow because it's too late now. However, I thank you in the name of us all for being such a wonderful audience, and I wish you well. Godspeed.

188. The Italian *Come un baston da pollaio!* is a Florentine figurative expression meaning "an extremely filthy person or thing." Zingarelli 2006 (Bologna: Zanichelli, 2005), 1369.

Bibliography

Primary Sources

Works by Flaminio Scala

Il finto marito. Venice: Andrea Baba, 1618. Reprint: *Il finto marito, commedia.* Venice: n.p., 1619. Modern edition in *Commedie dei comici dell'arte,* edited by Laura Falavolti, 225–365. Turin: Unione tipografico editrice torinese, 1982. Cited as Falavolti.

Il teatro delle favole rappresentative. Venice: Giovan Battista Pulciani, 1611. Modern edition by Ferruccio Marotti, 2 vols.: Milan: Polifolo, 1976. Partial translation in *The Commedia dell'Arte of Flaminio Scala,* ed. and trans. Andrews, q.v.

The Commedia dell'Arte of Flaminio Scala: A Translation and Analysis of Thirty Scenarios. Edited and translated by Richard Andrews. Lanham, MD: Scarecrow Press, 2008. Includes *The Theater of Tales for Performance* at 1–320. Cited as Andrews, *Thirty Scenarios.*

The Husband. In Andrews, *Thirty Scenarios,* Day 9, at 41–52. English translation of *Il marito.*

Il postumio: Comedia del signor I. S. posta in luce da F. S. detto Flavio, Comico Acceso. Lyon: Appresso Jacomo Roussin, 1601.

Manuscripts

Archivio di Stato di Firenze: Mediceo del Principato [ASF MdP] 5150. Letters of Benedetto Blanis Hebreo to Don Giovanni dei Medici.

Archivio di Stato di Venezia [ASV], Notarile testamenti: Beacian Fabrizio, b. 56, n. 236, 3 cc. unnumbered.

Other Primary Sources

Academy of the Intronati. *The Deceived.* In Giannetti and Ruggiero, *Five Comedies,* 205–84.

Andreini, Francesco. *Le bravure del Capitano Spavento.* Venice: Giacomo Antonio Somasco, 1607. Second part: *Le bravure del Capitano Spavento: Divise in molti ragionamenti in forma del dialogo,* Venice: Somasco, 1618. Modern edition by Roberto Tessari: Pisa: Giardini, 1987. Excerpts in Marotti and Romei, *La commedia dell'arte,* 2:212–302.

Andreini, Giovanni Battista, et al. *Comici dell'arte: Corrispondenze.* Edited by Siro Ferrone, Claudia Burattelli, Domenica Landolfi, and Anna Zinanni. 2 vols. Florence: Le Lettere, 1993. Cited as *Corrispondenze.*

———. *La ferza contra l'accuse date alla commedia.* Paris: Nicolas Callemont, 1625. Excerpt in Marotti and Romei, *La commedia dell'arte,* 2:489–534.

Andreini, Isabella. *Fragmenti di alcune scritture della signora Isabella Andreini Comica Gelosa, et academia intenta; Raccolti da Francesco Andreini Comico Geloso, detto il Capitano Spavento, e dati in luce da Flamminio Scala Comico, e da lui dedicati all'illustrissimo signor Filippo Capponi.* Venice: Gio. Battista Combi, 1617.

Aretino, Pietro. *Aretino's Dialogues.* Translated by Raymond Rosenthal. Introduction by Margaret Rosenthal. Toronto: University of Toronto Press, 2005.

———. *Sei giornate: Ragionamento della Nanna e della Antonia, 1534; Dialogo nel quale la Nanna insegna a la Pippa, 1536.* Edited by Giovanni Aquillecchia. Bari: Giuseppe Laterza, 1969.

Aristotle. *Poetics.* Translated by Kenneth McLeish. London: Nick Hern, 1999.

Barbieri, Nicolò. *La supplica, discorso famigliare a quelli che trattono de' comici.* Venice: Marco Ginammi, 1634. Modern edition by Ferdinando Taviani: Milan: Il Polifilo, 1971.

Bargagli, Girolamo, *La pellegrina.* Siena: Appresso i Florimi, 1618. Modern edition by Florindo Cerrata: Florence: L. S. Olschki, 1971.

Castiglione, Baldassare. *The Book of the Courtier.* Translated by Charles S. Singleton. Garden City, NY: Doubleday, 1959.

Dovizi, Bernardo, da Bibbiena. *The Comedy of Calandro.* In Giannetti and Ruggiero, *Five Comedies,* 1–70.

Ficino, Marsilio. *Sulla vita.* Edited and translated by Alessandra Tarabochia Canavero. Milan: Rusconi, 1995. Italian translation of Ficino, *De triplici vita.*

Giannetti, Laura, and Guido Ruggiero, ed. and trans. *Five Comedies from the Italian Renaissance.* Baltimore: Johns Hopkins University Press, 2003.

Lomazzo, Giovanni Paolo. *The Idea of the Temple of Painting.* Edited and translated by Jean Julia Chai. University Park: Pennsylvania State University Press, 2013.

———. *Rime ad imitazione de i grotteschi usati da' pittori: Con la vita del auttore descritta da lui stesso in rime sciolte.* Edited by Alessandra Ruffino. Manziana (Rome): Vecchiarelli, 2006.

Marotti, Ferruccio, and Giovanna Romei, eds. *La commedia dell'arte e la società barocca,* Vol. 2: *La professione del teatro.* Rome: Bulzoni, 1991.

Medici, Giovanni de', Don. "A Patron's Difficulties with a Troupe, 1620." Letter to Ercole Marliani, March 21, 1620. In Kenneth Richards and Laura Richards, *Commedia dell'Arte,* 76–79.

Pavoni, Giuseppe. *Diario descritto da Giuseppe Pavoni delle feste celebrate nelle solennissime nozze delli Serenissimi Sposi il Sig. Don Ferdinando Medici e la*

Sig. Donna Christiana di Loreno Gran Duchi di Toscana. Bologna: Giovanni Rossi, 1589. Excerpt in Marotti, *Il teatro delle favole rappresentative*, vol. 1, Appendix 2, lxxiii–lxxv.

Porcacchi, Tommaso. *Le attioni d'Arrigo terzo Re di Francia, 1574*. Excerpt in Kenneth Richards and Laura Richards, *Commedia dell'Arte*, 73.

Quintilian. *The Institutio Oratoria of Quintilian*. Translated by Harold E. Butler. 4 vols. Cambridge, MA: Harvard University Press, 1920.

Richards, Kenneth and Laura Richards. *The Commedia dell'Arte: A Documentary History*. Oxford: Basil Blackwell, 1990.

Rosetti, Giovanventura. *I notandissimi secreti de l'arte profumatoria, a fare ogli, acque, paste, balle, moscardini, uccelletti, paternostri, e tutta l'arte intiera*. Venice: per Francesco Rampazetto, 1555. New edition by Franco Brunello e Franca Facchetti: Vicenza: N. Pozza, 1992.

Secondary Sources

Andrews, Richard. "Introduction." In Scala, *Thirty Scenarios*, ix–lvi.

Bolzoni, Lisa. *The Gallery of Memory: Literary and Iconographic Models in the Age of the Printing Press*. Translated by Jeremy Parzen. Toronto: University of Toronto Press, 2001.

———. *Il teatro della memoria: Studi su Giulio Camillo*. Padua: Liviana. 1984.

Chai, Jean Julia. "Introduction." In Lomazzo, *The Idea of the Temple of Painting*, 1–41.

Dooley, Brendan. *A Mattress Maker's Daughter: The Renaissance Romance of Don Giovanni de' Medici and Livia Vernazza*. Cambridge, MA: Harvard University Press, 2014.

———. "Narrazione e verità: Don Giovanni de' Medici e Galileo." *Bruniana & Campanelliana* 14, no. 2 (2008): 389–403.

Dukore, Bernard F., ed. *Dramatic Theory and Criticism: Greeks to Grotowski*. New York: Holt, Rinehart and Winston, 1974.

Evangelista, Anna Maria. "Il teatro dei comici dell'arte a Firenze: Ricognizione dello 'Stanzone delle Commedie' detto di Baldracca." *Biblioteca teatrale* 9, no. 23/24 (1979): 70–86.

Ferrone, Siro. "Don Giovanni impresario." In *Attori, mercanti, corsari: La commedia dell'arte in Europa tra Cinque e Seicento*, 143–99. Turin: G. Einaudi, 1993.

Fitzpatrick, Tim. *The Relationship of Oral and Literate Performance Processes in the Commedia dell'Arte: Beyond the Improvisation/Memorisation Divide*. Lewiston, NY: Edwin Mellen Press, 1995.

Giannetti, Laura. *Lelia's Kiss: Imagining Gender, Sex, and Marriage in Italian Renaissance Comedy*. Toronto: University of Toronto Press, 2009.

Gitelman, Lisa. *Paper Knowledge: Toward a Media History of Documents*. Durham, NC: Duke University Press, 2014.

Goldberg, Edward. *Jews and Magic in Medici Florence: The Secret World of Benedetto Blanis*. Toronto: University of Toronto Press, 2011.

Henke, Robert. *Performance and Literature in the Commedia dell'Arte*. Cambridge: Cambridge University Press, 2002.

Jaffe-Berg, Erith. *Commedia dell'Arte and the Mediterranean: Charting Journeys and Mapping "Others."* Farnham, Surrey, UK: Ashgate, 2015.

Jenkins, Henry. *Convergence Culture: Where Old and New Media Collide*. New York: New York University Press, 2006.

Katritzky, M. A. *The Art of Commedia: A Study in the Commedia dell'Arte, 1560–1620, with Special Reference to the Visual Records*. Amsterdam: Rodopi, 2006.

Kerr, Rosalind. *The Rise of the Diva on the Sixteenth-Century Commedia dell'Arte Stage*. Toronto: University of Toronto Press, 2015.

Landolfi, Domenica. "Don Giovanni de' Medici: 'Principe intendentissimo in varie scienze.'" *Studi secenteschi* 29 (1988): 125–62.

———. "Su un teatrino mediceo e sull'Accademi degli Incostanti a Firenze nel primo Seicento." *Teatro e storia* 6, no. 1 (1991): 57–88.

MacNeil, Anne. "The Divine Madness of Isabella Andreini." *Journal of the Royal Music Association* 120 (1995): 195–215.

Maravall, José Antonio. *Culture of the Baroque: Analysis of a Historical Structure*. Translated by Terry Cochran. Minneapolis: University of Minnesota Press, 1986.

Marotti, Ferruccio. "Introduzione." In Scala, *Il teatro delle favole rappresentative*, 1:xiv–lxiii.

Pietropaolo, Domenico. *Semiotics and Pragmatics of Stage Improvisation*. London: Bloomsbury Academic, 2016.

Rocke, Michael. *Forbidden Friendships: Homosexuality and Male Culture in Renaissance Florence*. New York: Oxford University Press, 1996.

Saslow, James. *The Medici Wedding of 1589: Florentine Festival as Theatrum Mundi*. New Haven: Yale University Press, 1996.

Schmitt, Natalie Crohn. *Befriending the Commedia dell'Arte of Flaminio Scala: The Comic Scenarios*. Toronto: University of Toronto Press, 2014.

Stern, Laura Ikins. *The Criminal Law System of Medieval and Renaissance Florence*. Baltimore: Johns Hopkins University Press, 1994.

Tamburini, Elena. "I Comici Gelosi e l'Accademia della Val di Blenio." *Biblioteca teatrale* 97–98 (January–June 2011): 175–95.

———. Culture ermetiche e commedia dell'arte: Tra Giulio Camillo e Flaminio Scala. Rome: Aracne Editrice, 2016.

———. "Dietro la scena: Comici, cantanti, e letterati nell'Accademia romana degli Umoristi." *Studi secenteschi* 50 (2009): 89–112.

Ughi, Stefanella. "Di Adriano Valerini, di Silvia Roncagli, e dei Comici Gelosi." *Biblioteca teatrale* 3 (1972): 147–52.

Wootton, David. *Paolo Sarpi: Between Renaissance and Enlightenment.* Cambridge: Cambridge University Press, 1983.

Zingarelli, Nicola. *Lo Zingarelli: Vocabolario della lingua italiana [=Zingarelli 2006]*. 12th ed. Bologna: Zanichelli, 2005.

Index